PHILOSOPHY OF DREAMS

CHRISTOPH TÜRCKE

TRANSLATED BY SUSAN H. GILLESPIE

Philosophy of Dreams

Yale UNIVERSITY PRESS

NEW HAVEN AND LONDON

The translation of this work was funded by Geisteswissenschaften International—
Translation Funding for Humanities and Social Sciences from Germany, a joint initiative
of the Fritz Thyssen Foundation, the German Federal Foreign Office, the collecting
society VG WORT, and the Börsenverein des Deutschen Buchhandels (German Publishers &
Booksellers Association).

Published with assistance from the foundation established in memory of Amasa Stone
Mather of the Class of 1907, Yale College.

Yale University Press books may be purchased in quantity for educational, business, or
promotional use. For information, please e-mail sales.press@yale.edu (U.S. office) or sales@
yaleup.co.uk (U.K. office).

Set in Scala type by IDS Infotech, Ltd.
Printed in the United States of America.

Library of Congress Cataloging-in-Publication Data

Türcke, Christoph.
    [Philosophie des Traums. English]
    Philosophy of dreams / Christoph Türcke ; translated by Susan H. Gillespie.
        pages cm
    Includes bibliographical references and index.
    ISBN 978-0-300-18840-0 (cloth : alk. paper) 1. Dreams—Philosophy. 2. Dreams—
Psychological aspects. 3. Dream interpretation. I. Title.
    BF1078.T8713 2013
    154.6′3—dc23
                2013015739

A catalogue record for this book is available from the British Library.

This paper meets the requirements of ANSI/NISO Z39.48–1992 (Permanence of Paper).

10 9 8 7 6 5 4 3 2 1

CONTENTS

CHRISTOPH TÜRCKE'S *Philosophy of Dreams* covers a lot of ground—from Early Stone Age ritual to the impact of contemporary information technology on human cognition, from Aristotle and Georg F. W. Hegel to twentieth-century French theorist Jacques Lacan. This is challenging for the translator, who is unlikely to be expert in all these fields and who, moreover, must knit together the different vocabularies and perspectives of dissimilar disciplines, cultures, and eras. But all this pales in comparison with the challenge posed by the numerous works of Sigmund Freud, on which *Philosophy of Dreams* is based, and with which its author often begs to differ.

As Christoph Türcke rethinks and resituates dreamwork in his philosophical anthropology of human consciousness, he draws on works from all periods of Freud's extensive and wide-ranging writings.

Freud frequently revised and republished his works, then re-revised and republished them again. His most famous and influential work, *The Interpretation of Dreams*, which is central to Türcke's project, went through eight editions between 1899 and 1930. Between the first and fourth editions, the book mushroomed from 374 to 498 pages, finally coming to rest at 435.[1] Revisions tracked the evolution of Freud's thinking. Analytic practice elicited new examples, including new dreams. Freud's lively dialogue with fellow innovators in the field of psychoanalysis sometimes led to changes in approach. Commentators who emphasize the "immediate" and "personal" character of Freud's German are responding in part to the way the theories themselves arose—experimentally and in dialogue with others.

When it came to the translation of his works, Freud, initially, was remarkably cavalier. The first translation of *The Interpretation of Dreams* (1909) was by A. A. Brill, a friend of Freud's and student of the psychologist and Freud supporter Eugen Bleuler.[2] Brill attempted a cultural translation by replacing the German dreams of Freud and his patients with British equivalents—a wonderfully imaginative idea that did not find favor with critics. Confronted with the inadequacies of the first translation, Freud famously responded, "I would rather have a good friend than a good translator."[3] Characteristically, Freud's early translators all came from the circle of his acolytes and fellow pioneers in the new field of psychoanalysis. Their linguistic skills were assumed to be of secondary importance to their loyalty and personal experience of analysis. There was no expectation of a common standard of practice, language, or style.

All this changed with the institutionalization of psychoanalysis and the emergence of embattled factions within it. Under the control of the Institute of Psycho-Analysis, the translation of Freud's works into English was centralized and bureaucratized. Freud's disciple and biographer Ernest Jones organized what would become the twenty-four volumes of the *Standard Edition of the Complete Psychological Works of Sigmund Freud*, published between 1953 and 1974 and edited and translated by James Strachey, who also served as its indefatigable principal translator. Jones took the unusual step of creating a Glossary Committee, which he controlled. The Glossary Committee imposed a terminological consistency that, while arguably lacking in the original German, generally seems to have been supported by Freud himself when it came to the *Standard Edition*.[4] For many years, perhaps thanks in part to its editorial rigor, and in the absence of a critical edition in German, the English-language *Standard Edition* effectively served as the scholarly basis of much Freud interpretation, as well as translations into other languages. Freud's success in changing a whole climate of opinion may indeed have been due in part to the fact "that [Freud's] ideas were thoroughly promulgated throughout the world in the Standard Edition and in its many derivatives in other languages."[5]

In his translations, Strachey assumed a reliably moderate and rather ponderous, reserved tone. As he explained in his preface, "I am imagining Freud as an English gentleman of science, of wide education, born in the middle of the nineteenth century."[6] The result, admired by some, has also been the object of impassioned criticism, most famously by Jacques Lacan and Bruno Bettelheim. Lacan, in France, and Bettelheim, in the United States, argued that Strachey had distorted Freud's German by replacing his everyday language with Latin terms that made psychoanalysis sound "scientific."[7] As a means of rendering the new "science" acceptable to the American medical profession and society, the practice succeeded, and indeed psychoanalysis became more widely accepted in the United States than in Europe—where of course Freud's theories and Freud himself were extirpated and hounded out in the areas controlled by the National Socialist regime.

Thus, for more than sixty years the *Standard Edition*, with its heavy black volumes, ruled unchallenged in the world of Freud scholarship. But since the 1990s, a revolution in Freud translations has been underway. One reason for this is an accident of intellectual property law. British and European copyrights on the translations expired in different years (the British copyright in 1989, that of the EU in 2009), and this opened a window of opportunity for British publisher Penguin to embark on a new series of Freud translations. These translations, under the editorship of British psychoanalyst and essayist Adam Phillips, seek to provide a fresh, more literary approach to Freud. The series offers new translations by nonspecialist writer-translators, with titles that group Freud's work thematically. The "New Penguin Freud" has grown to fifteen volumes out of a projected twenty-four, some of which bear catchy titles like *The Psychology of Love* and *On Murder, Mourning and Melancholia*. Concurrently, psychoanalyst and neuropsychologist Mark Solms has been preparing *The Revised Standard Edition*, based on Strachey's work. *The Revised Standard Edition* is being published in the United States by W. W. Norton and is expected to appear in late 2014.[8]

For this translation of *Philosophy of Dreams*, the *Revised Standard Edition* and the important editorial corrections it will no doubt make unfortunately come too late. Nor, sadly, did I have access to the extensive glossary Professor Solms is developing. Yet Christoph Türcke's comprehensive, responsive critique of Freud's thinking about dreams and their importance for the emergence of human sociality seemed to require a reasonably consistent approach to the historical body of Freud translations. For the most part, therefore, Freud citations in the text are drawn from the *Standard Edition*, or rather from the proliferating reprints of its familiar volumes. In citing from the *Standard Edition*, I have, however, made a few changes. I agree with all the critics—from Lacan and Bettelheim to Adam Phillips and Mark Solms—that Strachey's translation of *Trieb* as "instinct" is an embarrassing mistake. German has a perfectly good word *Instinkt*, and English has a perfectly good word *drive*. With a couple of exceptions, therefore, where Strachey's *Standard Edition* says *Trieb* I have silently replaced the English word *instinct* with *drive*. I have straddled the line on the issue of "I" and "it" versus "ego" and "id" (as translations of German *ich* and *es*) by including both terms where it seemed feasible, and have silently undone Strachey's habit of creating hyphenated words for the terms psycho-analysis, dream-work, and many more of this type—a habit he himself, in retrospect, once said he found "tiresome."9 Where more far-reaching corrections were made, this is indicated in the notes.

The one notable exception to the selection of the Strachey *Standard Edition* as the point of reference for citing Freud's works is the Penguin Modern Classics volume titled *Sigmund Freud: The Unconscious*, translated by Graham Frankland as part of the edition overseen by Adam Phillips. Frankland's translation of *Triebe und Triebschicksale* as "The Drives and Their Fates" clearly carries the day over Strachey's "The Instincts and Their Vicissitudes." Citations from Freud's essays on "Formulations on the Two Principles of Psychic Functioning" and "The Unconscious" are also drawn from this volume.10

Bible translations are from the *King James Version*.

Thanks are due to Yale University Press's sharp-eyed editors Jennifer Banks, Margaret Otzel, and Kate Davis for their thoughtful review and for catching many small and large errors, and to Bard College colleagues Helena Gibbs and Garry Hagberg for their advice on psychological and philosophical questions. The College's librarians were invaluable in tracking down the seemingly endless number of works cited, demonstrating once again that in this era of electronic media and "concentrated distraction" (Türcke) we need them as much as ever.

PHILOSOPHY OF DREAMS

FOREWORD: THE EARLY STONE AGE IN US

TO ENGAGE WITH DREAMS is to descend to the underworld, to let go of everything solid offered by "established" customs and habits, forms of perception and thought, and dive down into the primordial world—the hallucinatory world of feelings and images from which human culture emerged with difficulty. For humans, there are two types of primitive world: the one we experience as young children, before we are fully acculturated, and the one humanity as a whole must have lived through, so that each individual may pass through it again in a foreshortened version.

It is quite evident that the primitive stage we live through as individuals never quite ends. No one is able to work through the hurts and wishes of childhood so thoroughly that nothing at all remains. Thus, each of us always continues to be a little bit of a child, no one becomes a 100 percent adult, and the ferment of our dreams is a constantly returning reminder of this fact. But what does this have to do with human prehistory? Does that history still bubble up, unmastered, in the dream life of the twenty-first century? Isn't it much too long ago? Certainly, it is unimaginably distant. But precisely this brings it into proximity with dreams: When we dream, time loses all sense of proportion for us. Something similar happens when we try to think back to the origins of humankind. Or can anyone come up with a concrete image of 2.5 million years? This is something even expert paleontologists cannot hope to do.

Although, by now, they have plenty of sophisticated biochemical methods with which to reconstruct a history from bits of bone, earthworks, and stones, that history remains so shadowy and indistinct that it never ceases to seem like a dream, while at the same time historical details can be reported quite soberly as scientific findings.[1]

In East Africa, in the area surrounding Lake Turkana, near Lake Victoria in a region of modern Kenya, roughly bordering South Sudan, Ethiopia, Uganda, and Tanzania, there lived a species of hominid—the name is *Homo rudolfensis*—who experienced something unprecedented. A long dry spell had pushed back the tropical rain forest and turned members of the hominid species in question into savannah dwellers. Meanwhile, the plants from which they drew most of their nourishment had become so tough, as a result of the drought, that *Homo rudolfensis*'s teeth could no longer break them down. They learned to pick up sharp-edged, conveniently sized pebbles. With their help, it was possible to cut up the refractory foodstuffs. And while this activity, carried out over thousands of years, became part of their flesh and blood, they discovered something that would have even greater consequences: it is possible to *make* pebbles sharp if they are not naturally that way. All that is required is to strike them with other stones in such a way that a sharp edge remains.

Homo rudolfensis had no idea of the long-term impact of this discovery. But with it came nothing less than the Stone Age. There were already apes that had learned to satisfy their hunger with the help of a detour that involved hitting a net with a piece of wood, or using a stick to reach a banana. They could achieve their aim only with the help of an object, not directly. But with the use of a stone to work on a stone—the very definition of the Stone Age—this detour stopped being just a sidetrack. It became the main track. Along the way, the desire for food took a new turn. In place of food, the new trend paid attention to the pebble. It had to be struck again and again, persistently and purposefully, until, following innumerable failed efforts and new attempts, it acquired the qualities that made it suitable for cutting up food. The entire motor behavior of the organism had to be adapted to this task.

In this process, attention was not only diverted from the food to the tool; attention also took on a new intensity and persistence. The pebble was the recipient of a level of interest that food itself, as long as it could be broken apart by teeth and fingernails, had never received. To first prepare a tool and then use it to prepare food, and to spend much longer and work much more intensively on the first action than on the second one that was actually its goal—what an enormous displacement and condensation of drive energy this demanded! We can legitimately speak of a revolution in nature's storehouse of drives. It launched a process of self-taming that was unprecedented in natural history, a practice of deferring the satisfaction of drives, of persistence and patience, to which beings who are controlled by their drives subject themselves only under the greatest duress, never voluntarily. Obviously, it was a matter of life and death. Either find a way to assist the jaw, or perish.

The pebble tools, simple blades and scrapers, that were found near Lake Turkana are the modest memorials to a struggle for survival that lasted several hundred thousand years—and the first traces of culture. Culture began as a survival strategy, and at first it developed extremely slowly. A lot may have happened during this primitive era, but it is practically impossible to identify any single event or action. Only what was repeated innumerable times, so that it became established as a skill, or even a technique, can even be registered—after it has long since, over a period of thousands or hundreds of thousands of years, turned into a *type* of event or behavior. The ancient Greek word *typos* has the primary meaning "blow." Its original sense is the activity of aiming a blow, like the one a stonemason or sculptor uses to let a meaningful shape emerge from a stone. Later, it comes to designate the meaningful shape itself. Viewed in this way, the pebble tools are archetypes in the most literal sense of the word: the first types in which the development of culture took concrete form. They also allow us to see clearly what archetypes consist of. They may be primordial and ancient, but they are anything but sudden or spontaneous. On the contrary, the older they are, the more effort was required to learn and produce them, and the longer the time it took for them to emerge.[2]

For the dimensions of archetypical time, ten thousand years is the smallest meaningful unit of measurement. A difference of a thousand years is usually impossible to discern. The most competent experts can easily be off by ten or fifty thousand years, and, measured against the tempo of cultural development, even that often doesn't make much of a difference. Consider: a million years after the first pebble tools, culture had advanced no further than to several varieties of hand axes and a use of fire about which we know nothing more. A million years after that, there were still no humans in the more narrow sense. Brain volume developed only slowly, along with the proportions of the skull and skeleton, the shapes of the hand and foot that are typical for Neanderthal and *Homo sapiens*. Only with the latter—the youngest hominid—does the word *human* really begin to apply. Humans became an anatomically stable species only something like 200,000–150,000 years ago, with the basic physical equipment that in the case of the Neanderthals remained largely unchanged until their extinction (ca. 27,000 years ago), and that in the case of *Homo sapiens* still exists today. This made possible something no other species ever accomplished: the condensation and displacement of the drive energy that initiated culture's own process of condensation and displacement, and that thus made it possible to form natural materials that would not only *do* something else, namely procure food, but also *stand for* something else—that is, mean something and take on the character of a sign.

The displacement from the creation of means to the creation of signs—this marks the emergence of human beings in the narrower sense. It also becomes palpable in a phase that we can identify only long after it began to be practiced. The transition may have taken forty or fifty thousand years. We have something that allows us to study this quite well: graves. On one hand, they are containers for preserving group members, that is, means. On the other, they are much more than that. The person who buries relatives doesn't just entomb them. He beds their mortal remains in a space that was specially prepared for them and that, from now on, is not supposed to be touched. This is a solemn act. It is a celebration of something, even if we don't know exactly what. And to celebrate something means to point to it—to mean something. Graves are means that are charged with heightened significance, and to this extent they are also signs. Ornaments, sculptures, and wall paintings, finally, are primarily or exclusively signs. They have been produced, with enormous effort, specifically in order to mean something and to give a sense of the enormous importance accorded to giving meaning to nature.

Even in this case, as with the earlier creation of tools, it must at first have been a matter of life and death—only now at the level of collectively practiced rituals. The cultic dimension of culture opened up. This may have occurred 50,000 years ago, or perhaps even earlier if the suspicion should prove correct that 70,000 years ago a snake cult was already in existence in the Kalahari Desert.[3] In any case, the Neanderthals, some

40,000 years ago, already possessed highly developed grave sites and burial rites. Bodily ornaments, sculptures, and paintings can be shown to have existed only for the last 30,000 years and only for our species. They are the reason we are called *Homo sapiens*. Our species' *sapientia*—the Latin term means "wisdom"—is the great riddle that confronts paleontologists, before which they stand in awe. It is, so to speak, the keystone of the Early Stone Age. Large brain volume, erect posture, manual skills, a tendency to defer gratification of drives—all this does not explain the singular achievement of this displacement, which opened the sphere of meaning to *Homo sapiens*.

This riddle does not only interest specialists. "Research on hominids is also research into ourselves. It touches our substance," said Friedemann Schrenk.[4] In point of fact, the basic physical equipment that *Homo sapiens* acquired ca. 200,000 years ago, the neuronal connections that became established in his brain, are the same ones we still carry around with us today. The Early Stone Age is inside us. We don't need to know anything about it as long as it merely provides the peaceful foundation. It matters to us existentially as soon as this foundation is stirred up.

This is exactly what modern advanced technology does. It does not leave the past in peace, even the most distant past. Its gaze may be mainly fixed on the future, but in doing so it also conjures up the Early Stone Age. Not only in the sense that it gives paleontology a wealth of precise methods, so that carbon, potassium, or DNA analyses allow us to make breathtakingly precise observations about the age and composition of bone, stone, and earth samples. Highly developed technology has an archaeological dynamic of its own. What do geneticists do? They don't only analyze and record genetic endowments, they interfere in them. Genetically modified foodstuffs have long been in circulation. There have been individual instances of hair-raising experiments. "In 1986, scientists took the gene that produces light in a firefly and inserted it into the genetic code of a tobacco plant. The tobacco leaves began to glow." Others "fused together embryo cells from a goat and from a sheep, and placed the embryo they fused they into a surrogate mother who gave birth to a goat-sheep chimera."[5]

To the acute danger that emanates from such manipulations for the present and the future is added their retroactive influence on the most distant past. They cross species boundaries that have become solidified in the course of millennia. They return nature to the state in which these boundaries were not yet firm—and draw them differently. Thus they excavate natural history, so to speak, and revise it; the term *revisionist history* takes on an entirely new dimension. This is especially critical when the revision has to do with human beings—not just for the purpose of fighting disease but to correct the human genetic inheritance. This amounts to "excavating" humankind's basic physical endowment, subjecting it to a kind of archaeological treatment. Nanotechnology has something similar in mind. If it should succeed in introducing tiny tubes into the brain to create new neurological pathways, in order not only to make a detour around defective nerve cells but also to gain access to brain regions that are supposedly underutilized, then this is also disturbing the natural history of the brain, with the nanotubes serving as tiny archaeological spades.

In the course of these efforts, which are still in their infancy, we tend to forget that modern media technology has already been busily engaged in mental archaeology for more than a century. In 1895, the Lumière brothers projected the first films in Paris's Grand Café. They didn't actually show much. A single take, about three minutes in duration, showed scenes of workers leaving their factory at the end of the workday, or a train entering a station. Only the event itself, nothing else. But the audience watched as if spellbound. A few even leapt up in fright because they thought the train that was entering the station was coming straight at them. Their misperception resulted from films' creation of a novel lack of optical distance. In the cinema, the spectator sees through the eye of the camera. His eyes are much less his own than in the theater. It is as if he enters into its gaze. Its images become his images; they get under the skin of his conscious awareness, because they are images of an eye without consciousness, an eye that sees without a filter, as it were, without feeling, remembering, or thinking anything—and that in this way opens up a new visual world. The new world is full of details, sequences of events, and connections that the eye without a camera would never notice, in other words a world of "unconscious optics,"[6] and simultaneously a world of unreflective immediacy. Its images have the intensity of dream images, which also appear to the dreamer as completely real and inescapable. Of course, these *aren't* dream images. They are much too sharp and precise for that, and often much too carefully arranged. But they roll past like a dream turned inside out, which gives the dream images a sharpness and precision they normally would not have on their own. The montage technique also represents a sharpening of what dreams do. The camera's focused and assembled images follow each other with the immediacy of the scene changes in dreams, but more abruptly. Each time, there is a little jolt, and each of these jolts has a twofold effect. First, it casts an immediate spell over the viewer. But then it immediately lets him drift off again, into a living dream life that is difficult to define—alongside the film and yet within its force field. Siegfried Kracauer noticed this early on. "Once the spectator's organized self has surrendered, his subconscious or unconscious experiences, apprehensions and hopes tend to come out and take over. Owing to their indeterminacy, film shots are particularly fit to function as an ignition spark. Any such shot may touch off chain reactions in the movie-goer—a flight of associations which no longer revolve around their original source, but arise from his agitated inner environment."[7]

The cinematic viewer is self-evidently awake; otherwise he would not be able to follow the film. Nevertheless, his waking state has descended quite some distance in the direction of dream and hypnosis. The boundaries between sleep, dream, and the waking state, which are already blurred, have become a good bit more blurry since the invention of movies. True, films are no longer anything exceptional or unfamiliar, or even a particularly elevated form of entertainment. The time is long since past when people looked forward all week to their weekend visit to the cinema. Moving images are part of the high-tech world of everyday. They not only color all our free time, they have also taken over the world of work. The coordination of entire processes of production and administration runs on screens. One consequence is that the individual sequence of images leaves a less-deep impression than in earlier cinematic eras. At the same time, the cinema has become one ingredient in a ceaseless audio-visual bombardment that constantly submerges words in images and pulls the senses abruptly back and forth between different scenarios, all of which demand our attention.

These scenarios set the rhythm of our modern experience of the world. They produce "concentrated distraction"[8] on a global scale, twenty-four hours a day. Young people are nowhere more persistent than when they are sitting in front of their activated screens—two to five hours a day is the global average. Foolish the person who believes all that to be without any more profound dissociative effect on the motor, sensual, perceptual, and mental apparatus. Just as customs can slacken, so can forms of concentration and coordination, representation and thought. After all, they themselves are nothing but habitual activities that have become sedimented as second nature. It is not necessary, as Jacques Derrida did, to call for their "de-sedimentation,"[9] Permanent audiovisual barrages are already busy doing this all day long. This is precisely what their mental archaeology is about. In this book, I pursue the suspicion that all this is not without success, that it is actually on the point of stirring up the Early Stone Age in us, which this foreword describes. It is stirring up the layers of thought that are the dregs of the millennia-long labor of *Homo sapiens*, the very thing his nerves struggled so hard to lay down—and that since then have given the impression that they have "always been there."

The dregs of a pot of coffee don't taste good, but the coffee owes all of its taste to them. And coffee only tastes good as long as the dregs stay at the bottom. The same is true of thought. Its dregs are an unappetizing precipitate of blood, sweat, and exertion. And yet, all imagination, all cleverness, all the mental originality that *Homo sapiens* has ever come up with are in the dregs, and can only rise to the top thanks to the fact that they sank down at an earlier point in time. Thought has no bottom other than this paleontological one, no new model for which it may be exchanged. If it is disturbed, if it stops being the peaceful, reliable subground of thought, then thought itself is threatened in an unprecedented way. Nothing could be more superfluous than to add to the threat, and pride ourselves on presenting the scientific community with the greatest possible number of literary or aesthetic creations in a de-sedimented, deconstructed state, like trophy animals we have felled.

An entirely different stance is called for when it comes to the dregs of thought. I would like to call it "regard," with a by-no-means-unintentional side glance at the breadth of meaning this term has in the writings of Emmanuel Kant. Regard, for one thing, contains the idea of regarding, of paying careful and detailed attention to a thing. It also always means "respect." Not affection or love. Kant saw that clearly. The moral law that he wished to commend to humanity was much too strict, in his view, to be loved. The dregs of thought are certainly not lovable. This layer, as will be shown, is a dreadful brew—and nevertheless quite precious. Without it there is no such thing as humanity.

To the extent that thought is mired in this brew, we can scarcely imagine it in a way that is primitive enough; and yet "primitive thought activity" is exactly how Sigmund Freud defines dreams.[10] This notion is the starting point of this book. Anyone who wants to understand what thinking is must begin by trying to grasp what dreaming is. Nowhere does human thought appear in such a primitive form as in the dream— even now, in the twenty-first century. At the same time, dream life itself remains open to new influences. In the last century, all kinds of items from industrial culture were deposited there. Fundamentally, this has not changed a thing when it comes to the primitive nature of dreams; dreams in highly developed cultures are still incomparably more confused and less capable of dealing with reality than the waking life of even the most primitive peoples ever discovered. To this extent, dreams, even those of the contemporary era, achieve a dimension of antiquity that no ethnology has ever managed to reach. On the other hand, the most simple and prim- itive dream constructs of which we are aware are themselves, to a consid- erable extent, already cultural artifacts. The dreams that our most ancient mythology ascribes to kings, heroes, hoary forefathers, or gods are already early flowerings of human narrative art. And children, who have the privi- lege of having the tales of their earliest dreams attentively stored in memory, are already members of highly developed cultures. Our dreams may delve down to primitive antiquity, but never nearly so far that even a single one would take us back to the origin of humankind. They are, nevertheless, signposts to that origin. In the following pages, we will attempt to discover whether they are not also something more: failed attempts and ciphers that render it, to a certain extent, legible.

One of Freud's greatest discoveries was that the things we experience as dreams and are able to recover in conscious awareness are merely "manifest dream content"—a facade. What is decisive is what goes on behind the scenes, the inner life of the dream, which succeeds in surrounding itself with this facade. For Freud, a dream's inner life consists of two mechanisms. In a rather schoolmasterly way he calls them the dreams' "two foremen."[11] Their names are noteworthy: "condensa- tion" and "displacement." Yes, these two concepts were already mentioned above. They were slipped in incognito, as it were, to help understand the forces of distraction and concentration in the human species without which pebble tools and graves—in a word, culture—could hardly have come into existence. We note that these are concepts that stand at the very center of Freud's theory. If there was anything Freud was proud of, it was the discovery of condensation and displacement. To have crystallized them out as evidence of the so-called "primary process" of the psyche and distinguished them from the "secondary process" (which is nothing but a cover for the primary process and attempts to make it acceptable to the outside world) was high on the list of his life's accomplishments. "I believe this distinction represents our most profound insight yet into the nature of nervous energy."[12]

It is all the more astonishing how little Freud made of this insight. It revives when he is interested in finding better interpretations for the dreams of his patients, easier resolutions for their neuroses—generally everywhere that he is trying to understand the psychic "apparatus" from whose depths the symptoms emerge. But as soon as he looks beyond his patients and their individual prehistory and turns his attention to the prehistory of the species, when he engages in intensive ethnological studies and focuses on the so-called "savages or semi-savages" as "direct descendants and representatives" of earlier humans and thus as a "well-preserved picture of an early stage of our own development"; when he ultimately even takes the risk of tracing all taboos and cultural parameters back to the murder of a powerful father, whom the primal horde is said to have hung in an act of collective violence[13]—then his most profound insight is barely mentioned. There is a strange blind spot here. If it is true that dreams are primitive thought activity, then like it or not the foremen of the dream must also be the foremen of all human thought, indeed of culture as a whole. But Freud never managed the breakthrough to this logical conclusion, and on this score ethnopsychoanalysis is hardly less tentative than he was.

This was no oversight. We need only imagine for a moment that when Freud was writing *The Interpretation of Dreams* he had become aware of the broad implications of condensation and displacement as the creators of culture and thought, and had devoted himself unreservedly to the task that results from this insight. Psychoanalysis would have taken an entirely different turn. It would have become much more anthropology, cultural theory, and epistemology than it already was. And above all, Freud would have had to become a philosopher and almost entirely give up his profession as a physician, something for which he neither felt intellectually qualified nor was prepared to do, for the sake of his patients and himself. After all, his life and material existence depended on the analytical cure. There was no way for him to judge whether venturing into these more distant regions of fundamental philosophy would be of any use to his practical work with neurotics, or how far condensation and displacement would actually take him. His most profound insight into the essence of nervous energy was too great a challenge and threatened the treatment he had founded. In this way, his most profound insight is also the biggest intellectual obligation that he assumed and that he left to posterity. Obligations are claims. Whether or not you are capable of satisfying them, they demand satisfaction. And the obligation we are talking about here becomes all the weightier, the further high technology's mental archaeology advances. Who is supposed to raise its profoundly deep workings up into the realm of collective consciousness? Who will defend the dregs of thought against their de-sedimentation, if not a psychoanalysis that has spilled over its boundaries toward philosophy, or a philosophy that has an inner ear for psychoanalysis?

The person who decides to take on this challenge should, however, be prepared for the reproach that he is engaging in mere speculation. But what do we mean by *mere*? It is time to rehabilitate speculation. Ordinarily, nowadays, what is meant by the word is nothing but a specific form of unsupported conjecture—the winner of the next soccer game, or the future of the stock market or real-estate prices. Speculators are thought of as people who make a profit from these uncertainties: traders, profiteers, big shots. But actually, literally, *speculator* means "a person who looks, a scout, an investigator." *Speculari* means "to catch sight of something that is not openly visible." Thus it can also mean to espy, or spy, and also to research. The ideal of the speculator is the detective who, with the aid of a few clues, draws an absolutely certain conclusion about what has actually occurred. Ordinarily, the conclusions we draw have only a certain degree of plausibility and are obviously not immune to errors, but this doesn't mean that everything that is merely deduced is automatically dubious. Many things that cannot be analyzed in the laboratory or on the dissecting table nevertheless do not behave otherwise than deductive thinking predicts. Every court of law that draws conclusions based on the evidence is acting speculatively. Without a confession on which to base its verdict, it can nevertheless convict the guilty party beyond the shadow of a doubt.

Paleontology would have nothing to do if it didn't constantly attach entire chains of conclusions to its rare finds. The regard for the dregs of thought that we wish to develop here does not even have any physical finds with which to bolster its arguments. It must learn to treat ancient texts as its finds, as the remains of much more ancient things that the texts themselves don't mention. This would be a hopeless undertaking if the bottom layer of thought did not also have a certain inner dynamic; we could call it the instinctive logic of the nervous system. It will prove to be our partner in the speculation that is about to unfold here, and will occasionally make certain connections so inescapable that we may say, even if the facts to which we have access don't suffice on their own as proof, that as far as human judgment can discern it simply cannot be any other way.

The way to the underground of thought will be traversed in three steps. The first leads into the center of the dream. Whoever dives into it and allows himself to be borne along by its internal logic will arrive at the prehistoric era in which the dream was not confined to sleep, when even during waking hours there was no other form of thought. To track it down, a second step is required—a step downward, to the particular life of the drives from which it emerged. The point at which dreams became specifically human is the animalistic nadir and midpoint of the entire inquiry. From it follows the third step: laying bare the drive dimension in the creation of words, and showing how word and dream interpenetrate. The dream "speaks," and language also "dreams."

This structure results in the following three chapters: "Dreams," "Drives," and "Words." At the entrance, unmistakably, as if waiting for us, stands Freud. He is, so to speak, the Virgil of this book. But he will lead where he does not wish to go.

CHAPTER ONE

Dreams

THE MENTAL AND THE PHYSICAL

PEOPLE ARE SITTING SOCIABLY around a fireplace. At the feet of the gentleman of the house, a hunting dog lies comfortably stretched out, sleeping. Suddenly it gives a muffled bark. "He is dreaming," says the gentleman. "That is his hunting voice." And the assembled guests begin to fantasize about what the dog might be "hunting." A deer or a fox? We will never know. The dog cannot formulate in words whatever it was that made him bark in his sleep. But of that highly developed mammal's dream there are not only external signs; we have proof from the neuroscience laboratory. It was first proven for human beings in 1953. Aserinsky and Kleitman found that during normal nighttime sleep, every ninety minutes or so, there appear short phases of heightened brain activity accompanied by rapid eye movements (REM). Most of the experimental subjects who were awakened during a so-called REM phase confirmed that they had just been dreaming. With this, it seemed clear: REM states are dream states.[1] And since REM phases have also been shown to exist in sleeping dogs, cats, and other mammals, the conclusion seemed inescapable: they also dream.

Soon, science came up with the causes. Deep in the brain stem, in the so-called pons region that forms a bridge between the spinal cord and the base of the scull, they discovered a formation of nerve cells that releases a chemical messenger called acetylcholine. It initiates the REM phases. But it has also been shown to activate certain higher regions of the brain. Evidently it excites them so they produce images. For when its effect has ended, after a few minutes, the dream also ends. The subject sleeps dreamlessly until the next REM phase is reached. This provided a simple physiological explanation for the entire activity of dreaming. Dreams are biorhythmically produced, the result of a kind of neural chance generator in the cerebellum that at regular intervals stimulates the cerebrum to produce more or less confused images. They make no sense. There is nothing about them either to understand or to interpret.

Naturally, that was overly hasty. Not everyone who was awakened from REM sleep, as it turned out, was able to recount a dream. On the other hand, there were others who experienced dreams outside REM phases. People were even found who, due to damage to the pons, were incapable of REM sleep but still had dreams. Others had a completely intact pons area but dreamed nothing at all. In their cerebral cortex, above the eye sockets, a particular nerve bundle had been damaged that ordinarily conducts impulses from the midbrain to the higher parts of the brain and that can always be seen to be particularly active when the organism is "appetitive," that is, full of desire for external objects that are meant to relieve the inner tension of its needs. This pathway for wishes also proves to be constitutive of dreams. The same is no less true of the "occipital-temporal-parietal" transition region just behind the ears, in the cerebral cortex. It plays an essential role both in the conversion of concrete perception into abstract thought and in the retention of concrete perception as abstract thought. If it is injured, human dreaming is also damaged beyond repair.

Obviously, dreaming is a very complex process that is brought about not only by the cerebellum but to at least the same extent by the cerebrum. It is not merely, as the REM scientists believed, the confused form of appearance of a cyclical, diffuse stimulation, but is to no lesser extent a process of wishing, thinking, and remembering. All these enter into a synthesis in the dream. Neuropsychology is always only capable of identifying sites in the brain that are particularly active when this synthesis is occurring; it can never say *how* it came about. For that, there is no other way to approach the dream than from the inside, from the perspective of proprioception, and to describe the "work" that its production has cost. In this process, one cannot escape Freud's interpretation of dreams. REM science seemed to have rendered it obsolete, but now, to the contrary, the new neurophysiology has given it a new basis.[2]

At the same time, we have to relate Freud's interpretation to the new discoveries. Here, the example of the dreaming dog is helpful. It shows that dreaming is not exclusively human. To grasp what is specifically human about dreaming, we first need to concern ourselves with its animal basis. In one respect, Freud did just that. His *Interpretation of Dreams* has a whole section on "The Somatic Sources of Dreams."[3] In it, he distinguishes between "somatic stimuli derived from the interior of the body," like thirst, digestive disturbances, and sexual tension, and "objective sensory stimulation" that comes from outside: cold, heat, smells, sounds, and so on. Freud treated the somatic stimuli with the greatest possible circumspection, even with a certain resistance; after all, he was surrounded by scientists who believed they could causally derive the entire life of dreams from them, as if dreams were always direct copies and symbolizations of physical and nervous stimuli. This led to some bizarre claims. "The human body as a whole is pictured by the dream imagination as a house and the separate organs of the body [as] parts of the house. In 'dreams with a dental stimulus,' an entrance hall with a high, vaulted roof corresponds to the oral cavity and a staircase to the descent from the throat to the esophagus."[4] Precisely the insistence that a strict causality reigns between somatic stimuli and mental states leads to the most arbitrary associations. Thus, the philosopher Johannes Volkelt, attempting to found a strict science of dreams, came up with the following: "Thus the breathing lung will be symbolically represented by a blazing furnace, with flames roaring with a sound like the passage of air; the heart will be represented by hollow boxes, or baskets, the bladder by round, bag-shaped objects or, more generally, by hollow ones."[5] And the other leading theoreticians of the dream who emerged in the final years of the nineteenth century—Karl Scherner, Ludwig von Strümpell, or Wilhelm Wundt—are not all that different. They present themselves as conscientiously methodological adherents of causality, but when it comes to reducing complex dream structures to simple bodily stimuli, they succumb to an interpretive arbitrariness that rivals that of shamans.

Freud has no difficulty indicting them for thoroughgoing failure to recognize that dream construction is independent of bodily stimuli. But does he not make things a bit *too* easy, with this independence? It is only relative, after all. Sometimes he forgets this. Then, for example, he even goes so far as to claim that *"dreams are not somatic but psychic phenomena."*[6] Here, the "somatic sources of the dream" are wrongly denied. The so-called "psychic" is treated as an independent substance—mortal, admittedly, and inhabiting a body; dependent on the metabolism and nervous activity of the former, influenced and constrained, but nevertheless viewed philosophically as a separate being with its own laws, an *ens per se*, or being in itself. Here, Freud almost indulges in metaphysics. But it is by no means necessary to think of the soul as something substantive in order to ensure its independence. It is enough to perceive it as the achievement of a specific balance that exists in higher organisms. Balance is something extremely amazing; it is never fully comprehensible or deducible. Namely, it is not simply an effect of physical causes but consists in the trick of bringing bodily organs, in opposition to their own gravity, into a higher, quasi-floating relationship with each other. Little children accomplish something like this when they learn to stand or walk. Tightrope walkers turn it into a virtuoso performance.

Just as there are motor achievements involved in maintaining a state of balance, there are achievements in sensory balance as well. Here, somatic stimuli and nervous stimuli emerge from the everyday process of their natural discharge and are gradually brought into the coordinated, floating state that we then call "mental experience." Here too it is true: the balance, at best, can be described in general terms, but *how* it is made possible and becomes reality is something we cannot explain. If it is practiced frequently enough, however, it becomes so habitual that it seems quite automatic, as if it were the achievement of a special mental substance. Western metaphysics was completely taken in by this appearance. From Plato to Hegel, the soul, at least the soul endowed with reason, the so-called spiritual soul (*Geistseele*), is seen as something grounded in itself and is consequently assumed to have its own essence. This is what is known as "hypostatization." It is true that balance is something admirably self-regulating and never fully deducible from the things being balanced; hence the soul, or psyche, as a balancing act of the soul, is something qualitatively different from the body. On the other hand, this balance is nothing other than a particular relationship between what is being balanced. In other words, the soul is merely a special aggregate condition of the physical.

Why, in *Homo sapiens*, this aggregate condition has moreover assumed the specific quality that we call "mental" will become clear in the course of this chapter. For now, I would merely like to point out that the "psychic" does not constitute a separate domain. Psychoanalysts who want to reserve it for themselves and would like to limit neuroscientists to expertise about the "physical" are merely promoting the old hypostatization of the soul with new means. Why are they afraid of the insight that the "mental" itself is nothing but the achievement of balance? They ought to recall that the founder of their discipline was himself a neurologist—a neurologist, admittedly, who gradually became convinced of the inadequacy of neurology but who, after all, was not a simple convert. Freud the psychoanalyst never stopped being a neurologist. Thus, he also never overcame a certain vacillation. When he was describing psychoanalysis in contrast to theology, he always presented himself as a tough natural scientist with no illusions. When he was contrasting it to neurology, he became a decipherer of images and symbols—with a certain susceptibility to core elements of philosophical idealism. The vacillation was not only his personal problem. It is part of psychoanalysis itself; after all, psychoanalysis is nothing but neurology that has outgrown itself. All attempts to tie it firmly to one side or the other, as if it were "really" a hermeneutics that occasionally misunderstood itself as natural science, or "really" a clinical practice that occasionally wandered off into cultural theory, are diminutions based on a logic of identity—exactly like all the efforts to identify the soul as either clearly bodily or clearly nonbodily.

This way lies siege mentality. Neither psychoanalysis nor neuroscience is free of it. Recent efforts to overcome it are all the more welcome.[7] The moves toward reconciliation of the two disciplines are not path-breaking or pioneering acts, however; they are nothing but an overdue reflection on the origins of psychoanalysis—its emergence from neurology. With this development, however, the origin of dreams in "somatic sources" is once again at issue. As was indicated above, it must be taken somewhat more seriously than Freud took it. Where should dreams have come from, initially, when they began to form in more highly developed organisms, if not from the somatic? What, other than somatic stimuli, makes dogs dream? At first, an animal level of dreaming must have been generated from somatic sources. Only then can dream life go its own ways and balance itself out into a complex, floating structure; only then does the individual dream not derive directly from bodily sensations; only then does Freud's critique of his contemporaries' dream research hit its target. And bodily and nervous stimuli never become entirely irrelevant to dreaming. Freud himself was the best example of how effective the animal base level is, even in highly cultivated human beings.

"For instance, there is a dream that I can produce in myself often as I like—experimentally, as it were. If I eat anchovies or olives or any other highly salted food in the evening, I develop thirst in the night which wakes me up. But my waking is preceded by a dream; and this [dream] always has the same content, namely, that I am drinking. I dream I am swallowing down water in great gulps, and it has the delicious taste that nothing can equal but a cool drink when one is parched with thirst. Then I wake up and have to have a real drink."[8] Here, two physical needs have come into conflict: thirst and sleep. But sleep, Freud says,

> is a state in which I want to know nothing of the external world.
> . . . I put myself to sleep by withdrawing from the external world
> and keeping its stimuli away from me. . . . So when I go to
> asleep, I say to the external world: "Leave me in peace: I want to
> go to sleep." On the contrary, children say: " 'I'm not going to
> sleep yet; I'm not tired, and I want to have some more
> experiences. . . ." Our relation to the world, into which we have
> come so unwillingly, seems to involve our not being able to
> tolerate it uninterruptedly. Thus from time to time we withdraw
> into the premundane state, into existence in the womb. At any
> rate, we arrange conditions for ourselves very like what they
> were then: warm, dark, and free from stimuli. Some of us roll
> ourselves up into a tight package and, so as to sleep, take up a
> posture much as it was in the womb. . . . If this is what sleep is,
> dreams cannot possibly form part of its program. . . . There
> ought to be no mental activity in sleep; if it begins to stir, we
> have not succeeded in establishing the fetal state of rest: we
> have not been able entirely to avoid residues of mental activity.
> Dreaming would consist in these residues.[9]

Actually, all Freud is trying to do in this remarkable passage is to make dreams comprehensible as an "intermediate state between sleeping and waking."[10] In the process, he provides an almost mystical version of sleep. He takes the fetal position as an image, accidentally cloaks the prebirth position it resembles in a little metaphysical hyperbole by calling it "premundane," and then says, of this preworld, that it is a place to which no one is able to return after birth but that we nevertheless intend whenever we go to sleep. In this way, the preworld is transformed into a kind of vanishing point of sleep. But then Freud's characteristic sobriety returns. He uses three simple adjectives to characterize the preworld: "warm, dark, and free from stimuli." That an organism likes warmth makes good sense. But why dark and free from stimuli? Lack of stimuli is simply uninteresting, in other words, sleep is deadly boring. And yet we long for it. The need for sleep is paradoxical. How can freedom from stimuli be something we long for? How can it be a stimulus for us?

Obviously, stimuli do not only attract; they also require effort. They are attractive—but only to the extent that they can be worked through, that the organism is in a position to turn them into relaxation. In other words, the organism doesn't enjoy the stimulus as such but rather its discharge. It "makes thirst enjoyable," as a famous beer advertisement says. As soon as the nervous system is no longer in a position to discharge the stimulus, that stimulus becomes a burden. The nerves don't hold up indefinitely under the stress of interesting things. It is too tiring. To this extent, sleep is a state of resignation—but it is its own special kind of relaxation. Not the one that the waking nervous system intends, but merely a substitute for it, which results when the nerves are not strong enough to discharge tensions on their own. But the substitute shows what the discharge aims for: the blissful relaxation that would be felt if all stimuli were to be absorbed.

Seen in this way, sleep is the interpreter of the waking state; naturally, only for a waking consciousness. Consciousness learns to understand itself better when it understands what sleep is after. Not for nothing is it halfway between death and blissfulness. Depending on the circumstances, it can mean one or the other, or both. As a resting state, it represents the goal of all longing and wishing. But it only represents it; it isn't it. Its relaxation lacks something. It lacks the satisfaction of the successful discharge of stimuli. The sleeper commits no sins. But he also doesn't enjoy anything. We cannot enjoy sleep as such but only remnants of the waking state *in* sleep—that is, certain dreams, or the feeling of refreshment we have after deep sleep, not sleep itself. Strictly speaking, we cannot even experience sleep. We experience *something* during sleep when we dream, but not sleep itself. Sleep as anesthetic or as a continuous state, for example in a coma, resembles death. A healthy body doesn't stand sleep for very long. It wants to experience something.

The paradox of sleep gives a first hint of the paradox of drives. To desire something or to be eager for something means to want the complete discharge of tension; only it would offer complete satisfaction. But at the same time the desiring person also wants to experience this state, to enjoy it. But this is an absurdity. As long as an organism is alive, the release of tension is never complete, for life *is* tension. Even during sleep, the release of tension is not complete. Breathing, circulation, digestion, and the working through of tensions are significantly reduced, but they don't cease. Thus, sleep demonstrates what it is that the organism attempts to achieve but doesn't succeed in achieving. It is rest without the spice of experience, and to this extent it is not happiness, no matter how much an unhappy person may long for this rest. In sleep, where the organic discharge of tension comes closest to its perfection, it is not experienced; where it is experienced, it is far from perfection. Imperfection is part of happiness. Perfect happiness, or, theologically speaking, eternal bliss, mystical union, is like squaring the circle. That it is impossible doesn't trouble the life of the drives, which still desire it. For purely physiological reasons, humanity is therefore incapable of getting rid of theology. The paradox of sleep shows precisely this. On one hand, it is far ahead of the waking state: a cipher for what the waking state longs for. On the other hand, it lags hopelessly behind: the state of the most profound resignation.

Dreams are caught in the middle of this paradox. Sleep is never wholly sleep. Withdrawal from the waking state never succeeds completely. However much the discharge of tension may be reduced, it doesn't stop entirely. This is why dreams exist. They are remnants of the waking state during sleep—a kind of tribute to the waking state. The more vigorously we dream at night, the worse we sleep. From this, people had always concluded that dreams disturb sleep, until Freud discovered that the exact opposite is true. Dreams impose themselves whenever sleep is threatened with interruption at a moment when the nervous system is not sufficiently recovered. "*Dreams are the guardians of sleep and not its disturbers.*"[11]

Freud's own thirst dream is a perfect example of this. His sleep is disturbed by thirst. The dream of drinking is the attempt to get rid of the disturbance. Only when it has failed does the sleeper wake up and go get a drink. We cannot exclude the possibility that the dog barking softly in its sleep is experiencing something similar. A feeling of thirst or hunger or an external noise threatens to disturb its sleep. This leads to an association—however vague—with food or prey, which causes the bark, and thus ensures that Fido goes on sleeping. It is not coincidental that the simple thirst dream, which most obviously derives from a somatic stimulus, serves Freud as the occasion for one of his most fundamental and consequential definitions of dreams: "If I can succeed in appeasing my thirst by *dreaming* that I am drinking, then I need not wake up in order to quench it. This, then, it is a dream of convenience."[12] Finally, he comes to this bold conclusion: "All dreams are in a sense dreams of convenience."[13] There is only one question he doesn't ask himself: how is it even possible that an organism is able to acquire this kind of convenience for itself? How can thirst, during sleep, lead to the perception that the person is drinking something?

Only through repetition. The organism must have felt thirst countless times and then have drunk something. More than this: it must gradually have formed a firm association between the two things—thirst and drinking. In other words, it must have been in a position to retain the repetition. But how could it do that? Repetition seems to be the most self-evident thing in the world. But it is one of life's greatest mysteries. For now, let us note just this much: Repetition retained is repetition that has become intelligent; it is memory.[14] But memory is one of the wonders of the world. It has no separate organ in the brain; it is not a container or storage space into which we put contents. Memory is an elementary neural achievement involving millions or billions of nerve cells working associatively, in other words, as an assembly. That individual nerves react singly and in isolation without involving other nerves is something that practically never happens. Links are constantly being made between single cells and entire cellular regions, by means of vertiginously complex chains of neurochemical reactions. It may be merely metaphorical, but it is not inappropriate and hence is a general habitus among neurologists to call these chain reactions "pathways" and "networks." The elementary neural function—discharging stimuli so the organism isn't tormented by them—takes place along these pathways.

Obviously, organisms, as a consequence of their gravity, have an inertia that is not only physical but also, to a certain extent, physiological. They have a tendency to repeat things that have succeeded in the past and to take the path of least resistance. This is also true of nerve cells. They know nothing of the pathways they are creating in the nervous system, but they are the elements out of which the pathways are created. And once a pathway has been established, it is easier to establish it the next time. Because the discharge of stimuli is so bothersome and uncomfortable, it tends to follow the path of least resistance. Neurobiologists call this tendency "process memory."[15] In other words, in the beginning, memory is nothing but a procedure: establishing pathways through the nervous system, extending, solidifying, networking them, and thus providing the organism with a certain repertoire of behaviors. Animals too must gradually establish the ways they respond to threats, heat, cold, thirst, hunger, flora and fauna, and so on. This gradual establishment is memory in the making. It is made through repetition, and repetition is never undertaken voluntarily. Organisms only go along with it to the extent that they are forced to do so. But that they go along with it means, at the same time, that they make it as easy as possible for themselves. The repetition follows a path that has already been established; it lies down in a bed that is already made. Inertia, repetition, and memory form an elementary unit. Indeed, memory itself is initially nothing but the injection of convenience into an inconvenient situation.

The memory work of the brain is not only associative in the purely neurological sense that nerve cells form assemblies and whole networks of traffic systems; memory is also experienced associatively. Initially, this is just as primitive as behaviorism says it is. If a dog has had its food served often enough together with the ring of a certain bell, it will associate the sound of the bell with the food. It takes the sound for food. By reacting to the sound with the same activation of the salivary glands with which it reacts to food, it lets us know that for it sound = food. This equivalency is memory. It is more or less the same with thirst. Thirst wants to be stilled. In other words, thirst = drinking. To be thirsty is equivalent to seeking the shortest route to the next spring. This poses no difficulty for an organism that has done this innumerable times before—unless the usual spring is unavailable. It is also true that drinking stills thirst. The equivalency is created in order for it to be taken away.

Memory emerges in order that its causes may disappear—and with them the memory itself.

This primary intention of memory is vividly illustrated in Freud's thirst dream. The dream is only possible if thirst and its association with drinking have become such a firm part of his memory that it occurs even in sleep. The thirst is real. But the organism reacts by stilling it in its imagination. What has been done often enough in fact is replaced by an imagined action. The organism repeats it but in a way that is more convenient for it. The dreamer has the experience of drinking without having to get up. The imaginary stilling of his thirst takes place for the sake of his rest, so he can continue sleeping, and this makes the elementary function of memory clear: it is, first of all, a sedative. The imaginary discharge of the stimulus can't replace its real discharge; sooner or later the thirsty person will wake up, after all. But the fact that the imagination is able to do this for a limited time shows that, for an organism that is capable of dreaming, the imaginary satisfaction of a need is not just fake[16]: it is also satisfaction by means of the imagination.

With this, the organism demonstrates a remarkable transformation that memory is able to carry out: from procedural (or process) to declarative memory, in other words, from repetition to retrieval. Repetition is not confined to redoing or reexperiencing things the organism previously did or experienced. It can also occur in such a manner that it retrieves something from the past—naturally not in the immediate sense, for the past is past, but rather by making it visually, acoustically, or linguistically present. True, the retrieval that makes things present to memory is always imaginary, yet it is only through this imagination that we know about things that are past. Only in this way is the past, is history, present. As something *merely* past, it would have disappeared without leaving a trace, it would not even be namable; in a certain sense it would not even be past—hence, not dreamable, either. Only where the work of memory is translation in a completely literal sense—that is, as translation from repetition to retrieval—can bodily stimuli be transformed into the images we find in dreams. Dreams are on the borderline. On one hand, they repeat: I reiterate the experience of getting up and getting myself a drink. On the other, they merely retrieve: after all, I am merely dreaming what I have always done, getting up and drinking. On one hand, the satisfaction of the drive is merely imaginary. On another, it is more: it is hallucinatory.

HALLUCINATION

Hallucinations are familiar to us only as pathological phenomena—as "perceptions without corresponding stimuli from without."[17] All our sense organs can be affected by them, but most of the time they consist in hearing voices and seeing figures that no one else observes and for which there are no evident causes in the vicinity of the affected person. Similar things can occasionally be experienced under the influence of intoxication or extreme fatigue. In such cases, the energies we normally use to process stimuli are weakened, and this encourages the emergence of states of perception that escape supervision by the waking consciousness. In the case of schizophrenia, they frequently even ignore it. "The *impression of reality* made by hallucinations usually leaves nothing to be desired. What the patients see and hear is unassailable reality for them, and when hallucinations and reality contradict each other they mostly conceive what is real to us as unreal. It is of no avail to try to convince the patient, by his own observation, that there is no one in the next room talking to him; his reply is that the talkers just went out or are in the walls or speak through invisible apparatus."[18]

Hallucinations are borderline states. It is as if they had gotten stuck somewhere in the process of transition from perception to imagination. They are no longer the one and not yet the other, and thus, once again, they are also both. It is difficult to say whether the perception is being distorted *into* imagination or distorted *by means of* imagination. In any case, the force is lacking to separate perception and imagination. To this extent, even very modern hallucinations are primitive states. From the perspective of the theory of memory, they retain, within themselves, the transition from repetition to retrieval. This is the archaic era during which memory began to be specifically human. Its first foray into the sphere of retrieval, of representation, is hallucinatory. It is here that the specific activity begins that the Germans call *Einbildung*. Today this word is used almost entirely in its colloquial senses of "fiction" or "conceit." But in the eighteenth and nineteenth centuries, *Einbildung* still had the literal sense of its word roots *ein* ("in") and *Bild* ("image")—in other words, the process of creating an interior image of exterior circumstances and events. For Kant, the *Einbildungskraft* ("imagination," in the literal sense in which English also retains the same roots) was one of the elementary powers of thought.[19] Carl Gustav Jochmann understood all of human cultivation

(German *Bildung*) as the result of *Einbildung*.[20] It is very enlightening to consider this literalism, as long as we don't forget that this "imagining" is no different from walking or talking, insofar as it must first be learned, and with considerable effort. The first attempts are inevitably awkward, confused, and diffuse, still inwardly and outwardly incapable of keeping representation separate from the thing that is being represented. In this first phase, imagination is hallucination, is "primitive thought activity"[21] in its most primitive stage. The obverse is also true. At this stage, all thought was hallucinatory; there was no other kind. Hallucination is thought's first form, the ancestor of all waking consciousness, all reason.

We contemporary humans have enormous difficulty accepting this because we cannot experience hallucinations without having them collide with a waking consciousness that reflects reality. Schizophrenics don't just hallucinate, either. They labor under the impossibility of reconciling their hallucinations with waking consciousness. And if their hallucinations don't collide with their own waking consciousness, they collide all the more with those of their fellow humans, doctors and guardians, who have no desire to share their obsessive ideas. Even in cases where their own or other people's waking consciousness is unable to beat back the hallucination, waking consciousness cannot be unthought. The hallucinations are seen through its lens and communicated in its language. That there were periods in which all thought was hallucinatory, in which hallucinations constituted the mental norm—it would be difficult to make this situation plausible if there were not a remnant of hallucination that we all experience: dreams. Normally, hallucination has no chance when it is confronted with an intact waking consciousness. But in sleep, it comes alive. Dreams, it is true, are merely hallucination's remainder, are what rise up and are permitted when our wakefulness is in remission. They are not hallucination's authentic primal state in human history. But this remainder allows us to guess at what hallucinations originally were: protective techniques. They open up a space for imagination and, with it, an imaginary interior space in which the human being is not entirely at the mercy of the stimuli assailing him or her from outside. It becomes possible to start bringing these stimuli under control by imagining them—transporting their image inside this space. Imagination, in this process, does two things: it displaces external stimuli to the inside, and in the process it condenses them. That is, it doesn't "copy" them but condenses them into tightly concentrated, significant impressions.

Here, the two concepts come into play that for Freud contain the whole "secret of dreams": displacement and condensation. They are the "foremen" of dreamwork. And dreaming, for Freud, *is* work. We don't dream merely for our pleasure but in order to get rid of something. Dreaming is thoroughly effortful, even it if prevents something that is even more strenuous, namely sleeplessness. True, at first Freud does not seriously associate his thirst dream with work. Everything seems to be right on the surface. It goes like clockwork; he can produce the dream experimentally. No attention is paid to the fact that organisms have had to engage in extremely hard neural labor before they became capable of even the most primitive dreams. And yet, one can only be awed by the artistry of the thirst dream. A person manages to stay asleep for quite some time, despite his thirst, by imagining what he would otherwise be doing: getting up and going to get a drink of water. He places this action inside an interior experience and does not at all experience exactly the same thing as he would if he were actually to get up. In imagination, the individual phases of the action—rolling over, pushing the sheet aside, letting your feet glide down to the floor—are telescoped, as the course of the action is condensed into a more or less clear "going to get a drink of water."

Freud gave marvelous examples of condensation elsewhere. Often, in a dream, different people are combined into a single person. "A composite figure of this kind may look like A perhaps, but he may be dressed like B, may do something that we remember C doing, and at the same time we may know that he is D."[22] Or we dream apparently senseless words, which nevertheless are revealed to be quite significant combinations of other words: the word "Autodidasker" turns out to be a blend of the words *author* and *autodidact* with the name Lasker,[23] and so on. There is also the famous Freudian slip in which " 'facts came to *Vorschwein* [a nonexistent word, instead of *Vorschein* (light)]. . . .' In reply to inquiries he [the speaker] confirmed the fact that he had thought these occurrences ' *Schweinereien*' ['disgusting,' literally 'piggish'production]."[24] This is a perfect example of condensation and also shows that it is an essential spice of jokes. But in his own thirst dream, it does not attract Freud's attention. That not even this simple dream could have occurred without the reciprocal collapse of displacement and condensation into a single experience escapes him. For him, the thirst dream is simply banal. The dream only becomes interesting to him where it goes beyond its simple basic form and not only openly reveals what he wants but begins to conceal it, to disguise itself and speak in riddles; where the content of the dream becomes a facade behind which something else lurks. Only then does Freud speak of displacement and condensation, call them the two foremen of the dream, and track down their work the way a detective would. What he understands by dreamwork is only the work that takes place *in* the dream. But dreamwork is first of all the work *leading up to* the dream. In order for displacement and condensation to act as foremen within the dream, they must already have been active, namely as pathbreakers in the direction of the dream, without which there wouldn't be one. This preliminary work does not attract Freud's attention. He doesn't ask about the conditions of possibility of the dream; what interests him is what happens in the dream itself. Let us observe him for a moment as he interprets one of his favorite dream examples.

"A lady who, though she was still young, had been married for many years had the following dream: She was at the theater with her husband. One side of the stalls was completely empty. Her husband told her that Elise L. and her fiancé had wanted to go too, but had only been able to get bad seats, three for 1 florin 50 kreuzers—and of course they could not take those. She thought it would not really have done any harm if they had."[25] What does this dream mean? The patient doesn't know, nor does Freud. His theory, however, is: She knows it, after all, but doesn't have access to this knowledge. He, the analyst, can open the way to what she cannot reach only by posing pointed, persistent, patient questions. What occurs to you in connection with this dream? She has to give an account of this, first in general, then in all the details. He is betting on the fact that the dream will reveal itself through a process that is similar to the dream: association. My dreams undoubtedly occur in me. But is it I who have them? Don't they, rather, come to me? Shouldn't we say "it dreamed in me," rather than "I dreamed"? Something similar takes place in the case of my ideas. It is not so much that I have them as that they come to me. *Something* occurs to me.

Ideas cannot be completely regulated. They have their own stubborn ways, which means two things. For one thing, they are contrary, that is, they come when it suits them, not me. For another, they have their own sense, their own logic, over which I do not have complete control, even though this logic is taking place inside me. For Freud, this contrary/ uncontrollable element in waking consciousness parallels the contrariness of dreams. If, afterward, when the dreamer is awake, he freely associates with the dream and manages both to remain strictly focused on the details of the dream and to allow in everything that occurs to him in this context, then he will, more or less automatically, go back down the path that the composition of the dream has taken. The things that occur to the dreamer unwrap the cocoon of the dream. And, sure enough, here come the ideas. Well, on the day before the dream, the woman who dreamed it learned of Elise L.'s engagement. The previous week she went to the theater with her husband, ordered their tickets in advance, paid an additional charge, and then had to observe that the hall was half empty, whereupon her husband teased her for being in too much of a hurry. The analyst proceeds to ask about additional details. Where do the 1 florin 50 kreuzers come from? Also from the previous day. Her husband gave his sister 150 florins, for which the sister immediately bought a piece of jewelry. The three? It occurs to her that Elise L. is three months younger than she is.

More ideas are not forthcoming, but those he has are enough for Freud to set the puppets dancing. First, he sees the confirmation of one of his ground rules: no dream without the remains of the day. By this he understands an event from the previous day. It can be utterly trivial, but it gives the person who experiences it more to work on than she at first realizes. The experience is carried over into sleep, but unprocessed, as a potential sleep disrupter. In the present case, there are two remains of the day: Elise L.'s engagement and the 150 florins that the sister-in-law immediately turned into a piece of jewelry. And since, for the patient, these remains of the day suggest more than mere information, they are joined by additional things: the visit to the theater a week before, an additional number (three), and illogical statements like "of course they could not take those" and "it would not really have done any harm if they had."

What Freud accomplishes in the interpretation is to sniff out the common source of irritation from the dream that has been recounted and the associations that come with it. In the dream we are considering, it is hidden inside the times that are mentioned. Elise L. and her fiancé had also wanted to go but came too late; there were only "bad seats" left. But, as the context soon makes clear, Elise L. and her late ticket purchase are only the other side of what is actually at issue. The dreamer has been unable to wait. Just like her sister-in-law, who immediately had to spend the gift of 150 florins on a piece of jewelry, she has been in too much of a hurry and wasted the extra charge for the theater tickets. In reproaching her for her hastiness, her husband has not suspected how right he is. She has married too soon—him. She has taken a "bad seat," one for 1.50 florins, one-hundredth of what her sister-in-law has thoughtlessly squandered. The hundredth is also a reversal; it stands for a hundred times. It would have been a hundred times better to wait: the result would have been a husband who was a hundred times better.

The dream that was told is the "manifest dream content." But behind it there lies a concealed motif; in Freud's terminology it is the "latent dream thought."[26] In the present instance, it is crystallized in the phrase "too much of a hurry." The dreamer herself cannot permit herself to have this thought. It would threaten her entire life situation. But it plagues her. And the information that Elise L., who is only three months younger than she, has gotten engaged, touches precisely this sore point. When she is awake it doesn't come up. But in sleep, when the waking consciousness drifts downward toward zero, it springs to life. This does not mean that it is able to unfold freely. Even in sleep, there is still sufficient control that it can only appear in a censored form that is made unrecognizable. "Dream censorship" makes sure of that.[27]

It too belongs to Freud's great discoveries. Waking consciousness ordinarily does not even notice that it is constantly censoring its thoughts. But it can only think logically to the extent that it denies itself all illogical and unsuitable thoughts. No logic is free of censorship. But censorship is not only logic. It is "custom" in a radical sense of the word: the totality of the rules that are inscribed in a nervous system in the course of acquiring the habits of society. These kinds of basic rules were originally laid down in the form of prohibitions. The biblical Ten Commandments show that quite clearly. That you should "Honor thy father and thy mother" means that you should *not* injure, insult, or behave rudely toward them. To "Remember the Sabbath day, to keep it holy" means not to do anything ordinary or banal that could desecrate it. "I am the Lord thy God" means "Thou shalt have no other gods before me." And the other Commandments are already formulated as prohibitions: make no graven images, do not kill, commit adultery, steal, or bear false witness against your neighbor.[28]

There is another famous example from antiquity in which the prohibition has effectively become second nature to an individual. Socrates, as Plato describes him, talks about an inner voice that he thinks he has heard from "my early childhood" in certain situations in which there is a decision to be made. He calls it *daimonion* (resembling a god), "a sort of voice which comes to me, and when it comes it always dissuades me from what I am proposing to do, and never urges me on."[29] What speaks to Socrates there—audibly or inaudibly—is naturally his own voice. All the same, he experiences it as a higher authority that objects when he is on the point of doing something unconsidered. It is his reason, so to speak, but not in the form of Logos, that is, unfolded into well-considered thoughts and argumentative speech, but folded into an intuition that does not cease having its impact even in situations where there is no time for calm consideration. The *daimonion* is the perfect example of a censoring authority.

Censorship is custom that sits deeper than any waking reflection. Even in sleep, it is still on the lookout. It does, however, have a specific historical index. The censoring power of the Ten Commandments has become much weaker. Only the prohibitions against murder and theft are still strictly binding. In today's neoliberal context, the ritualistic rules that the Christian West once impressed upon its members, as decisive for their salvation, no longer form part of the hard core of culture. Instead, other rules have been inscribed, for example: You must always be fit, reachable, and flexible. The new rules can become the hard core of censorship without ever having been officially promulgated. Whenever the wish appears to spend a few days without one's cell phone and Internet connection, the neoliberal *daimonion* advises against it.

The censorship is imposed by the individual herself. But at the same time it is also the form in which a particular society is present in the individual. This was true even for Socrates. The authority that censored him was not actually Athens, and yet Athens was present within it—somewhat like the negative of a photograph. Inner, personal censorship, by the way, resembles external, political censorship to this extent: as long as it functions perfectly, it goes completely unnoticed. It becomes noticeable only when it is infringed upon. The sleeping state is an excellent example of this. There, the control of waking consciousness is loosened to the point where forbidden thoughts arise. But enough control remains that these

YBP Library Services

TURCKE, CHRISTOPH.

PHILOSOPHY OF DREAMS; TRANS. BY SUSAN H.
GILLESPIE.

Cloth   273 P.

NEW HAVEN: YALE UNIVERSITY PRESS, 2013

AUTH: ACADEMY OF FINE ARTS, LEIPZIG. TRANS. FROM
GERMAN. ON THE ORIGINS OF CULTURE, ETC.
LCCN 2013-15739
  ISBN 0300188404   **Library PO#** FIRM ORDERS

		List	30.00	USD
8395 NATIONAL UNIVERSITY LIBRAR	**Disc**	14.0%		
App. Date 5/07/14 HUMANITIES 8214-08	**Net**	25.80	USD	

SUBJ: 1. DREAMS--PHIL. 2. DREAMS--PSYCH. ASPECTS.
3. DREAM INTERPRETATION.
AWD/REV: 2013 COYB
CLASS BF1078   DEWEY# 154.63   LEVEL ADV-AC

YBP Library Services

TURCKE, CHRISTOPH.

PHILOSOPHY OF DREAMS; TRANS. BY SUSAN H.
GILLESPIE.

Cloth   273 P.

NEW HAVEN: YALE UNIVERSITY PRESS, 2013

AUTH: ACADEMY OF FINE ARTS, LEIPZIG. TRANS. FROM
GERMAN. ON THE ORIGINS OF CULTURE, ETC.
  LCCN 2013-15739
  ISBN 0300188404   **Library PO#** FIRM ORDERS

		List	30.00	USD
8395 NATIONAL UNIVERSITY LIBRAR	**Disc**	14.0%		
App. Date 5/07/14 HUMANITIES 8214-08	**Net**	25.80	USD	

SUBJ: 1. DREAMS--PHIL. 2. DREAMS--PSYCH. ASPECTS.
3. DREAM INTERPRETATION.
AWD/REV: 2013 COYB
CLASS BF1078   DEWEY# 154.63   LEVEL ADV-AC

thoughts are able to make themselves felt only in roundabout ways and in masked form. The masked appearance of forbidden thoughts—this is the manifest dream content, the experience of dreaming that the dreamer subsequently attempts to grasp in words but that often remains unclear to him, as something strange, a riddle. All this is quite proper, says Freud. The two foremen, condensation and displacement, make sure of this by composing the riddle.

The dream of the theater tickets can be viewed as a single great condensation. Disparate events are gathered together in a single scene and thus rendered unrecognizable: the visit to the theater, the news of Elise L.'s engagement, the gift to the sister-in-law. The combination of events does not occur haphazardly but targets a site of irritation; this is exactly what happened in the thirst dream. Except that there, the site was easy to identify, as the thirst that needed to be stilled. In the theater-ticket dream, on the other hand, it is coded. It is the over-hastiness that plagues the dreaming woman and that she cannot bring herself to admit. Condensation, in other words, has something of the quality of a constellation, whose elements are grouped around a center to which, as a group, they refer without focusing on any single object. Instead, every reference simultaneously disguises the center it points toward. This is not only condensation aiming at a center but also displacement pointing away from it. Displacement and condensation never work independently of each other. They are only two sides of the same game of hide-and-seek, during which the same things are simultaneously blurted out and kept secret. Blurted out, to the extent that they are expressed in manifest dream content, but kept secret by their disguise. What is actually meant is shifted, diverted onto something unimportant; for example, the wedding is diverted to the visit to the theater, the unsatisfying husband to the unoccupied seats in the stalls, the dowry squandered too early to the 1.50 florins. But the unoccupied seats could also stand for "unmarried," the 1.50 florins for the inadequate husband whom the dowry has gotten in exchange. Precisely because displacement always also implies condensation, the individual elements of a dream can be cathected[30] with a number of meanings.

If there is a regular method of interpreting dreams that we can identify, it consists in the patient search for commonality within a heterogeneous variety. In principle, this process is no different from that of a child who learns to interpret roses, carnations, orchids, and so on as flowers. That process is not exactly obvious, either. Roses and violets don't declare that they are flowers. Starting from the species, the child must deduce the genus, so to speak. For this, he needs a pinch of intuition. But the intuition required by the interpreter of dreams is more complicated. Like a detective, he must follow clues that lead through a tangled mass of dream elements and associations. The outcome of this sleuthing is neither a genus as it relates to species, nor a higher concept as it relates to lower ones; it is not even clear that it will always take a conceptual or comprehensible form. Freud did decide to call it "latent dream thought," but early on, before he became attached to this formula, he occasionally spoke more cautiously of "latent dream content."[31] We should be *even more* cautious and speak of the latent commonality as a motif. At first, it is nothing but the site of an irritation, radiating stimuli. The images and associations that it throws out seem to flicker; they are like tongues of fire licking at and through each other. This is what makes the manifest dream content so confused and full of gaps, with some things turning up two or three times and others missing altogether.

Dreams are not entirely lacking in rules, but the rules they contain are less strict than the rules of conceptual logic. If individual dream elements can mean different things—empty seats, for example, standing for both "unmarried" and "over-hasty"—then there is also more than one defensible interpretation. "Correct" and "incorrect" are far less unambiguous than they would be in a logical chain of propositions and conclusions. On one hand, this makes the interpretation of dreams especially difficult. It has many fewer secure points of reference than the interpretation of texts. The interpretation of dreams has much greater latitude—and a bigger margin of error. Even when the process tries to be methodically stringent, it remains relatively loose. The other side of this is that the interpretation of dreams is particularly difficult to evaluate. Is it reading into the dream something that the dream doesn't really contain? Is it leaving out or failing to incorporate something that cries out for interpretation? Are there a number of equally plausible interpretations? For all this, there are no clear-cut criteria. Moreover, some patients develop a sense for what the analyst wants to hear; they produce what Freud called *Gefälligkeitsträume*—"dreams that attempt to please." The analyst who fails to see through this, who overlooks his own emotional involvement in the patient's history and the fact that the hours spent in analysis are, above all, an event that takes place between the patient and the psycho-analyst, is likely to go wildly astray in dream analysis.[32]

Thus, the interpretation of dreams is highly susceptible to error, diffi-cult, and easy to misuse. Whether Freud's own attempts always hit their mark—as he worked to distill the driving, clarifying motif from within the mass of stimulation that is the dream—does not concern us here. But only because he did not avoid the risk of error and actually practiced regular dream interpretation was he able to gain access to the particular mental space of dreams. The interpretation may have remained dubious in every single case, but only stubbornly persistent interpretation was able to demonstrate that dreamwork is mental work. According to Kant, it is never possible, in the case of an individual act, to be absolutely sure that it is moral—but this does not alter the fact of the existence of morality.[33] The same is true here. It is impossible ever to be sure that an individual dream is comprehensively interpreted "correctly." But this does not alter the fact that there is a specific dream logic. Certainly there is also a layer of the dream underneath this logic, where the dream is so tangled and fleeting that nothing distinct can be derived from it. But as soon as dreams have reached the level of intensity where they have become images that their dreamer is able to recount—images that move, irritate, or stimulate ideas in him, without being completely trans-parent—they display the basic characteristics of primitive thought activity: a manifest content, and behind it a latent motif that an inner censor wants to conceal, along with certain powers of translation that reveal it, never-theless, in a form that is mashed together, abbreviated, masked, and distorted.

Since Freud's discovery of this fundamental structure of dream logic, no serious engagement with dreams can fail to take it into account. This applies even in the case of one of Freud's dreams that is very famous but that is said to fall outside the Freudian coordinates. The chemist August Kekulé, by his own admission, owed his greatest scientific achievement, the discovery of the benzene ring, to a dream. "During my visit to in Ghent, in Belgium, I stayed in an elegant bachelor apart-ment on the main street. . . . There I sat, and tried to write my textbook, but it wasn't going well; my mind was on other things. I turned the chair toward the stove and fell into a half-sleep. The atoms, once again, were cavorting before my eyes." This had happened to him once before, when, on his way home from intensive professional conversations about chemistry, he had fallen into "a dreamlike state." "My mental eye, sharpened by repeated images of a similar sort, now distinguished larger images of diverse forms. Long rows, often more compactly joined together. Everything in motion, twisting and turning like a snake. And look, what was that? One of the snakes grabbed its own tail and the image spun mockingly before my eyes. I awoke as if struck by lightning; this time, as well, I spent the rest of the night working out the consequences of the hypothesis."[34]

We don't learn very much—neither how the image of the snake that grabbed its tail was able to waken the dreamer and become his "hypothesis," nor what the "other things" were that occupied the scientist's mind as he sank into "half-sleep," nor what effect the gaze into the stove might have had on him. There is no graspable remainder of the day, no urgent latent motif, no evident censor, but instead a dream image that was already in circulation in ancient Egypt—the Ouroboros, the mythical serpent biting its own tail. With this, for Carl Gustav Jung, everything became clear: one of the eternal symbols that lies buried in the deepest strata of every human soul revealed itself to the scientist in his dream and pointed the way forward. "Thus Kekulé's vision of the dancing couples, which first put him on the track of the structure of certain carbon compounds, namely the benzene ring, was surely a vision of the coniunctio, the mating that had preoccupied the minds of the alchemists for seventeen centuries. It was precisely this image that had always lured the mind of the investigator away from the problem of chemistry and back to the ancient myth of the royal or divine marriage; but in Kekulé's vision it reached its chemical goal in the end, thus rendering the greatest imaginable service both to our understanding of organic compounds and to the subsequent unprecedented advances in synthetic chemistry."[35]

The Freudian psychologist Alexander Mitscherlich was not prepared to accept this kind of mysticism. He proposed an alternative interpretation that begins with Kekulé's "bachelor apartment" and the confession that he had faithfully followed the advice of his respected teacher Liebig: "If you want to become a chemist . . ., you must ruin your health; a person who doesn't ruin his health by studying, nowadays, gets nowhere in chemistry."[36] This leads the Freudian to the following interpretation:

Why shouldn't we, as the most powerful motivation, take into account the great deprivation of sexuality and love of a man in his best years, as the impulse for the image of the serpent that "mockingly" presents itself to him? However tempting it must have been for Kekulé . . . to give in to pleasure, as desire and fantasy suggested to him . . ., such wishes were equally forbidden. To ruin your health—the orders from the powerful father specified that you were supposed to do this, not in dangerous liaisons, but in the service of a personified and beatified science. When he feels the desire to stray from the path of virtue, the dreamer jumps back as if on the brink of an abyss, and denies his night-time hopes of a love feast. . . . A warning, an alarm, that said: Wake up, work, don't believe in wraiths, only work can give you satisfaction! . . . The fact that the symbol of coupling, the serpent, appears is due to the sexual exigency of the researcher, not the still undiscovered structure of benzene. That the image of the serpent that bites its own tail can also be read as a benzene ring is pure chance.[37]

All this, once again, sounds quite familiar, in a Freudian way. We have a latent motif and a censor; the lack of remains of the day hardly matters. But, with a wave of the hand, one of the decisive Freudian determinants of dreams has been eliminated—that it is primitive thought activity. There is no need to argue that young August Kekulé's drives must previously have been so distorted by prohibitions and renunciations that it was possible to attach them to chemical structures in the way that others can only attach them to manifestly sexual objects. Even if we don't know what "other things" were going through his mind, he had not gotten as far with his textbook as he wished. He took this frustration with him into his half-sleep. There, it attached itself to a latent motif of a related kind, namely the wish to understand the benzene ring, and in his half-sleep something relaxed—the censor. Here, true, we must define "censor" more broadly, in a way that includes more than just sexual morality. If the censor, as defined above, is the totality of the rules to which a partic- ular nervous system has become habituated in the course of its social training, then elementary scientific standards are naturally part of it. What Thomas Kuhn called a "paradigm" is an excellent example of mental censorship. When Copernicus questioned the Ptolemaic worldview, with the earth at its center, he touched on an elementary instance of censorship within Western culture, on which the psychic economy of an entire society relied. This is why Copernicus, Galileo, and Bruno were so unendurable. And, on a lesser scale, less dramatically, it was evidently part of the paradigm of nineteenth-century chemistry that benzene had the form of a chain.

When someone who takes a powerful but unsatisfied scientific drive to bed with him, not only is sexual morality loosened; the scientific paradigm also softens, and in this state, for Kekulé, the brooding that continued as he was falling asleep—perhaps encouraged by a flickering coal stove—transformed itself into an image that, as a waking chemist, he did not accept. Only the dreamer could interpret it. Only he could suddenly see clearly that his dream image prefigured a possibility that was not envisioned by the scientific paradigm, and that he immediately set about transforming into reality. To what extent his dream image may also have had a sexual basis, perhaps because it showed him his stunted libido, or whether it forbade him to grasp his "tail,"[38] it is hard to say. It would have been necessary to ask him. In any case, the Freudian coordinates do not in the least require us to reduce Kekulé's dream to a crude sexual scenario and ignore its meaning for the understanding of productive imagination.

SYMBOL AND ALLEGORY

If we emphasize the primitive thought activity, then, when we look at dreams, a thoroughly philosophical foundation appears almost spontaneously. In the concept pair "manifest"-"latent" the old distinction between appearance and essence lives on, as it has persisted since Plato. It says: We can only perceive the world the way it appears to us. But appearances are always only an exterior—appearances of something that itself does not appear. In philosophy, then, this hidden element within appearances, which can only be grasped speculatively (that is, in thought), and not by means of the senses is called "essence," "substance," or "the thing in itself." The latent motif in dreams can also only be approached by means of thoughts. Whether the latent motifs are "essences," in the strict philosophical sense of the term, will be explored later; but what is essential about dreams, their source or core, is beyond doubt.

Given that he has strayed into philosophical territory, Freud is speaking in terms that are strikingly metaphorical. The scene he sketches resembles an illegal border crossing. Here you have a shady fellow named Motif who wants to steal across the border. The customs officer or censor does not allow him to pass, but two foremen, who are actually more magicians or touts than serious workers, provide him with a disguise that will allow him to slip through customs. Naturally, there are no actual munchkins sitting around in his interior mental space, spying and playing tricks on each other. Their names are metaphors—but for what? For what the nerves do, that is, for quite specific accomplishments. In their case, neuroscience not only cannot say how they function, it cannot even localize them in the brain. Neuroscience works with different parameters. Motor and sensory functions, feelings, perceptions, memory, language—for these it is able to identify the dominant brain region. But condensation, displacement, censorship are orthogonal to all of these; they participate in all these parameters and are identical to none. They are synthetic achievements of the nerves, more precisely: moments of a single action of the nerves, called synthesis. Without such synthesis, there is no thought, not even the primitive thought of dreams.

In dreams, what happens is not like a factory with a division of labor, where various functions work together. Rather, there is a plot underway in which the four participants merely serve as different aspects of a single participant. Displacement is nothing but another aspect of condensation, condensation another aspect of displacement. The censor acts as an agent that opposes both these forces; it neither displaces not condenses but rather controls—yet it is only the control that makes for something being displaced or condensed. Thus, we can't say that condensation and displacement are working at the instigation of some shady motif, we must say that they are both working just as much at the instigation of the censor. As the wish whose disguise they tailor is *their* wish, the censor is also *their* censor. They can only work against it because they are saturated with it. In the work of the foremen, the censor works against itself. It becomes reflexive. The riddles of the dream are acts of the dreaming organism outsmarting itself. What it is unable to express it expresses, nonetheless, in disguised form. This process of working with and against each other, with the multiple tensions that are located within the synthetic action of the nerves, evidently cannot be approached except through metaphors. But as long as we remain conscious of the fact that they don't clear up the mystery of this neural accomplishment, but only concretize it, there is no objection to using them, with caution.

The use of metaphors, in this case, is congenial to the topic. After all, primitive thought activity is an image-creating process. In the "brief interpretation of dreams" that Freud presents in his lectures, he places special emphasis on this. After the description of condensation and displacement, he writes: "The third achievement of the dreamwork is psychologically the most interesting. It consists in transforming thoughts into visual images." Freud notes parenthetically that not everything that is a thought becomes an image in the dream, and that visual images are not the only ones that are possible. We can also dream voices, smells, tastes, and touches, and to this extent we can also have "images" of them. But visual images "nevertheless . . . comprise the essence of the formation of dreams."[39] We already encountered a prominent example of this. "I was in too much of a hurry," in the dream of the theater tickets, turned into a half-empty hall or "bad seats." Other examples: "The dreamer *was pulling a lady* (a particular one, of his acquaintance) *out from behind a bed.* He himself found the meaning of this dream element from the first idea that occurred to him. It meant that he was giving this lady preference." The idea of preference, here, is based on a verbal pun—the German noun for preference, *Vorzug*, is related to the verb *vorziehen*, meaning "to prefer or pull out." "Another man dreamt that *his brother was in a box* [*Kasten*]. In his first response '*Kasten*' was replaced by '*Shrank*' [cupboard], and the second gave the interpretation." The German word for "armoire," *Shrank*, is related to the verb *einschränken*, which means to restrict: "His brother was restricting himself." Or: "The dreamer *climbed to the top of a mountain, which commended an unusually extensive view.*" But the first thought that occurred to him was not related to his mountain climbing. Rather, he thought of the fact that one of his acquaintances was the editor of a newsletter called *Rundschau*, a word that in German means "survey" or "view"—literally "looking all around." (The syllable *view*, with its visual association, is also retained in English *review*.) The review published by the dreamer's acquaintance dealt with links to distant parts of the world.[40]

The workings of the dreams that are reported here in such a lapidary fashion do not astonish us nearly as much as they should. Artists draw on all their powers of concentration, all their gifts and skills, to translate a subject into an image, and it may take them weeks or months to complete it. During sleep, something similar happens as if all by itself. In the wink of an eye, as it were, words are translated into images that might never have occurred to the dreamer when awake. Without knowing how she does it, the dreamer produces a translation that is both primitive and original. There is only one drawback: It cannot be carried across from sleep to the waking state, and it cannot be elevated to the status of "art."[41] The translation is original only when motivated by a state of elementary need, an acute drive to form an image. According to Freud, it is only *thoughts* that harbor this drive, and only forbidden ones at that. In the dream, they start into motion—so away with them, to the next best hiding place. The act of translation that is accomplished in this way is a makeshift cover-up: the movement is more one of flight than of artistic creation. Still, we cannot comprehend how displacement and condensation can manage this with such speed. It costs effort to be constantly looking around for suitable hiding places, and thus it is a relief when there are familiar ones to be found right nearby, which offer an easy way out. First, diffuse dream images are spontaneously generated, and some of them become codified and elaborated through repetition. Among the self-evident things that a culture generates, along with a web of rituals and customs, is an arsenal of familiar images that offer the dreaming organism reliable places of refuge and make the game of hide-and-seek that is dreamwork more comfortable and convenient: dream symbols.

Early on, in his studies of hysteria, Freud came up with a concept of the symbol that could almost be described as physiological, as he learned to read the specific images assumed by colds, vomiting, paralysis, or neuralgia. For example, there is the patient who recounted how her husband said something that she found deeply hurtful: "She then suddenly grasped her cheek, crying aloud with pain, and said: 'That was like a slap in the face.'"[42] In this case, the patient herself had come up with the link between her recurring attacks of facial neuralgia and the hurt that was their basis. But ordinarily the physical symptom does not reveal the cause to which it is a response. It is a symbol, in the sense that it is an image of something else and directly steps in for it. It covers over the thing that is imitated, expressing it only reluctantly and in a mediated way—by attempting to suppress it to the point where it becomes unrecognizable.

In the same way that specific illnesses develop within a given cultural context, becoming the preferred places for traumatic pain to flee to, there is also, according to Freud, a stock of hallucinated images in which painful thoughts take preferential refuge. But where, in the case of hysterical neuralgia, the idea was to understand the symptom as an image, here the key is to understand the images as symptoms. And when certain dream images keep cropping up and troubling different individuals, although they have absolutely no idea what these images mean, then the physician is obliged, according to Freud, to jump in and "interpret these 'mute' dream elements ourselves." And lo and behold: "In this way we obtain constant translations for a number of dream elements. ... A constant relation of this kind between a dream element and its translation is described by us as a 'symbolic' one, and the dream element itself as a 'symbol' of the unconscious dream thought."[43]

"Symbolism is perhaps the most remarkable chapter of the theory of dreams," Freud adds. At any rate, it proves to be the most dubious, as soon as the stock of symbols is examined. "The range of things which are given symbolic representation in dreams is not wide: the human body as a whole, the parents, children, brothers and sisters, birth, death, nakedness—and something else besides."[44] And this "something else" is the key to everything. It is the sexual symbols. Freud provides the long list, which even today has not stopped growing. The male genitals can be symbolized by all long, upright, sharp, and intrusive objects, such as sticks, umbrellas, knives, pistols; the female genitals by everything hollow, including cavities, grottos, trunks, or rooms; coitus by riding, flying, stair climbing, mountains, and so on.[45]

There is nothing that has contributed more to Freud's fame than the sexual symbols. In the vulgar reception of psychoanalysis, they are precisely what he didn't want—jokers that can be played wherever someone doesn't know what to say next or needs a quick, uncomplicated worldview. Freud neither denied that there are other dream symbols, nor failed to demand the greatest possible caution in interpreting the sexual ones. They are only allowable as "a supplement,"[46] when the patient's work on the associations that he himself brings to his dreams stalls. But wherever Freud's wide-reaching theoretical and therapeutic work begins, it gravitates, as if by magnetic attraction, to the sexual symbols. For him, they are symbols par excellence. He insists on their contextual dependence, and yet nevertheless he calls them "stable translations."[47] But for whom are they stable? First of all, for Freud himself. His own life and family milieu seemed constantly to reaffirm them. And without a doubt, upper-class bourgeois Vienna around 1900, as so vividly described by Stefan Zweig in *The World of Yesterday*,[48] was a virtual biotope for the flourishing of the very type of neuroses whose treatment coincided with the birth of psychoanalysis. Freud, it is true, thought far beyond his native Vienna. He called the entire world of myths and fairy tales, popular culture, maxims, and jokes as witnesses for his vocabulary of symbols. But his examples are far too selective to be extrapolated to all of humankind. Almost all the jokes, sayings, and popular turns of phrase that he cites as evidence come from central Europe. That the symbolic content of the Polynesian or African rites and myths he cites in his ethnological studies should follow exactly the same translational logic that was common in the Viennese biotope around 1900 is something that, in Freud, never rises above the status of a claim.[49]

With the formulation "stable translations," Freud named not so much a proven set of facts as a personal fixation. Above all, one thing is not certain—that "sexual symbol" always has to mean "symbol for sexuality." It can just as well stand for the opposite, for sexuality as a symbol of something else. Even a cursory look at Greek mythology, with which Freud had been familiar since his school days, provides relevant examples. When Hesiod tells us that Cronos castrated his father, Uranus, he is not referring symbolically to a sexual practice but describing it in a completely straightforward way, so that it, as a onetime event, also provides the narrative condensation of a historical process that is hardly recoverable in its details: long-lasting tribal feuds in which a Cronos tribe or clan was victorious over a Uranus tribe or clan; or the Cronos cult defeated the Uranus cult and probably did many more things to the vanquished than just castrating them.[50] The love affairs that Zeus had with Metis, Themis, Eurynome, Demeter, Leto, Hera, Semele, Alkmene, and so on[51] are not just expressions of sexual relations under early patriarchy but echoes of the thoroughgoing, region-wide victory of patriarchal tribes over matriarchally organized tribes around the Mediterranean— whereby Zeus's occasional rapes probably represent relatively gentle images of the way in which the Zeus tribes attacked the old mother gods. The myth of the sacrifice of Iphigenia before the Trojan War undoubtedly contains a narrative condensation of the archaic custom of offering the divine protector a virgin before setting off to war.[52] To see, in this ritual sacrifice, nothing but a sexual symbol—for example for the ritual deflowering of which there is evidence throughout the Mediterranean region—would not occur to anyone but a few overdetermined Freudians. Whereas ritual deflowering during a sacrificial celebration makes quite good sense when it is understood as a symbol for an archaic ritual, long since taboo, in which virginal blood also flowed, just a lot more of it, and the virgin ceased being a virgin in a different sense, namely by being slaughtered.[53]

Just as we must get used to the double meaning of the term "sexual symbol," we also have to ask ourselves whether what Freud understands by a dream symbol deserves to be called a symbol at all. Freud's renegade crown prince, Carl Jung, had asked that question once, when the master's tendency to reduce everything to sexual symbols began to make Jung uncomfortable. This couldn't be all there was! Had Freud possibly gotten stuck on something relatively superficial, namely the kind of symbols that were only makeshift disguises, symptoms, signs for something else? Had he failed to dig down to the deep level of symbolism? This is the suspicion lurking at the source of Jung's own theory of symbols. "For instance, the old custom of handing over a sod of turf at the sale of a piece of land might be described as 'symbolic' in the vulgar use of the word; but actually it is purely semiotic in character. The piece of turf is a *sign*, or token, representing the whole estate. ... Every view which interprets the symbolic expression as an analogous or abbreviated expression of a known thing is *semiotic*." Signs are always mere external substitutes and covers for something internal, which is separate from them. In the symbol, this internal thing itself speaks. It finds its way to its optimal revelation. "Every psychic product, in so far as it is the best possible expression at the moment for a fact as yet unknown or only relatively known, may be regarded as a symbol, provided also that we are prepared to accept the expression as designating something that is only divined and not yet clearly conscious." Genuine symbols do not disguise anything. "A symbol is alive only in so far as it is pregnant with meaning. But, if its meaning is born out of it, i.e., if that expression has been found which expresses the sought, expected, or divined thing still better than the hitherto accepted symbol, then the symbol is *dead*." Except that, for Jung, symbols that die like this, or sink down to the level of signs, are not genuine symbols at all. The genuine ones—for example the cross, the mandala, the serpent that bites its tail, or the Hero—are immortal, pregnant with meaning, inexhaustibly giving birth to meaning, and do not cease representing "the inexpressible in an *unsurpassable way*."[54] Real symbols, for Jung, are not external indications of neediness and lack but manifestations of profundity and fullness. So he builds a psychic underground garage for them, which spreads out underneath all individual development and which eternally and unchangingly contains the archetypical basic characteristics of human beings. In his terminology, it is called the "collective unconscious." The primal symbols arise from it. There are some symbols that no one can invent or construct, but that erupt in ever unchanging form, unpredictably and without any motive, from inexpressibly unconscious depths. They don't stand for anything, they represent nothing, and they are indistinguishable from the psychic primal ground that rises up in them. The symbol and the thing that is symbolized glide over into each other, to the point where they become indistinguishable.

What Jungians, however, generally fail to recognize is this: if the symbol turns into the thing itself, then it is no longer a symbol. In the end, Jung's supposed deepening of the theory of symbols is essentially the fire sale of symbolism. Freud was well advised not to follow him there. Without saying it explicitly, Freud keeps the primary meaning of "symbol" alive. The Greek *symbolon* is actually a shard. It was the custom, when a friendship was ritually confirmed, to break a small clay tablet into two parts. Each of the two friends took one piece along on his life's journey, and when the friends, or their descendants, met again, the clay tablet could be reconstructed by fitting the two broken edges together, thus affirming the friendship. The primary layer of meaning of *symbolon* thus includes both the break and the wish for an unbroken union. When Freud began to read hysterical paralyses and neuralgias as "memory symbols," he perceived them as psychic fragments. In the process, he had a particular kind of symbolization in mind, namely the transformation of ideas into visual images. To understand the logic of this process, we may start by imagining a female figure that adorns the portals of innumerable churches and town halls. She stands with a sword in her right hand and a scale in her left and with a blindfold covering her eyes. For the person who doesn't happen to know that she goes by the name of Justice and embodies a certain concept of righteousness, she will remain a mystery.

But the moment her identity is explained to him, the mystery is solved: Justice punishes the unjust (sword), but only after carefully weighing both sides (scales), in a way that is free of corruption and favoritism (blindfold). What the concept says, the image says again, differently—in a different medium. It lends the concept a sensual force that the concept does not have by itself, but it doesn't actually broaden its meaning. On the contrary, it is only understandable for the person who is already in possession of the concept.

"Justice" is the classic case of an allegory. Goethe, whom Freud valued so greatly, says, "Allegory transforms the phenomenon into a concept, the concept into an image, but in such a fashion that the concept should always remain limited and complete, to have and to hold in the image, and expressible in it." In other words, Goethe considers allegory to be a conceptual art—and thus the lesser form of visual representation. It lacks a fully developed imagistic sense of its own. For him, it is less a special case of symbolism than its fire sale. Art is supposed to be symbolic, not allegorical, dedicated to ideas, not concepts. "Symbolism transforms what appears into an idea, the idea into an image, in such a fashion that the idea in the image always remains infinitely effective and unreachable; and, though it be expressed in all languages, remains inexpressible."[55] For Goethe, the idea has a much higher status than the concept. It is the common vanishing point toward which concepts and sensuality converge, the still unnamed element in both of them—something that is yet to appear, something nameless, whether in a joyful, fearsome, or uncanny sense. If a rose symbolizes beauty; a laurel wreath, fame; a lion, strength or fright; a painted landscape, peaceful or raging nature; a portrait of a human face, torment or compassion—the words are merely approximations. They all signify something that words don't manage to reach: the idea. Symbols don't cover up ideas. The symbol is quasi transparent; it allows the idea to shine through, thanks to its quality as an image. For this, the symbol needs no conceptual leg up. Its own image content is what reveals the idea, allows it to be present, in effect—but as something remote, as the "unique phenomenon of a distance, however close it may be,"[56] to cite Walter Benjamin's famous definition of the "aura," which reads like a variation on Goethe's "idea."

Freud's dream symbols are not like these. They have the character of allegory. We may rate allegory higher then Goethe and Weimar Classicism did; we may grant it its own kind of expressivity, as a kind of puzzle or sign of decline, as Benjamin did, in particular.[57] But this doesn't change one fact: Allegories are derivative. The concept or thought is already there and is then reinserted into the image. It is coded in the image, and only if you know the key, the code, can you unlock it. Dreams are also derivative. The organism, in sleep, falls far below the achievements of waking thought. In the dream, says Freud, it is like "replacing a political leading article in a newspaper [by] a series of illustrations," as if we were "thrown back from alphabetic writing to picture writing."[58] With abstract words, we can occasionally draw on a concretely imagined content that has faded in them. For example, we can see in the German word *besitzen* (to possess), the act of a real body sitting (*sitzend*) on it.[59] But what is to be done with words whose image content is near zero, for example with "past" and "future," or with abstract relationships like "because," "therefore," "although," "but," "insofar?" What about "yes" and "no?" In dreams, it is if they have all been boiled down, reduced to a formless, fermenting mass that is only more challenging for their interpreter.

It is well known that images are subject to one fundamental limitation. They can only exist in the positive "yes" mode. Hence the huge irritation when René Magritte painted a pipe and under it the sentence *Ceci n'est pas une pipe* (this is not a pipe).[60] The tricky thing is that this sentence itself is part of the painting, not merely its title. So is it the *image* of a sentence? Or a *real* sentence, which says, "This is not a pipe; it is only a painting of one?" Or does it simply demonstrate that an image that denies its own existence is a monstrosity? Naturally, Magritte did not overcome the image's inability to negate itself, but all the same his unfathomable play on "yes" and "no" showed that images can make this incapacity vivid as their own lack, and can indicate that they actually want to say "no" to themselves. With this, he found an artistic form for an internal image-conflict that continues to surface, in acute form, in dream images. Often, these images are especially emotional and intrusive—a sure sign of the fact that a stormy "yes" or "no" is announcing itself in them.

Dream images are less able than external images to be purely neutral in what they say. Recall Freud's patient who, in his dream, saw his brother as a box and immediately interpreted the box as a cupboard and the cupboard as an image that meant "self-restricting." It is quite likely that the dreamer was wishing for something: either that the brother should hold back (or be less demanding of him, the dreamer) or that the brother should *not* hold back (for example just accept everything his wife did). Thus, every image in a dream can mean either "this is how it is," or "this is how it is, but I don't want it to be this way," or "it is not like this, but this is what I wish for." The dream cannot clearly distinguish between what is and what ought to be.[61] And here, Freud's great talent is to keep on asking and poking persistently at the elements of the dream, holding them up for comparison, experimentally and under contradictory assumptions, until they finally fit together and release a latent thought. For him, this was obviously also an intellectual pleasure of the first order.

A special role is accorded to reversibility. It not only occurs between affirmation and denial but characterizes dreamwork as a whole. "We find in dreams reversals of situation. . . . Quite often in dreams it is the hare that shoots the sportsman. Or again we find a reversal in the order of events, . . . like a theatrical production by a third-rate touring company, in which the hero falls down dead and the shot that killed him is not fired in the wings till afterwards. . . . Or there are dreams where the whole order of the elements is reversed, so that to make sense in interpreting it we must take the last one first and the first one last."[62] For Freud, the reason why all this is such an inalienable part of dreams is that, in his view, dreaming as a whole is a movement of reversal. The dreamer turns back—back to a primitive state that, in his waking state, he has left far behind him. "The dreamwork thus submits thoughts to a *regressive* treatment and undoes their development."[63]

With this, the allegorical aspect of dreams is very strongly foregrounded. Freud looks at dream images primarily in terms of the extent to which they are submerged thoughts. Can they then also be the opposite—wishes rising up? One should not criticize Freud for this—after all, he himself is the pioneer in expressing this insight. Or has anyone else worried more perspicaciously about the hidden movements of wishes that emerge in sleep, to find their fulfillment in a hallucinatory image? Doesn't *The Interpretation of Dreams* bet everything on showing that all dreams are wish fulfillment—even anxiety dreams?[64]

But here we must be very careful. *The Interpretation of Dreams*, which consistently portrays the human being as "the animal that wishes,"[65] always focuses on a specific kind of wishing, namely on wishes that, before they can appear, have always already been suppressed. These are not just emotions that are pressing for release but emotions that are already saturated with the knowledge that they are not supposed to exist. What is meant are primarily early childhood emotions, for example, incestuous desires for physical union with a person's closest relatives. In Freud's account, it is only by being forbidden that such a desire, in principle, becomes a wish, just as, in the biblical myth of the Fall, it was only the prohibition of eating from the tree of knowledge that awakened the wish to do so. Here Freud, the sober materialist, has inadvertently stumbled onto a figure of thought characteristic of philosophical idealism, namely, that the spirit constitutes nature. In our case, the thought generates the wish. It not only gives it its identity but becomes identical with it, in the state of being "unconscious." "Unconscious" does not mean only the sum of everything we don't know, whether because we haven't learned it or because we happen not to be thinking about it at the moment. Rather, the unconscious, in its specifically Freudian sense, is very much known, indeed known so intensely as to be a source of vexation. The technical term for this is "repression." It is knowledge in the state of denial, as a thought that has been repressed into a state of preawareness. A thought that has been repressed in this way, for Freud, is now nothing but a wish. This means that the reverse is also true. The unconscious wish always already has the form of a thought. In pulling off this sophisticated trick, turning thoughts into wishes and vice versa, Freud is practically Hegelian. No wonder his one-sidedly allegorical perspective on dreams never appears to him as a limitation. The wish that rises up to the status of a dream image, and the thought that sinks down to the status of a dream image seem to him to be one and the same thing. Hence the unquestioning talk of "latent dream thoughts."

That, in many cases, the structure of dreams functions allegorically is undoubtedly correct. But it cannot have begun allegorically. Before thoughts can sink down to the level of images, stimuli must first have created the images, and from these images, thoughts must have arisen.[66] And, in the long-ago era when the primitive, hallucinatory imaging process began whose remainder we experience in dreams, there was nothing except images. They were the miserable beginning of the activity of thought—as well as its highest point. The fleeting, flickering, blurred images that are generated at this level are not disguised thoughts but rather attempts to give some kind of shape to diffuse bursts of stimulation. To the extent that we can even speak of thought, it consists of nothing but this image shape itself. To the extent that it is pregnant with intellectual potential, that potential exists solely in the form of the image. But it has not yet been born; it is still far from being explicitly thought, far from being conceptual. In its primary stage, the generation of hallucinatory images cannot be regressive but must have been progressive—an embryonic form of what in Goethe is called "the symbolic." And only from here, from the point at which a wish rises up that is definitively not yet a thought that has sunk down, can we grasp the primary process of imagination—not from the relatively highly developed culture of allegorical dreaming.

REVERSAL

But it is not only the allegorical slant of Freud's concept of reversal that is so striking. His approach is also obscured by a lack of clarity that reaches to the very center of the theory of dream structure and requires us to do a bit of philological detail work. When Freud speaks of the foremen of dreams, he generally mentions two, and in the big chapter on dreamwork he treats them in a way that is nothing if not schoolmasterly: "A. The Work of Condensation,"[67] and "B. The Work of Displacement."[68] Then we are promised "two further determinants which exercise an undoubted influence on the choice of the material which is to find access to the dream."[69] But these two requirements do not constitute sections C and D. Only more than 160 pages later does Freud arrive "at last . . ., at the fourth of the factors involved in the construction of dreams."[70] This is "Secondary Revision," which we can skip over here. But by now Freud is already at letter I. What has become of the third element of dream structure? Freud does not devote only one section to it, as he does to the other three; it gets a whole half dozen. "C. The Means of Representation in Dreams. D. Considerations of Representability. E. Representation by Symbols in Dreams—Some Further Typical Dreams. F. Some Examples—Calculations and Speeches in Dreams. G. Absurd Dreams—Intellectual Activity in Dreams. H. Affects in Dreams." It is immediately obvious: these titles do not produce an ordered sequence of ideas. More-general and more-specific perspectives are mixed up together, and the third factor in the construction of dreams has almost disappeared. It only shows up in one of the titles: "Considerations of Representability."[71]

But is it even a separate factor? After all, what have condensation and displacement done, when they give a specific disguise to a latent motif that has to slip by the censor, other than to take its representability into consideration? In fact, Freud introduces this consideration, his third factor (or foreman), merely as a variant of the second one, displacement. "The displacements we have hitherto considered turned out to consist in the replacing of some one particular idea by another in some way closely associated with it. . . . We have not yet referred to any other sort of displacement. Analyses show us, however, that another sort exists and that it reveals itself in a change in the *verbal expression* of the thoughts concerned. In both cases there is a displacement along a chain of associations; but a process of such a kind can occur in various psychical spheres, and the outcome of the displacement may in one case be that one element is replaced by another, while the outcome in another case may be that a single element has its *verbal form* replaced by another," usually in the form of "a colorless and abstract expression in the dream thought being exchanged for a pictorial and concrete one."[72] This is supposed to characterize the "consideration of representability" and justify it as an independent third factor. But what has been described is nothing but another kind of displacement—one that exchanges the sphere of words for that of images, instead of simply replacing one image with another.

In the previous section, incidentally, Freud had written rather extensively about exchange, namely the expression of a wish or thought by means of its opposite, although this was examined under a different heading, namely reversal. The special interest Freud exhibits in this phenomenon also motivated him to add the following passage to a later edition of the work (1909): "Incidentally, reversal, or turning a thing into its opposite, is one of the means of representation most favored by the dreamwork and one which is capable of employment in the most diverse direction."[73] There can be no doubt: Reversal also shows "consideration of representability." But what is the status of reversal itself? Obviously it plays a central role. The linguistic exchange that replaces something abstract with something visual and concrete is nothing but a form of reversal: replacement, a dream's return to the primitive language of images. Yet Freud does not want to give reversal the status of a separate factor in the construction of dreams. Instead: "Considerations of Representability"—something completely nonspecific. The *whole* of dreamwork is beholden to this consideration. To list it, along with condensation and displacement, as a separate factor in dream construction is like putting dogs, cats, and mammals in the same category. "Consideration of Representability" is a stopgap solution, nothing but a cipher for something that has no status as a factor in the construction of dreams.

Perhaps the lectures, written fifteen years later as a cleaned-up, transparent, shorter version of *The Interpretation of Dreams*, can offer answers? At first glance, it seems so. Again, condensation and displacement are explained as *the* mechanisms of dreamwork, and then we read: "The third achievement of dreamwork is psychologically the most interesting. It consists in transforming thoughts into visual images."[74] But what is the third achievement? Is it comparable in importance to condensation and displacement? And is the construction of dream symbols, for which Freud previously reserved a separate chapter, part of this third achievement, or is it something distinctly different? Next, he discusses absurd dreams and how dreams deal with contradictions. In this connection, as in the more extensive *Interpretation of Dreams*, he points to reversal as an especially clever trick of dreamwork. Considering the emphasis he places on this, it should actually be considered a further, fourth achievement. All the more astonishing is his short summary of dreamwork: "The achievements I have enumerated exhaust its activity; it can do no more than condense, displace, represent visually and subject the whole to secondary revision."[75] There is no more talk of reversal. It has great relevance in Freud's interpretation of dreams, but somehow it doesn't have a proper place. It remains a cloudy, dark spot in a theory that aims for maximum transparency. It is well known that whenever Freud came across dark spots, he would become suspicious that they might conceal something important. Why shouldn't we learn from him and be similarly suspicious?

In the following, I shall express a general suspicion. My suspicion is that, taken together, condensation, displacement, and the dark spot contain a lot more than the secret of dream construction—namely, nothing less than the secret of the construction of thought and culture and of the development of humanity. To what extent we will be able to prove this remains to be seen. But we stand a chance of coming close only if the basic thesis of *The Interpretation of Dreams* is put to the test: that "*every* dream is the fulfillment of a wish,"[76] and nothing else. In the case of the thirst dream this is evident, and in sexual dreams it can be even crasser and more obvious. The dreamer has an orgasm, even physically, although he doesn't hold the person he is dreaming of in his arms. Here, the boundary between imaginary and real wish fulfillment becomes especially blurry. We might be tempted to say that if a wish is experienced as fulfilled, it makes no difference whether it is satisfied by real objects or imagined ones; what matters is the subjective experience. But there is no pure subjectivity. There is always *something* that is experienced, be it figures, colors, tones, atmospheres or smells, and so on. And we cannot experience something without thinking, at the moment of experiencing it, that it is real. Dreams are no different. To dream something is to experience it, at that moment, as real. It *is* like that. The dream doesn't want to be only a dream. Thence the disappointment when you wake up, are not holding the dreamed-of person in your arms, and are forced to admit that the dream may have been wish fulfillment but was only hallucinatory. Displaced from a real object onto an imagined one, the wish fulfillment was ersatz satisfaction. But you only know that after you wake up. The dreamer herself has no idea of ersatz. Only in the brief phases of "secondary revision,"[77] which interferes in a dream that is already underway and attempts to smooth and shape it in such a way as to conform to the censor, does the thought "it is only a dream, after all" sneak into the dream. These phases of dreams have been called "lucid dreams," because the dreamers clearly realize that they are dreaming. They could just as well be called "borderline dreams," because they are located on the border of wakefulness. Where the dream is in its element, however, its nature includes being experienced as *ens realissimum*.

A large number of simple, noncoded dreams can satisfactorily be understood as wish fulfillment. But what about all the dreams that are accompanied by unpleasant feelings, feelings of anxiety, embarrassment, or helplessness? Simple, says Freud. Here, the dream censor enters the picture. Children's dreams are largely free of censorship. But because their wishes are largely incompatible with culture—wishes to touch and taste excrement, incestuous wishes to possess the mother or father—they are forbidden and, in time, forbid themselves. But if these wishes pop up during sleep, according to Freud there are two possibilities: either they are so disguised that they can pass the censor, or they already censor and punish themselves at the moment of their expression, so that instead of pleasure, what is felt is anxiety. For example, we have the respected older woman who, in a dream accompanied by a powerful feeling of embarrassment, offers an officer corps a "service" that proves to be shorthand for "sexual services." And Freud's analysis shows that she feels for her son, who happens to be doing his military service, a love that is not without a massively incestuous dimension.[78] She has a profound wish and simultaneously wishes not to have it. This conflict between her wishes is expressed not only in the subsequent shame she feels about the dream but also in anxiety and anguish during the dream itself.

Thus, according to Freud, anxiety dreams prove absolutely nothing that would contradict the wish-fulfillment function of dreams. On the contrary, the more anxiety a given dream content evokes, the more forbidden is the wish expressed in it; the more necessary it is to disguise, reject, or deny it; and the more probable that it refers back to those oral, anal, incestuous emotions of early childhood for which Freud coined the term "libidinous." In short, dream anxiety is nothing but the transformation of forbidden libido and, to this extent, a star witness for the theory of the dream as wish fulfillment.

This was Freud's claim up until the First World War. Then large numbers of traumatized men returned from the front. Freud was in no hurry to treat them. He had little direct contact with the veterans. But the reports that reached him about them and their dreams were enough to undo his entire dream theory. Was it possible that these people, who woke up night after night, trembling and bathed in sweat as a result of dreams in which they rehallucinated the explosions and shredded corpses they had previously experienced in the war, were simply punishing themselves for their forbidden erotic emotions by means of coded castration dreams? Freud could not seriously claim this, and he was much too intellectually honest to try. Thus, he had to admit that, along with the anxiety that in dreams represents encoded libidinous wishes, there is another kind of dream anxiety, a completely unencrypted anxiety about dying. In *Beyond the Pleasure Principle*,[79] he undertook the first great attempt to understand this anxiety. It is different from the anxiety that stands for erotic wishes, but it has something in common with it. Both are reaction formations, one to forbidden inner emotions, the other to powerful shocks that attack from outside. And, as Freud analyzed the relationship of shock and anxiety, he reverted completely to being the neurologist he had been when he began his medical career.

Nervous systems are constantly at work responding to stimuli. And they have the peculiar habit of preserving the nerve synapses across which stimuli, including unpleasant ones, have been successfully discharged, and turning them into pathways. Anxiety is the condition in which the return of tormenting stimuli is anticipated. In other words, anxiety is an elementary form of memory. To be anxious is to remember pain or embarrassment that has been experienced before and to get ready to experience more of it. Getting ready, here, means not wanting to experience a new pain in the same way as the old one. It means seeking to confront it more effectively by mobilizing the nerve pathways that were created during previous attempts to discharge the pain, so as better to absorb the new suffering. To this extent, says Freud, anxiety is not just the same as fright. On the contrary, "there is something about anxiety that protects its subject against fright and so against fright-neuroses."[80] Fright, in contrast, strikes without any preparation. Here, the protective anxiety is lacking. An overdose of stimuli has burst in, in the form of a shock, without there being any system in place to absorb it. And where there has been no preparation, the nervous system helps out with postpreparation. This is how Freud explains the dreams of the traumatized veterans and accident victims. They "are endeavoring to master the stimulus retrospectively, by developing the anxiety whose omission was the cause of the traumatic neurosis."[81] In other words, by constantly repeating the shock situation in a hallucinatory fashion, they attempt to create a system that will absorb and discharge it, ex post facto.

Admittedly, these dreams have little need of interpretation. There is no latent dream thought to be expressed and concealed by a manifest dream content. There is no forbidden wish that can be uncovered by asking pointed questions. Dream content and dream thought collapse into one; everything is right on the surface. Like the thirst dream, the fright dream is a one-dimensional, flat, primitive form of the dream; it offers no intellectual challenge to the psychoanalyst. What it does offer is a broadside against the general theory that dreams are wish fulfillment— at least to the extent that wishing necessarily implies an underlying dimension of infantile eroticism. The latter, though, is an opinion that resonates through Freud's work like a basso continuo. However much his views on the number and character of the fundamental drives may have changed over the course of four decades, there is always one basic assumption: where there is a wish, there is Eros (or libido), at least as understood in a very broad sense, as striving for unity. Viewed in these terms, even the death drive, which Freud believed he had discovered in *Beyond the Pleasure Principle*, and which he made responsible for the compulsive repetition of traumatic shocks—is erotically conceived as a striving to return to a lifeless primal state—the place from which all life comes.[82]

But if all wishing is defined erotically, the fright dream doesn't fit the theory. We look in vain for an erotic impulse in it. It contradicts the thesis that Freud insisted on for decades and fought for tooth and nail, namely that *all* dreaming is wish fulfillment. Thirteen years later, in his "Revision of the Theory of Dreams" (published in 1933 as part of the *New Introductory Lectures on Psychoanalysis*), Freud went so far as to admit this, but he did so in a way that didn't cost him anything. "We should not, I think, be afraid to admit that here [in the case of traumatic fright dreams] the function of the dream has failed. I will not invoke the saying that the exception proves the rule: its wisdom seems to me most questionable. But no doubt the exception does not overturn the rule." And then, with a little terminological maneuver, he immediately tries to reduce the exception to the rule. Instead of calling the dream "the fulfillment of a wish," he suggests simply calling it an *"attempt* at the fulfillment of a wish."[83] All of a sudden, the traumatic fright dream fits in perfectly. It can be booked as a failed attempt at wish fulfillment. All other dreams, on the other hand, even anxiety dreams, appear to be successful attempts. The fact that wish fulfillment in dreams is always only hallucinatory, and is thus never 100 percent successful, is covered over—and the traumatic fright dream is not taken seriously. It becomes an exception, a fringe phenomenon, a not quite fully illuminated dark spot that nevertheless in no way prevents us from continuing with the interpretation of dreams, just as before.

How different Freud's tone was in *Beyond the Pleasure Principle*! Under the influence of his recent discovery that the dreams of traumatized war veterans shattered his wish-fulfillment theory, he came up with a literally earthshaking supposition, when he stated that the traumatic shock victim's repetition compulsion, which makes him return repeatedly to the situation in which he experienced the shock, was "more primitive, more elementary, more instinctual than the pleasure principle which it overrides."[84] Moreover, it made it necessary "to grant that there was also a time before the purpose of dreams was the fulfillment of wishes."[85] Here, there is no mention of a mere exception; it is more of an abyss. If, indeed, there was a " time before," in which things were "more instinctual" (a comparative form found nowhere else in his writing) than they are in the underlying erotic layer, then it is a different "time before" than the infantile one that continues to haunt adults and make them neurotic. Then we are looking at a different time dimension in the history of our species—the "Early Stone Age in us." Freud, with a sure instinct, saw it blaze up in the traumatic fright dream, where it admittedly represented an acute danger for the starting point of his research and analytic practice, which until then had been entirely sexuality-centered. Hence, he never seriously allowed this dimension of time before to affect him, and only fixed his attention on the primitive activity of thought after it had long since passed through the primary stages of primitiveness.

Let us take a closer look. There is a certain logic to the development of retrospective anxiety as a means of overcoming shock. It is literally a physio-logic. At first glance, it appears completely illogical. A traumatic shock is a horrible thing. Is it not absurd for an organism to constantly repeat this horror, instead of avoiding or fleeing from it? Obviously, the organism is driven by the need to rid itself of the shock. Neurologically, in repeated new attempts, pathways are created, broken in, deepened, over which the painful surplus of stimuli can be discharged. From the point of view of the theory of experience, a fright that is constantly repeated gradually loses its fearfulness.[86] We begin to grow accustomed to it. It acquires a certain familiarity, particularly since, as it is repeated, it no longer bursts in upon us suddenly but appears specially performed, at the dreamer's behest. The frequent repetition of the performance is the attempt to play it down, to make it bearable or normal, and thus ultimately to make it go away.

Dreams that hallucinate traumatic war experiences, over and over again, are expressions of the wish to be preserved from fright. They are star witnesses for wish fulfillment—just not the Freudian kind, which is premised on the condition that wherever there is a wish, there is Eros. Here, by contrast, we have a wish fulfillment that is "more instinctual" than the erotic drive—the wish to rid oneself of fear. Where fear attacks, all pleasure comes to an end. But fright, trauma, pain cannot be experienced without the simultaneous wish to have them stop. "Woe entreats: Go! Away, Woe!"[87] If Freud had made allowances for this previous, more primal, more driven dimension of wishing, this "more primitive" time of the pleasure principle, as he himself described it, if he had allowed it to touch him, his theory that dreams are wish fulfillment would not have been endangered for even a moment. His own reflections on fright, horror, and anxiety are precisely what taught us to see the dreams of war veterans and accident victims as desperate attempts at rescue. They reveal the ex post facto development of anxiety as a neural trick to render the horror harmless. Once the latter has struck, running away is useless. You carry it with you everywhere you go. And it is much too powerful to be ignored or repressed. Repression always requires two things: the power of repression and a thing that allows itself to be repressed. Repression is not a primal mechanism of the psyche. It has a chance only in zones of moderate stimulus. Full traumatic assault makes a mockery of it and permits only one response. Those who are affected are forced to repeat it for as long as it takes to lessen its sting.

At the origin of all human meaning, in light of everything we have said, stands a huge contradiction. Repetition means affirmation, strengthening, celebration. However, the repetition of traumatic fright occurs in order to get rid of it. The repetition seeks to get rid of itself, as it were. In other words, the repeated affirmation of horror occurs for the purpose of its negation. By gradually making it ordinary, bearable, familiar, it makes it into its opposite. *It reverses it.* This much we can derive without any difficulty from the simple dreams in which war veterans, night after night, are tormented by visions of the explosions, attacks, and assaults they previously experienced at the front. These dreams are attempts at self-healing. Naturally not sufficient ones. The dreamers need further therapeutic help. Nevertheless, their nightmares are a relatively high cultural achievement. Traumatic repetition compulsion, acted out in a dream, is repetition compulsion that has become hallucinatory, sublimated, weakened. It would never have gotten to this point had there not been previous, much rougher forms. These previous forms are to be investigated—the "primitive" time that traumatic repetition compulsion experienced before it became capable of assuming the shape of a dream. For this, we need to take a step back.

SACRIFICE

Stone Age hominids, who ranged in hordes across forests and savannahs, who had learned the art of creating stone axheads and making fire, and who, as a result, were in a position to prepare all kinds of food and to nourish themselves with plants, cadavers, and animals—why were they not satisfied with their achievements? Why did they start to transfer the persistence and patience they had acquired making stone tools to the much more elaborate production of things like graves, images, and ornamentation, things that are not edible but are only intended to *mean* something? Why did they make these things into the central focus of their lives? Why did they surround them with strict rituals whose performance must have cost them the arduous self-control required for endless repetition? Why did they do this to themselves? What in the world drove them to give nature a "meaning"? We do not know the answer. There were no cultural anthropologists present. There is only one thing we can say with certainty: no entity under the sway of drives does something like this for fun and pleasure, but only under the most extreme pressure.

Perhaps, in this case, it was a certain bodily disproportion that built up the pressure, over a considerable period of time, namely the size of a brain that is excessively large in relation to the body. No other species has such an elaborate nervous system as *Homo sapiens* (and the extinct Neanderthals); none has such a high degree of sensitivity to stimuli. Similarly, no other species has been similarly forced to deal with this sensitivity, to find ways to discharge tormenting stimuli. Necessity is the mother of invention, but invention does not occur everywhere there is need. In the case of *Homo sapiens*, it is true that the need associated with the overly large head was combined with favorable conditions for invention, for example unusually functional organs for grasping and a constellation of larynx and vocal chords that made it possible to model and modulate sounds. But all these are merely the essential physical preconditions for giving meaning to nature. They do not explain how it happened. Here, there will always be a gap. It is never possible to say how the sphere of meaning opened up. All we can do is identify conditions without which it could not have done so.

Among them is traumatic repetition compulsion. Not that the hominids were uniquely troubled by traumatization. The entire animal kingdom is subject to it. But only one species arrived at the unheard-of physiological trick of putting up protection, after the fact, against something it had been unable to avoid or flee from beforehand. Traumatic repetition compulsion is flight that takes place after the event has already occurred—flight in the wrong direction, not away from the fright but toward it, to the place where it attacked, into the suffering being's own interior, its nerve center. In other words, traumatic repetition compulsion is an elementary form of self-absorption. It is subjecting yourself, once again, to whatever overcame you from outside in the traumatic situation. At first, this will hardly have been anything other than a rough and diffuse echo of elementary forces of nature, for example when a hominid collective that was shocked by a noise made noise in turn. Or when, after being buffeted by storms, earthquakes, or wild animals, the group made a special attack on its own weak, defenseless, or wounded members. The beginnings of this repetitious type of action may only be guessed. But the regular forms that developed from it can be identified. It may have taken thousands of years before they assumed firm contours. In any case, traumatic repetition compulsion only becomes graspable, for the first time, after it has already assumed regular forms over a long period. And for these forms there is an established concept: sacrifice.

The meaning of sacrifice for early humanity[88] can scarcely be overestimated. As soon as Early Stone Age settlements assume an orderly form, they are grouped around a center—a mountaintop, a stone, a stake, a fireplace, graves. Center means sacrificial center, and burial, in the beginning, is not sharply distinguished from the act of sacrifice. Wherever we come across mythological traces of early humanity, that is, ancient layers of narrative, sacrifice is either the central event itself or the driving motive behind the story. The Greek verb *rezein* is the verbal memory of this state of affairs. It means both "to make a sacrifice" and also, in general, "to do, to be active." Thus, it expresses the fact that making sacrifice is the essence of human action, the specific human activity per se. Killing—this is something animals also do, and sometimes to their own kind. But ritual killing, in a solemn gathering at a specific place according to an established schema—this is a specific, exclusive characteristic of human beings.

Sacrificial victims are at the heart of the matter. It is not frogs and snails that are sacrificed but the most precious thing people possess—humans, later also large mammals. This is not something that is done for amusement, but only when there seems to be no other way to get help. Obviously, it is an attempt to relieve some kind of affliction. But what about sacrifice makes it capable of bringing relief? It only reenacts horror and suffering, it *does* the very thing it is supposed to provide relief from. This is absurd. Sacrifice cannot be understood at all, other than from the perspective of traumatic repetition compulsion. To get rid of the natural horror that has befallen it, the hominid horde falls upon itself. From among the living beings by which it sets the greatest store, it selects a few and, together, slaughters them. In this way, the group plays down the horror of nature by organizing, practicing, and staging it itself, by giving it, in the process, the firm rules that we call ritual. The word *ritual* comes from Sanskrit *rta*, which means the same as "solid existence, support, truth, right." Where there is *rta*, there is security, everything is done "the right way." At first, ritual and sacrificial ritual are identical. All rituals are descendants of the ritual of sacrifice.

At the beginning of the creation of ritual, the elementary mechanisms that Freud would later claim for the construction of dreams are already at work. That traumatic repetition compulsion turns fright into its opposite was already shown. It is reversal in pure form: affirmation of horror. But this affirmation can always only be ritualized in a particular place. Ritual is always characterized by a bounded space, within which it can take place without interruption.[89] It must be a peaceful place. The horde must enter it in harmony and perform the ritual in harmony, otherwise it is not *rta*. On the ground of this harmony, it must break off a piece of the natural horror, as it were, and perform it as a sort of concentrate of itself. And in the process, two things occur. Its manifold forms of appearance are *condensed*, in the ritual space, into one. And it is *displaced* from its manifold places of appearance into the ritual space.

There they are: condensation and displacement. Without them, says Freud, no dream comes into being. Now we can add something else: without them, it is not even possible to constitute the ritual space. And here we can see for the first time how it all coheres. Their coherence is embedded in a third thing: *reversal*. Dreams don't show this directly; they are already too much of a secondary phenomenon for that. Dreams show how condensation and displacement function, but not the violent act of reversal that originally jolted them into action. In dreams, this violent act has already become routine. It's as if it got lost in them. Thus, Freud remarks that reversal is present throughout the dream; in his mind, it is essential. But he was not able to localize it. In his dream theory, it remains a dark spot, a function without a place of its own, trailing along in the wake of condensation and displacement.

Emotionally, Freud was quite correct in sensing that reversal is a dark spot. After all, it has its origin in what it found most terrifying: fright and horror. It is like the original vortex of fright—and at the same time the pivotal moment in human development, the first glimmer of humanity. Only in the vortex of stimuli that is the reversal of fright do condensation and displacement come into being. They are manifestations of the trans-formation of fright and horror into their opposite, by means of repetition. Only through condensation in a representative form do fright and horror become graspable. Only by displacement into an undisturbed, ritual space do they become predictable. Condensation and displacement are the two elementary means that reversal has at its disposal in the attempt to concentrate fright and horror by means of continuous repetition,[90] within a ritual space, and to gain control of them there.

Admittedly, this taking hold was at first merely fictional, and from our standpoint of today, completely absurd—as if the forces of nature should have become even a tiny bit more sparing of Neanderthals and *Homo sapiens* due to the fact that the early hominids had begun to construct a protected space in which to gain control over them. Nevertheless, with the creation of this type of space, something begins that is otherwise unheard of in natural history—the great process of internalization. "The history of civilization is the history of the introversion of sacrifice," Adorno and Horkheimer write in *Dialectic of Enlightenment*.[91] But the sacrifice itself is already introversion, is pulling and condensing fright and horror into a protected space. Horror was brought into this space in the form of an image, it was *imagined* into it. This is the primal form of imagination—contraction in space. It is an external process, perceptible by all the senses and affecting everyone, a collectively suggestive act in an identifiable place, which becomes a protective space only through the act itself. It is the first space of imagination but not yet an imagined space.[92]

To condense and displace fright into this space means giving it a bounded, condensed, exemplary form of proceeding. "Exemplary" means, on one hand, that an example is made, a pattern is created for an action that can be carried out again and again in the same way; a ritual is practiced. On the other hand, the collective as a whole begins to differentiate itself from its individual members, the "exemplars." It repeats the traumatic event, does it to itself, but does so in an exemplary way, which means to selected individual members of the clan. In this process, it cannot avoid developing a mode of selection. We don't know how this began, but we do know that casting lots was one if the earliest magic practices. Certainly, it was not introduced first for the purpose of dividing up booty and land, as a practice linked to a victory; rather, it was initially an emergency measure to avoid being destroyed by natural horrors, as the book of Jonah accurately reminds us, when the crew of a ship that is in crisis on the high seas draws lots "that we may know for whose cause this evil is upon us." The lot falls to Jonah; he is thrown into the sea so that it will grow calm.[93] It is difficult to imagine that the lottery could have its origin anywhere but in the collective's decision on which of its members it should visit the natural catastrophe. To find this out, all that is needed is to toss a branch, a leaf, a pebble,[94] or some other light object with an unpredictable trajectory into the air above the heads of the assembled collective. The person near whom it lands, whom it sticks to, or to whom it points is the chosen one. All eyes are fixed on him or her. This is the gaze that consecrates to death, the elementary form of the evil eye.

Next comes the preparation of the chosen one. Its origins are also unknown. Perhaps the collective originally fell upon him, as is still the case in Euripides' tragedy, where a swarm of maenads (Bacchae) attacks Pentheus, the ruler of Thebes, and he is torn to pieces by his own mother.[95] It is, however, known that stoning was among the archaic rituals performed by a collective against individual members. Stoning can both kill the person in question and reduce him to a state in which his killing can be celebrated without any resistance.[96] And everyone can participate. It thus fulfills one of the conditions of ritual killing. The collective must carry it out unanimously. No one is permitted to interrupt the process. The protected space is a site of strict unanimity and inviola-bility, except for those who are responsible for it—the chosen ones. And no one is allowed to exempt himself. Everyone must raise his hand against the chosen ones, to participate in bringing about their deaths. The ritual assures collective participation. Everyone has to take part, and everyone is implicated and affected. Implicated as perpetrators and affected, first of all, in the sense that they could have been a victim and that they themselves have barely escaped death at the hand of the collective. Affected, in addition, because they have to tear out a piece of their own hearts when they slaughter one of their own. It is horrible for them to have to do this, but they have no choice. Even when traumatic repetition compulsion is transformed into ritual, it still does not cease breaking in upon individuals with the violence of a natural reflex.

Two kinds of signs of this impact on the individuals thus affected have become associated with the ritual killing of one's own relatives. One, which may have an earlier origin but can only be reconstructed from fragmentary narratives and later forms, is the mysterious sign with which God is supposed to have marked Cain, "lest any finding him should kill him."[97] The "mark of Cain" makes sense only if the fraternal murder with which it is connected was not an individual crime of passion, as the story of Cain and Abel suggests, but a collective ritual deed, a human sacrifice.[98] It is the sign of the perpetrators, who are affected by the death they cause and from which they themselves have escaped, the sign of their guilt and their having been spared. It is the first hint of the emergence of a specifically human affect, in which shame, mourning, and relief are all inseparably intermingled, but which has the character of the above-mentioned first glimmer of humanity. The other sign of the affect is archaeologically verifiable: burial. People surely did not come up with it out of some sudden irruption of hygiene or piety, but out of need. The ritual of the collective killing of a member of the clan was less horrible when a second ritual followed, which showed the victim the excess of affection that had previously been withheld, and laid his earthly remains under the earth in such a manner that his blood no longer "crieth . . . from the ground."[99] Burial too is clear evidence of the initially inseparable emotional mixture of shame, mourning, and relief—a hint at the way traumatic repetition compulsion, which at first aims at nothing more than the intermittent release of an unbearable excess of stimuli, in the course of its ritualization, begins to become the ground of a specifically human feeling.

The content of the last three paragraphs is an idealized historical sketch—constructed from evidential clues but by no means arbitrary. Certainly, it leaves many things open, for example, how the early hominid collectives were structured; whether, in the beginning, they fell upon a single member or an unspecified number of them; whether this involved only members of their own clan or those of other clans, or certain animals;

whether selection procedures other than the casting of lots were used; what other kinds of collective killing practices there may have been apart from stoning; what marks of selection there were besides the mark of Cain and the burial, and so on. In short, the sketch is extremely incomplete. This changes nothing about the fact that the historical process, in its basic characteristics, can hardly have occurred otherwise than the few lines of this sketch indicate. Its conclusions are not merely hypothetical. It is beyond dispute that ritual killing was constitutive for early humankind and that its logic is one of traumatic repetition compulsion; that humans could not have done this without condensing and displacing the act into a ritual space, nor without turning, in concentrated form, against their own flesh and blood; that the killing of fellow clan members was the core of the ritual, which made a selection process inevitable; that the ritual killing of animals was already a replacement for it, and not the other way around; and that ritual slaughter of humans was an idea that at some point led to the practice of slaughtering animals. It is an unchanging part of the signature of old mythological narrative layers that they talk about replacing human sacrifice by animal sacrifice. Where human sacrifice occurred in high cultures, for example among the Aztecs, it represents a return of the repressed, for which specific historical circumstances have prepared the way, as a new invention that might somehow invalidate the historical logic of sacrificial substitution—the replacement of human beings, successively, by animals, plants, and finally metal objects, in order to be free of the pressure of sacrifice.

For the moment, talk of human sacrifice is still premature. The archaic ritual killing of clan members first had to achieve the specific status of a sacrifice, and the road to this point can only be sketched out if the remarkable process of internalization that began with the constitution of a ritual space is first examined a bit more closely. Internalization, as has already been shown, began externally, when the natural horror that had been experienced was placed, or "inbuilt," in a delimited and protected space. On one hand, this move was fictional. The real natural forces that shatter the human collective are not such as to be able to be influenced in the slightest by the creation of ridiculously small protective spaces. But on the other hand it is extremely real. The entire fright and horror that strikes the collective really *is* compressed into these protective spaces. In them, the collective gives itself a representation of the entire fright and horror of nature. Not that nature is only terrible; it affords innumerable living beings many moments of peaceful comfort and well-being. All enjoyment is first enjoyment of nature. Sunshine, starlight, the sound of the sea, birdsong, ripe fruits, comforting warmth, refreshing coolness—they are all gifts of nature. Nevertheless, the entire wealth of its beneficence is not what makes nature worth mentioning, or, initially, before there was regular language, worth representing. Only traumatic fright and horror were capable of that.

REPRESENTATION

To represent something to oneself—what this means, initially, is something as hallucinatory as it is performative. It is no accident that the attempt to put the ritualization of traumatic repetition compulsion into words almost automatically conjures up theatrical terminology: to *play down* the horror, to *produce* it, *stage* it, or *present* it. Human beings "are only wholly human when they are playing," says Friedrich Schiller,[100] with which he means, by playing, the unforced behavior in which humans find themselves in cultivated harmony with nature. But Schiller's sentence has an archaic subtext. Becoming human starts with the beginning of the development of rules of the game. The word *play* feels a bit out of place in this context. The thing for which the rules are being made is bloody serious. Nevertheless, its regulated conduct already also has the aspect of performance. In the ritualization of traumatic repetition compulsion, the collective is, in fact, at the origin of theater. In repeated new attempts, each more compressed and concentrated than the previous one, it reenacts the experience of fright and horror. It plays it down. In the process, it is as remote from reality as it is saturated with reality. On one hand, it hallucinates the real, natural horror in an abstruse manner. On the other hand, it celebrates it in frightfully concrete form. The representation it creates for itself is in equal measure hallucination and real action. The imagination, at first, has a very physical aspect. It is the power that ritually informs the play of human muscles. In the exercise of this power, the compulsion to repeat becomes intelligent, so to speak. From a naturally occurring repetition, occurring as a reflex, it becomes transformed into a reexperiencing. The collective brings back past horror—it imagines it. It begins to remember it by bringing it back to life in its bodily movements. Thus, it transforms it into performance. The performative achievement of memory, with which memory begins to become specifically human, can also be called presentation, representation, or re-presentation.[101]

To represent means to make something that is absent present. What is absent is, first of all, what is past, but past in a particular way: a past that in a certain sense is not past at all, because it naturally doesn't stop causing pain. Its re-presentation serves the purpose of making it really past for the first time, sending it into retirement, as it were, where it no longer torments or makes anxious or uneasy. The past thus proves to be something paradoxical. On one hand, it is only there as long as something previous is remembered. Something that is unnoticeably past, without leaving a trace, has simply vanished—it is not part of the existing past. On the other hand, the existing past is always incomplete; we may think of it as the undead past. Completely past is only what no longer touches or moves anyone—what has been utterly forgotten, the past from which we have been delivered in favor of an undisturbed present. "For . . . the former shall not be remembered, nor come into mind, [but ye shall be] glad and rejoice for ever. . . ."[102] This, in the words of an Old Testament prophet, is the vanishing point of representation. We represent that past so it can vanish completely. We memorialize, in order not to have to remember. At its origin, human memory was the attempt to get rid of the past. It came about in order to forget.

Latin *representare*, literally "to make present again," is helpful here, as it underlines the theatrical aspect of what we are discussing. Representatives are performers. They play a role. And if it is a collective that they are playing, they play a leading role; they are the prominent or chosen personages in whom an amorphous and dispersed mass, whether it be a clan, a people, or a nation, becomes condensed and graspable. Today, the word *representatives* is associated primarily with the appearance, made effective through media, of dignitaries, political representatives, and people who act important.[103] Originally, *representatio* was a kind of collective self-defense. In the beginning it is above all the "chosen" who are the representatives. The collective groups itself around them. Their exemplary, ritual killing condenses and displaces fright and horror into a protected space, distills it into action, thus representing it and making it graspable. In this concrete sense, it is its essence. But the latter is still far from being a mental concept; rather, it is a physical act that is condensed into an image—the scene in the most absolute sense.

The Greek word *skene* refers to an enclosed space in which the decisive action takes place and attracts the greatest possible attention, and then, derived from this meaning, to this action itself. The *skene* is not a tableau, a still image, but one that is in motion—and very well suited to correct two historical prejudices. One is the claim that the first images were standing images—the sculptures and wall paintings with which *Homo sapiens* began to manifest its specific powers of representation some thirty thousand years ago; while moving images are said to have been added only much later, at the end of the nineteenth century, with the invention of the cinema. The other prejudice states that images were at first reproductions of objective models, before they, more or less simultaneously with the invention of film, became nonrepresentational—modern abstract art. We can now see that almost the opposite is true. Images began as moving images. And the individuals who set the scene had to gesticulate, dance, make noise, scream, in order to even be able to stand their own image-making and image-becoming. Ritual killing, for all its participants, is a hugely physically and emotionally moving image. And yet it is not a copy of anything concrete. It has no model. Instead, it represents something intangible, namely fright and horror. It turns it into something imaginary. The original function of the image is to transform something that is not visual into something that is imaginary, as a representation of the unrepresentable, a grasping of the ungraspable.

This, precisely, is what representation means. In it, something becomes graspable that we are otherwise unable to grasp. Copying, by comparison, is already secondary. There is a graspable shape that is copied. The earliest images that have come down to us, for example, the anthropomorphic statuette with the head of a lion, from Hohlenstein-Stadel in Württemberg; or the animal images on the walls of the Chauvet Cave, are ancient, around three millennia old, and yet they are copies—testimonials from a relatively late stage of human imagination. By then, the performance of moving images must long since have become part of human flesh and blood. Only then could the capacity develop to retain, from moving but ritually fixed images, specific significant elements that were captured in a new, incomparably more static fashion, namely in stone, ivory, or wall painting. It is quite possible that from the first moving images until the first still images, a similar amount of time passed as from the first still images until the present. Even if there is still much puzzlement over the precise function of the first sculptures, reliefs, and paintings, one thing may be considered certain: They were created not to be contemplated quietly, reverently, and with artistic appreciation, but as fixed elements in a moving *skene*, or as props and scenery for the archaic representations the collective was making for itself.

Even today, when we look at these representations, we feel torn between admiration for the enormous self-taming and self-mastery that was achieved in the ritualization of traumatic repetition compulsion, and disgust at the horrifying form of this ritual. How fierce must the contradictory emotions have been for the participants themselves! They found a means of escaping unbearable fright and horror, but this means was almost as dreadful as the thing it was designed to overcome. The ritual killing of clan members can't stand to be unaccompanied. It is driven to surpass itself, and over the course of a long time this drive opened the way to an incomparable escape. Actually, the escape was already present in embryonic form in the ritualization itself. When the ritual discharges traumatic shock by turning it into a special performance, it takes on an intentional aspect. Latin *intendere* literally means "to stretch or tense oneself toward something." Actions that do this are goal oriented. As Aristotle put it so nicely, they have a "final cause" (*hou heneka*),[104] or, to put it more simply, a "wherefor." The "wherefor" of ritual killing is, at first, something concretely physiological—to obtain relief through the discharge of tension. But the constant repetition of ritual killing gradually enabled the collectives that suffered through it to arrive at another "wherefor"—one that offered them more than just a sporadic chance to catch their breath. By assuaging the horror itself, constant repetition lent it meaning. Ritual killing that has a meaning becomes easier to bear.

The opening up of this kind of meaning is a qualitative breakthrough that borders on the miraculous. How, where, and in what period it occurred, we do not know. But we can identify some of the things that were necessary for it to be able to take place. And it *did* take place. For this, the imagination had to accomplish something that later, in philosophy, was called *metabasis eis allo genos*: "transition to a new kind." It had to turn from a caterpillar into a butterfly, so to speak. Evidently, this happened in such a way that the ritual space in which it had imaginatively installed the horror became the base camp for an expedition into the unknown—into a new continent that came about only as a consequence of this expedition.

Condensing and displacing the multiplicity of natural horrors into the interior of the ritual space, and compressing them into clusters of moving images, had already made an impressive start on the road to internalization. But the moving images, however much they may have taken the form of concentrates and extracts, were naturally still extended in both space and time—an interiority that had not yet found itself. Imagination had to pull itself together once again, to work on itself a second time, as it were, before it was able to achieve a second-degree condensation and displacement that can be described only metaphorically—and that is itself a metaphorical process. *Matapherein* means "to carry across," and the carrying across that took place here displaced and condensed the contraction of natural horror, in the ritual space, into a contraction of the ritual space itself.

How this was possible we will hardly ever be able to determine in a seamless way. The only thing we may be sure of is that it did not happen voluntarily. Evidently, the drive to escape from the ritual killing gradually forced the imagination to take what it had already condensed and displaced into moving images, and to condense and displace it to a state of spacelessness—to bring spatially and temporally separate ritual figures together in a single point, by literally distilling them down to forms without any extension. This is a contraction of a contraction, to the point where condensation becomes disappearance. But condensation and displacement cannot advance to the second-level stage without reversal doing the same thing. A remarkable reversal of the reversal takes place. Namely, the flight forward, toward horror instead of away from it, which until now has been the secret of success of traumatic repetition compulsion, takes the form of a flight into the interior. Its forward movement simultaneously becomes a retreat. It carries out a "self-repulsion," as Hegel would have said,[105] a movement whose meaning can no longer be fully apprehended in terms of spatial parameters. Instead, it evaporates into something nonspatial. In the process, an astonishing event occurs: in the ritual space of imagination an imagined space is erected.

MENTAL SPACE

Only with this does the creation of interiority really come into its own.[106] It opens up "a room of one's own," to borrow from the title of a famous book—a space that did not exist until it was opened up by the imagination. Its opening up was its creation. And where this occurred, ritual killing literally assumed the qualities of "genius." It translated itself—crossed over—to the other shore of its own "genius." When the Romans used the word *genius* to refer to a guardian spirit that is already active at conception and at the birth of a human being and that accompanies him his whole life long, they were using a term in a way that had already been strongly individualized and humanized. Its more elementary form referred to the *genius loci*, the "spirit of the place." Not just any place but, at first, *the* place per se, where an action takes place that in Latin is called *operari* and can be translated as both "operate" and "sacrifice." To this extent, *genius* is an important word that, while it may be Latin, refers to something that is by no means restricted to ancient Rome. The authentic *genius loci* is a human breakthrough that belongs to more than one culture. It is the ritual of killing in a fleeting state, in two senses. On one hand, it makes it possible to evade the full impact of the act of killing; on the other, it represents the aggregate sense of killing in a state of evaporation, which is related to the ritual the way steam is related to water. It floats above the action, without the latter's concrete form and clear localizability. While the representation that the collective, as a whole, creates for itself in the act of ritual killing is common to all and is graspable in the most literal sense, the representation that now forms an arc above it has become ungraspable: imaginary.

Imaginary space can only open up within the space of ritual. But it does not open up empty. It is filled with representation of the "genius." In this representation, the imagination performs its second-degree reversal—a feat that deserves our wonder. Imagination turns itself inside out, as it were, from performative representation to mental representation. *Mental* derives from the Latin *mens*, which means "inner sense" or "power of invention," and from which the meanings "spirit" or "mind" are only secondarily derived. Let us, therefore, think twice before claiming that mental representation is the definitive origin of mind. Origins have their peculiarities. The person who wishes to see modernity as having its origin in the nineteenth century, and modern art in the twentieth, for example, is soon confronted with a *via moderna* in the waning years of the Middle Ages, and with surrealist-seeming images from the early Baroque period. If we seek the origin of the bourgeoisie in the Renaissance, someone may ask us why we won't allow the ancient Greek *polis* to count as early bourgeois? Wherever there are origins, there are precursors. This is especially true in the case of the mind. To what extent the capacity of some animals to recognize certain forms already deserves to be called mind need not concern us here. But certainly the specific level of mind that is characteristic of humans has been achieved at the moment when representation takes place, even if the individuals who are doing the representing have no idea, at first, what mind is. It suffices that the ritual they perform, the moving image they present, should represent something, that it repeats it and thus brings it back. The ritual is meaningful not just because it concerns life and death but also because it points to the absent thing that it re-presents, and thus exemplifies the paradox of the absent presence. Where something that is absent, and therefore not concretely graspable, nevertheless appears in a representation that both embodies and points to it, reality turns two-dimensional. It breaks apart into a graspable phenomenon and the ungraspable thing to which it bears witness. Wherever this kind of two-dimensionality opens up, meaning is created, and where there is meaning—whether in the form of an appearance that points to an "essence," a specific thing that points to a generality, or a signifier that points to a signified—there is mind. Mind is not a separate substance, but an act of meaning in which the thing that is meant is never immediately present but always only intended or thought of. In performative representation, this occurs via gestures and the voice. This is mind, or "spirit" in Hegel's vocabulary, that is external to itself. With the breakthrough to mental representation, it becomes internal to itself. Meaning erects its own space, the space of the imaginary. From now on, this will be the space of the mind. Gesture and voice are now only the external, if always indispensable supports for its inner movement; they are no longer the media of its occurrence.

We may therefore state with certainty that there is a pre-mental mind. The mental is nothing but the mind's own sphere, an imagined, imaginary space—a non-space that, at the same time, never loses its spatial associations.[107] The result: It is experienced as a fulfilled space—fulfilled in the very sense that in it a desperate wish is fulfilled, even if only in an imaginary, hallucinatory fashion—the wish to escape from the horror of ritual killing. The spirit, or "genius," is not just a ritual that has fled but also the point toward which it flees, its aim. The ritual is performed for its sake. Moreover, it is experienced as if it bore its origin within it, as the thing that first constituted the ritual by demanding the ritual killing. The Greek word *chaos*, which originally meant "yawning abyss," and only later "empty space" (and by no means "disorder"), can be read in this context as the literal version of the *genius loci*. It is a man-eating abyss but, as abyss, also the ground for the ritual killing, its justification. The killing must be, because the abyss demands it. It gives it meaning. The killing becomes something beneficial; it can satisfy the "genius" and assuage its anger, as a higher power that hovers protectively over the ritual and the collective that carries it out. Ritual killing, which had begun long before as the merely reflexive repetition of unmastered horror, becomes much more bearable if it has a meaning or something to which the sacrifice of the chosen can be addressed. This addressee is the original form of what in philosophy is later called a "final cause" (*causa finalis*, or *Zweckursache*). It is a cause that works not by repulsion but by attraction. It draws things toward it. Its categorical attractive power is an establishing and simultaneously a justifying force. To establish *is* essentially to justify; this remains true today. Actions and sentences that can be grounded in a plausible "because" are justified and thus potentially lasting. Even today, a dearth of justification is experienced as a mental vacuum that exerts attraction, as a kind of abyss that opens up underneath the thing that is not justified. But before justification took on the form of the first statements and arguments, it had already been imagined for a long time, as a final cause that served to justify ritual. The "genius" is its archetype, the original ground that is simultaneously an original abyss.[108] Only when the ritual killing is performed for the sake of the "genius"-abyss, in its mental force field, does it become an offering to a god and assume the status of a sacrifice— a sacred event.[109]

The sacred, initially, is nothing but self-interpreting traumatic repetition compulsion that gives itself its own meaning. We should, however, not suggest that we are talking about some mechanical base-superstructure schema, as if the ritual had been fully developed first, and the "genius" had then been set on top of it. From the beginning, one purpose of traumatic repetition compulsion was the attempt to make the event easier to bear. This resulted in the protracted process of its ritual condensation and displacement. Implicitly, the urge to be able to endure the event always already contained within it the urge to interpret it. Thus, strictly speaking, the ritual is only complete when it has taken on the character of the "genius"—when it has given itself a higher being to which to address itself. Its elevation, in the form of the "genius," is already at work in the development of a fixed ritual structure, and is not just its product. Nevertheless, we can identify a clear temporal sequence in one respect. Where ritual actions become condensed and displaced into mental forms, there must already have been condensation and displacement of dramatic dimensions. Where mental representation arises, there must already have been performative representation. Only via the enormous detour of the performative could the mental become possible.

This also means that in the history of genres of thought and expression there is no direct road from sensual perception to mental representation. The belief that certain hominids somehow, at some time or other, came up with the idea, out of idleness or boredom, of conserving their sense impressions and thus ultimately making them last after their external sensual stimulus had faded away is a scientific fairy tale. Early hominids had not the slightest reason to do such a thing of their own volition. Mental space may be an excess of nature and the site of a new type of storage, but it is a product of despair, not luxury. It could never have come about without stubborn neural hard labor. Its opening up was an incomparable breakthrough. But once it had succeeded, there existed an unforeseen space in which mental representation could be exercised for as long as it took to become sedimented as the disposition of an entire species. And where this sediment, finally, is passed down from generation to generation, the road from perception to representation has been graded and leveled until it appears as if the long detour to its opening up had never existed. The new generation has only to walk down it, something that remains taxing, but that compared to the exertions of the road builders is a pleasant stroll. Children can grow from perception to representation as if this were an organic process that Mother Nature had always envisioned for them. Modern neurophysiology looks only at this organic process. It has no sense of the cost of the initial mental exercise or of the "genius" that was its first product, as it began to balance on the knife edge between representation and perception, the starting point of all the hallucinations that, even today, are what Bleuler's classical definition called them: "perceptions without corresponding stimuli from without."[110]

The "genius" is a misperception of this kind, on the part of the collective. The collective believes that it perceives it, together, when actually it is only collectively imagining it. Only when this imagination has acquired a certain durability and steadiness could it become aware of itself as a separate sphere and differentiate itself from the external world. Only then do representation and perception become separated from each other. Representation continues to require external perception; this is still true today. But representation ceases to be confused with the perception. Instead, representation supports itself on perception, like a crutch with which it learns to go its own ways, or, philosophically speaking, to develop its own logic.

Collective hallucinations, it is true, already contain the germ of individuality. They are brought forth collectively by all the participants. Nevertheless, they exist only insofar as each participant has them for herself, as her own imagination. When the imaginary space opens up within the ritual space, there are created, strictly speaking, as many imaginary spaces as there are individuals taking part. Except that these spaces are so open to interpenetration by others, through shared motions, gestures, or sounds, that they are effectively only *one* space that the many individuals share in such an undifferentiated way that their personal characteristics play no role. We should not assume that the first hallucinatory representations of the "genius"—and consequently the first hallucinations—already arrived at a clear distinction between singular and plural. What did they look like? We don't know. But everything speaks against their having had either clear contours or significant similarities with natural beings or events. The fleeting aggregate condition can probably be characterized most accurately with the word *specter*. Specters are shapes that don't quite have a proper shape. They are more or less what Rudolf Otto called Arab desert gods: "wandering demonstrative pronouns,"[III] in other words archaic numina that float around their collective more or less formlessly, and are only graspable where they themselves grab something—abruptly falling upon a terrible here and now. This here-now, in Otto, is called the "holy"—another word for what I have termed "genius." The "genius" or the "holy"—the two concepts are used interchangeably in the following—is the embryonic form of divinity, and precisely as such it is also shapeless, something in which characteristic traits that resemble humans or animals, individual and plural, have not yet assumed an identifiable form. And yet all the sublime representations, thoughts, and concepts to which human beings ever aspire have no other germ cell than this: the impoverished hallucination of the "genius."

DREAMTIME

At the origin of everything mental was hallucination. Dreams, on the other hand, at least specifically human dreams, first emerged from hallucinations.[112] They resemble hallucinations that have set, like the sun—that have sunk down into the mental underground. At the same time, this sinking down is only the other side of hallucination's ascent into developed, waking consciousness. The alternation of waking and sleeping states is common to the entire world of animals, it is true. But from the waking state of animals to that of humans there is no direct route, any more than there is a direct route from animal perception to human representation. The person who hallucinates may be awake, but the numbing force of primary hallucinations is a waking state that is greatly diminished. To work one's way out of it, to a state in which we are no longer completely at the mercy of this stupefying power but can relate to it wakefully and soberly, can treat the hallucinations as "material" and turn them into something that they themselves are not yet—namely lasting, reproducible representations with contours that don't immediately burst like soap bubbles when they meet the resistance of external nature—this self-development of hallucination can be called the "awakening" of humankind, in a sense that is metaphorical but by no means only metaphorical.

We will never be able to reconstruct its initial phase in detail, but here too there is an inner logic at work. The same way traumatic repetition compulsion became self-ritualized, resulting in a graspable form, primary hallucination could not help structuring itself and gradually, by dint of innumerable repeated collective representations, forming fixed images, like mental molds shaped from the amorphous mass of the "genius."[113] The resulting forms were by no means as firm and structured as the ones that would later be hewn out of stone or poured in bronze. They are fixed forms only in the sense that we call customary turns of phrase "fixed." In their fleeting aggregate state, they never stop oscillating and fermenting, and they are "fixed" only to the extent that they are always able to support themselves by ritual gestures and vocal sounds that are themselves unchanging.[114] And yet, the inner modeling of fleeting specters is the precondition for the ability to shape the first sculptures and wall paintings that we regard as the first objective evidence of the specific *sapientia* of *Homo sapiens*.

Primary hallucinations, in contrast, continue to ferment, if only because they are always trying to escape from themselves. Their content, the "genius," may be an escape, but it is a terrible one. Only as a man-eating abyss does it provide the "wherefor" of a ritual. Archaic hallucination has good reason to work on itself, a process during which the imagination becomes fully immersed in itself. It is not just that it creates an inner image of something external, by means of condensation and displacement; it is also capable, on its own, of further condensing and displacing the imagined material. At first, naturally, the inner molds that emerge in this process are only hallucinatory. But as they begin to transform the formless, wraithlike representations into shapes, they make the "genius" more graspable and gradually help to give the collective a graspable quality, too, in the dual sense that (1) the collective performs the ritual more intentionally, and (2) it also begins to develop the elementary forms of mental understanding. When the mental molds first emerged, they were inexpressibly weak, indistinct, and uncertain. They had to feel the resistance of external nature, to correct and differentiate themselves, and gradually, in innumerable iterations, to measure themselves against the outer world before they were fit to represent this exterior world in an interior space and in a form that could be preserved. Survival of the fittest is far more actively at work here than in the evolution of species.

True, mental fitness is "fitness" that has a specific orientation. The thought forms and concepts of *Homo sapiens*, seen from the perspective of the evolution of the species, are all namely self-corrections of hallucination—we could call them metamorphoses of hallucinations—a result of the desperate attempt to break free of themselves. The attempt failed, but it led to an unintended success: the turning of hallucination against itself. It too is a prime example of reversal. The flight of the mental away from itself turns back in the opposite direction—toward itself. With this, something qualitatively new appears in natural history—the paradoxical process by which victory is also defeat, the thing that wins out is also the thing that is overcome. And the result is that one thing, for certain, cannot happen: the thing that has been overcome cannot simply disappear. Hallucination that overcomes itself exceeds its own limits and is clarified into mental molds. But the latter cannot come into being without also separating themselves from the diffuse mass of hallucinations ("genius mass") from which they have emerged. This means that everything in the hallucinations that is not transformed into waking, conscious awareness is banished from waking consciousness—into a nonwaking but nevertheless mental state underneath waking consciousness. The mental space becomes two-dimensional. It separates into waking consciousness and its underground. And this underground becomes the collecting pool for whatever remains of hallucination. All the events that previously made up the forward position of the intelligence have become mere shadows of themselves, surpassed, outshone, suppressed, pressed together, decomposed, and covered up by the forces they had once called into being. And yet at the same time this mental underground remains the elementary mental site of an irritation that never stops twitching and flicking its way into waking consciousness—both as a disturber of the peace and as an elixir of life and basic nourishment of our mental representation of the world.

Between waking consciousness and its underground, in other words, there runs a boundary that is both strict and permeable. Like the forces of reaction and separation that are generated when two opposing streams of water meet, without consisting of anything except water or losing their capacity to pass through each other at any given point, this boundary is also, on one hand, purely mental—as imagined or imaginary as everything mental, and not anything that could be measured neurologically. Yet, on the other hand, it is the result of a turnaround that is accomplished with the greatest possible effort, without which no single clear representation could ever have emerged from the primal mass of hallucinations. For the creation of this boundary there is no more fitting term than "primal repression." The rise of waking consciousness, which is simultaneously the sunset of hallucination, is an act of repression par excellence—and comme il faut, namely repression that turns against itself. Only via this reversal, or turn against itself, was it possible for the representational world of *Homo sapiens* to emerge. This world itself is already a product of repression. Every waking contour that is drawn in mental forms is also the limning of a boundary between waking consciousness and its underground. Whenever we think, we also repress and censor. What Freud calls "primal repression" is only a special, late form of this.

He is thinking of the "initial phase of repression that consists in the psychic (ideational) representative of the drive being denied access to the conscious."[115] But when this "initial phase" occurs, true primal repression has long since taken place. The capacity to draw a boundary in mental space has long since become the capacity to reason, the seemingly self-evident basic equipment of *Homo sapiens*, as if it has always been part of his "nature" and never come at a cost. Consciousness and unconsciousness have become solid basic pillars of the "psychic apparatus," and it is only a matter of detail as to the location of the boundary between them, the ways stimuli painfully intrude into a highly cultivated waking state and are rejected and banished to the state that Freud calls "unconscious"—and that can now be better understood as the realm of suppressed hallucinations.

Ordinarily, we pay attention to submerged hallucinations only when they surface in sleep, as dreams, or in the waking state as slips of the tongue or delusions. But the waking state suffers from a blindness that almost seems like a kind of *déformation professionnelle* when it comes to the constant presence of this submerged hallucination, right under the surface, and to the finely detailed labor that it carries out, ceaselessly and with great fluency, on the edge of waking consciousness. We can compare the fact that in waking consciousness no mental representation is completely without its hallucinatory glow to the light of a candle in sunlight, which may all too easily escape our notice. There is no representation without image content, without a remainder of the sense perception above which representation has assumed its sublime place. And the disappearing truth remainder in representation is its hallucinatory spark, which both lights it on fire and glimmers out in it. Hallucination doesn't just rumble through the mental underground, dethroned and jumbled together as "such stuff as dreams are made on"; nor does it cease interfering in each of our representations—and thus constantly documenting that it is the unquenched inflammatory site of every representation or thought that is created. It is a past that does not die—the mental primitive era we are never rid of.

There is one old culture that imagines the primitive age of the world as "dreamtime." It is the world of the Australian Aborigines. In their myths, which were passed down only orally as late as the nineteenth century, an especially significant memory of the long process of hallucination's self-mastery has been preserved—admittedly in a form that does not distinguish between hallucination and dream, and that grasps "dream" less as a state of human consciousness than as a general state of the world. "Dream," in these myths, is only distantly related to the images that arise while we are asleep at night. The expression *altjiranga ngambakala*, which is customarily translated as "dreamtime," is already strongly metaphorical. It means something like "born of its own eternity," or "immortal," or "uncreated," and—derived from all these—something like "to see or dream eternal things."[116] It is linked, above all, to two characteristics of dreams. First, dreams know neither past nor future, but only the present. And then, dreams invent and are thus creative. Both these characteristics come together in dreamtime. On one hand, it is imagined as an earlier age, as time prior to the sequential order of things, before decay and death entered the world. On the other hand, it is seen as a time that continues to persist in a subterranean way, so that, in dreams or dreamlike states, one can dive back down into it and participate in its creative forces—the same forces that once wove the world. One of the most important Australian myths tells it as follows:

> During the dreamtime, the whole earth lay in a deep slumber.
> On her surface nothing grew, and nothing moved on her, and
> over everything there lay a great stillness. The animals, and the
> birds as well, still slept beneath the earth's crust. But one day the
> rainbow snake awoke from this great sleep. It forced its way up
> through the earth, and at the spot where its powerful body broke
> through the earth's crust, it pushed the rocks aside. Then the
> Great Snake began its wandering. It moved across the land in all
> directions, and as it wandered it left its traces in the earth, for its
> body formed the landscape in many places. . . . Now all the
> animals awakened, came into the light, and followed the
> rainbow snake, the great mother of all life, throughout the
> whole land. . . . Now the Great Snake proclaimed laws that were
> valid for all beings. . . . However, some beings did not obey, but
> created disorder and fought among themselves. Then the
> mother of all life became angry. . . . Thus, the sacrilegious ones
> were turned to stone; they became cliffs, hills, and mountains.
> . . . Then the Great Snake transformed the beings who obeyed

the laws into human beings, and she gave each of them his totem, from which the human was descended. Thus, the tribes and clans knew themselves by their totem. They were the descendants of the emus, the kangaroos, the black-headed python, and many other ancestors from the dreamtime.[117]

We can most likely consider the linkage of snake and rainbow as a dream image in which the fear-inducing image of the snake, which strikes so abruptly, loses its terror by being connected with the mild rays of a snake-like phenomenon in the heavens; and the deadly grip of the giant snake turns into a great, world-founding movement that embraces heaven and earth. The snake's windings through the countryside, which are supposed to have formed the mountains, valleys, lakes, and rivers, can be read as a mythical condensation in which the winding paths of the Aborigines, on their wanderings, melted into the snake cult that left its imprint on the entire continent. This coincides nicely with the fact that the snake also promulgated the "laws" and assigned the human beings, who only became human through their adherence to the laws, specific totems. Obviously the snake itself was the original totem animal and the laws were the cult devoted to it, while Australian totemism derived from a branch of the snake cult and its displacement onto other major animals of the continent.

That the myth pulled these events together in dreamlike fashion is beyond doubt. But where does it actually mention dreaming? It presents the emergence of the concrete, inhabited world as a general awakening from a dreamless world-coma, in which the snake plays the role of path-breaker and mother of all life. The snake's breakthrough to the surface of the earth is the starting signal for all living things to bestir themselves. The life they then begin is only dreamlike in the very general sense that in it wish and wish fulfillment are not yet clearly or widely separated but form a hallucinatory unity that, as yet, knows nothing of time and decay. But viewed in this way, every imaginary golden age or good world origin stands for a dreamtime, and what is special about the Aborigines is merely that, by borrowing generously from dream categories in their narrative of the origin of the world, they already practice a remarkably generalizing type of interpretation of dreams, which does not analyze concrete dreams so much as the phenomenon of dreaming itself. The

latter is translated into cosmic terms and suggested as the primal, benefi-
cent state of the world. In the process, the originally hallucinatory state of
mental activity is invoked, but in such a way that the thing that is remembered is immediately disguised and made unrecognizable by being transformed into its opposite. That mental state was indeed dreamlike, to the
extent that the representation of the "genius" was hallucinatory wish
fulfillment. But the memory of the fact that it was hair-raising was probably still part of the mental baggage of the Aborigines when they settled
Australia some seventy thousand years ago. Myths, however, are created
precisely in order to get rid of this kind of baggage. They recall unmastered experiences narratively in order to deconstruct their nightmares.
The rainbow snake is a figure for this kind of repetition. It recalls the
horror of an archaic snake cult—which was not a unique invention of the
Aborigines and was very likely among the things they brought with them
to Australia—and then transforms the snake into the mother of all life,
who is painted in delicate rainbow hues, and in the process becomes sedimented into an archetype around which a whole bouquet of myths is
gathered.

What has come down to us of all this—and let's not forget that the
Australian myths were passed on and developed in exclusively oral form
much later than the Eurasian ones, namely well into the nineteenth and
twentieth century—is far removed from the time of the Aborigines'
migration to Australia. It is at a level of narrative and dream culture for
which happiness has long since become more than the experience of
momentary protection, namely lasting harmony with the natural conditions of life, as a state marked by the hallucinatory primal unity of wish
and reality—a blessed unity. Once the hallucinatory original state of
things has been turned upside down in this way, the descent of hallucinations into the mental subregion of dream and the rise of waking
consciousness can also only be represented in a turned-around form—as
the decline of dreamtime. Why the blessed state was not tolerated is
something no narrative about the Fall from grace is able to make plausible. Even the Australian narrative can only provide a made-up story of
how the blessed now-time of the dream became ruined, how mortality,
death, and evil came into the world, and how the dream went underground and was covered over and disfigured by waking consciousness—
to such an extent that, since then, dreamtime has only been able to be

experienced sporadically, whether in sleep or in the rituals that bring it to mind and work toward its complete rehabilitation—toward a backward-leading approach to the blessed origin.

The Aborigines' dreamtime myths are anything but a primitive people's faithful reports of primitive times. They are cultivated screen memories of the origin of dreams. Parts of them virtually deserve to be considered as a theory of dreams. This makes clear, once again, from a different perspective, how much Freud's seemingly so simple thirst dream is dependent on certain preconditions. Condensation and displacement must already be operating automatically for it to take place. It can already be counted among cultivated "blessing" dreams, which we may by no means assume belong to the elementary stock of human dreaming. Once again, the question of origins raises its head. What did the first dreams look like? Here, once again, we have to say: we don't know—and nevertheless we can deduce some things from the physio-logic of dreaming.

Even humans from high cultures continue to combine many different kinds of things in their dreams, all mixed in together. Some dream elements are so confused that we can find no suitable words for them. But this only demonstrates how much dreams *need* the word.[118] Without it, they cannot be recalled and communicated. But if even verbally skilled beings occasionally have the experience that their words don't come close to the things they have dreamed, how laboriously must *Homo sapiens*, on the long road from stammering to speaking, have had to learn to call a dream a dream, and to distinguish between perceptions and representations. This is difficult for another reason, because dreams, from the moment of their inception, are individual, long before human beings know what individuality is. All humans dream, but each one dreams for herself. It takes time before humans are able to adapt the common language they have practiced during their waking hours to this individual experience, which can only be communicated in words and then only inadequately. Language must become mature enough for dreams. When it does, it first articulates dreams that are especially striking. The more moving, the more urgent the dream, the more dreamers need to unburden themselves in language from the pressure that the dreams exert, and the sooner they find words for them. Dreams become graspable where they break into language, as it were, where people use articulated sounds to create a breathing space for themselves vis-à-vis their dreams. And only when dreams become graspable are they recognized as dreams, that is, as special kinds of experience. Before that, they are only more or less indistinct experiences—not in need of language and therefore not worth talking about.

This is when both dreams and dreamers enter tradition as something markedly special, in terms of both the dream's content and the dreamer. But who are these markedly special dreamers? They too are "chosen," but they are no longer the individuals who were chosen by lot and marked for ritual killing. Rather, at a much higher stage of development, they are those individuals who have distinguished themselves by special powers, such as physical strength and mobility, mental acuity and decisiveness, or specific abnormalities. As an example, we should not underestimate either the great respect that archaic societies had for epileptic seizures, sleepwalking, and trance states; or the spontaneous capacity to see them as moving images, performative representations that allow the "genius," or the shapes that it has meanwhile assumed, to be present in unusually unmediated ways. In a broader sense, all the "chosen ones" to whom we refer are individuals with an ecstatic gift. Only the person who naturally possesses such a gift, or is thought to possess it, can hold the collective together as a ruler or shaman. And to the extent that humans have learned to count dreams among the ecstatic phenomena, dreams enter the circle of things that are experienced as meaningful, that is, fateful—and have consequently become capable of articulation as ecstasy turned inward. The dreamer sleeps; he has retreated from the outside world and is entirely self-absorbed, to the extent that in a certain sense he is not at all absorbed in himself, namely not in his right mind. In this state, he experiences something remarkable. He seems to leave himself and enter a state in which he sees, with closed eyes, something by which he feels immediately moved. Yet after he has awakened, his impression is: what I have seen is not *my* image. It is not *I* who have been dreaming; something *dreamed me*. The dream vision accosted me, sought me out.

Only when such visions have assumed the full intensity of the ecstatic and have developed a degree of intrusiveness that makes them break out in words, does the historic significance of the breakthrough of dream telling and tradition emerge. That this breakthrough preferentially occurred in rulers and shamans (to the extent that it is even possible to keep the two roles apart) is a function not only of their disproportionate gift for the ecstatic, but also, even more, of the social position resulting from it. They are the representatives of their collective. Their dreams are not a private affair: they dream as representatives of all the others. Only for this reason are their dreams absolutely meaningful. The salvation and damnation of the collective are at risk in them. Failure to pay attention to the dreams of the representative would be irresponsibility toward the fate of the collective. These dreams have to be handled with great care and circumspection. In them, being meaningful and demanding interpretation are one and the same. Inevitably, they are surrounded by the maximum possible amount of social attention, and ultimately, in Mesopotamian and Egyptian high culture, they lead to the emergence of a caste of dream interpreters who are responsible for the king's dream welfare, just as doctors and cooks are responsible for his bodily welfare. The idea, on the contrary, that one day ordinary people could have started to tell each other their dreams, could have taken it into their heads to inquire what it all might mean and develop interpretive schemata that were then picked up by the royal court and professionalized for the interpretation of royal dreams—this is completely anachronistic.

The interpretation of dreams can scarcely have begun other than as hallucination; it must have been bitterly necessary. The interpretation of a given dream already begins when it is captured in words. The dream that is recounted is no longer the dream that has been experienced. Through words, it has been given a certain shape, endowed with emphases and omissions, and—let us not forget—an escape valve. In the beginning, the interpretation of dreams has a literally physiological aspect. Their telling is a relief. The dream that has broken out in words loses something of its nightmarish quality. And only dreams that have been told, or already interpreted, can be further interpreted, that is, subjected to a secondary work of interpretation. Dreams that break out in words are usually in need of this secondary treatment. Just recounting them is not enough to reduce their nightmarish quality to a level that is bearable. Interpretation through telling must be joined by the interpretation of what has been told. And only this second, secondary, and seconding version is normally what we mean when we speak of the "interpretation of dreams." It began as a way of absorbing the shock of dream telling. This, however, means that dream telling, at its inception, was already what psychoanalysis later intended it to be, namely a source of relief.

GILGAMESH

How can we prove this? Again, only indirectly, by examining evidence. We have no access to the first dreams, nor even to the first ones that broke into words. The oldest surviving written descriptions of dreams derive from the second millennium B.C.E. They belong to a relatively late period of *Homo sapiens*, the high cultures of Mesopotamia and Egypt. Naturally, these are not authentic dream protocols but literary stylizations. It is all the more astonishing that, precisely in the most significant of these dream reports, everything points to the conclusion that their stylization is not some free narrative invention but the archetypal condensation of a thousand-year-old practice of dream interpretation. The literary work to which I refer is *The Epic of Gilgamesh*. Gilgamesh, the legendary ruler of Sumer, seems to have caused a great wall to be erected around Uruk, the capital of his kingdom. Consequently, he must have lived ca. 2,700 years B.C.E. He is the first human figure to have inspired a whole group of legends. His heroic deeds are closely interwoven with another enigmatic figure: Enkidu. There are strong indications that Enkidu was originally the ritual twin of Gilgamesh—the chosen one who had to die for the survival of the people or their kingdom—and Gilgamesh was his counterpart, the priest-king who had to carry out the killing. At any rate, Gilgamesh's lament for Enkidu, which sends Gilgamesh to the ends of the earth and even down to the underworld in the search for a means to escape his own death, provides a kind of basso continuo of the epic—and the cipher of a long-abandoned practice of human sacrifice that was so powerful that the epic still resonates with it even though it has long since covered it up. Enkidu's death has been transformed into the result of a fever, and his figure is so cleverly interwoven with Gilgamesh's that he turns up, in life, as the counterpart of the great king—first as his prehuman opponent, "born in the uplands" and so much his equal in strength that neither can vanquish the other in wrestling,[119] and then as his inseparable "brother," fellow fighter and . . . interpreter of dreams.

Gilgamesh and Enkidu set out together to do battle with Humbaba, the fearsome protector of the cedar forest—"his voice is the Deluge, / his speech is fire, and his breath is death!"[120]

[Gilgamesh climbed to the top of the mountain,]
 [to the hill he poured out an offering of flour:]
["O mountain, bring me a dream. So I see a good sign!"]

[Enkidu made for Gilgamesh a House of the Dream God,]
 [he fixed a door in its doorway to keep out the weather.]
[In the circle *he had drawn* he made him lie down,]
 [and *falling flat* like a net lay himself in the doorway.]

[Gilgamesh rested his chin on his knees,]
 [sleep fell upon him, that spills over people.]
[In the middle of the night he reached his sleep's end,]
 [he rose and spoke to his friend:]

["My friend, did you not call me? Why have I wakened?]
 [Did you not touch me? Why am I startled?]
[Did a god not pass by? Why is my flesh frozen numb?]
 [My friend, I have had the first dream!]

"[The] dream that I had [was an utter confusion:]
 [in] a mountain valley . . .
[The mountain] fell down on top of . . ."
. . . .
 Enkidu spoke to his friend, [gave his dream meaning:]
"My friend, [your] dream is a good omen,
 the dream is precious [*and bodes us well*].

"My friend, the mountain you saw [*could not be Humbaba:*[121]]
 [we] shall capture Humbaba, [him] we [shall *slay,*]
we shall [cast down] his corpse on the field of battle.
 And next morning [we shall see a good] sign [from the
Sun God.]"[122]

In his commentary, the German translator calls the scenes depicted
here an "ancient ritual."[123] In fact, the narrative transports the two heroes
back in time to the prehistory of Uruk, when it was not yet urban and
its residents carried out their cultic activities in mountain caves rather
than elevated, built temples in the center of the city. Still, the dream is
set among purely cultural achievements that serve as a kind of
cushion. There is a specially constructed "House of the Dream God,"[124]

and a door to keep out the "weather," or breath of the dream. A "circle" drawn around the sleeping hero (probably made of roasted flour, *Röstmehl*) is the archaic charmed circle to keep evil out. In addition, Enkidu takes up the position of a "net" in front of the hut, whereby it is unclear whether he is there to catch the right dream or to intercept the storm wind so that it enters the hut as a mild breeze. But all these preparations, culturally at a level that surrounds the dreamer with an entire dream administration, cannot prevent Gilgamesh from being in "utter confusion" and "frozen numb" when he awakens from his terrible dream. All the cushioning has not helped at all, a circumstance that may give us an inkling of the degree to which a striking dream was experienced as a force of nature. This is the moment when dream interpretation must go to work to achieve what all the preparations have failed to do—to turn the dream into a "good omen." Enkidu appears as the archetypical condensation of institutionalized dream interpretation when he announces that the collapsing mountain will destroy not Gilgamesh the dreamer but the monster Humbaba.

In the fourth tablet of the Gilgamesh epic, the "ancient ritual" is repeated five times, with almost identical wording. Only the dream world changes. So far, it has not been possible to reconstruct the second dream. Of the third dream, it is said,

> heaven cried aloud, while earth did rumble.
> The day grew still, darkness came forth,
> there was a flash of lightning, fire broke out.[125]

In the fourth, there is talk of a "Thunderbird," or lion-eagle, and repeated mention of a "mouth [of] fire" and "breath [that] was death."[126] The stiff, pedantic repetition not only underlines the ritual aspect of the process; it is itself a part of process memory—a repetition compulsion transmuted into literature, whose obvious traumatic content offers a profound insight into the ancient history of dreams. Everything suggests that the first articulated dream experiences—like primary hallucinations—are impressions of fright. Humbaba allows us to intuit something of the type of experiences connected with the first "genius" hallucinations. The monster is so terrible that he does not even assume animal or human characteristics. He remains a formless, ghostly horror, and his description consists only in the depiction of his effect: "His voice is the Deluge, his speech is fire, and his breath is death!" But the five visions Gilgamesh has of him, five attempts to capture his ungraspable nature even provisionally, are not so very different from the attempts that Freud reports in the cases of war-traumatized soldiers. Hand-grenade explosions, from the point of view of the person who experiences them, are not very different from collapsing mountains and roaring heavens. But the Gilgamesh epic seizes these experiences at the opposite end, as it were—not where they make their appearance in a highly developed society and lead to the doctor's office, but where their articulation first took shape in the course of human history. There, they appear in the opposite form. Fright dreams, which are so obvious to the psychoanalyst that they no longer give him anything to interpret, were once the very essence of the thing that cried out for inter-pretation. Interpretation, at first, was not intended to solve riddles but to prevent fearful events. What the fright dream attempted to do by producing hallucinatory images and retelling the dream in words, the words of the interpreter attempted to do by giving them a different content.

At first, the secondary words of interpretation were still entirely under the spell of the dream. They too participated in what Freud saw as the retrospective development of fear. Today, we are hardly capable of sensing how much fear was involved, and how much force, when dreams first stormed a waking consciousness that was still in the process of being constituted. At best, we can form an intuitive impression with the help of the oldest written testimonials, for example, from the fact that *The Epic of Gilgamesh* gives as much room to the fearsome dreams about Humbaba as to the victory over the fearsome Humbaba himself, namely an entire tablet. As *Homo sapiens'* waking consciousness struggled to achieve basic continuity and consistency, dreams must have been as threatening to the entire collective as certain hallucinations are nowadays to psychotics. And so emerging consciousness, in desperation, once again turned to the trick of reversal and reinterpreted the representatives of an unmastered hallu-cinatory prehistory as prophets of a still undecided future. The reinterpre-tation of the past as future, and of horrific images as "good omens," are one and the same. We should note, however, that in this respect the future is like a mental space; it only opens up when something takes refuge in it, in the act of interpretation. It is a flight forward, the escape that waking consciousness imagines in order to avoid being overtaken by its hallucinatory past. But it itself starts with hallucination. Where the interpretation of dreams begins, the great drama of hallucination's turning back upon itself is replayed in fast-forward. The great mountain that fell on Gilgamesh in his dream *will be* the defeated Humbaba. This is the archetypical example of this reversal—concentration of the primitive era of dream interpretation in a graspable form. Only in the actual practice of this interpretation—which evidently was linked early on with reading the flight of birds and the entrails of a freshly slaughtered sacrificial victim[127]—did humanity, for the first time, begin to see the future as a separate temporal dimension and grammatical form. Its perception began as the reflex response to an unmastered past.[128], [129]

Once words had been found for fright dreams, words were also found for dreams themselves. But the finding of words for dreams changed dreaming itself. It stabilized waking consciousness and the boundary that separated it from the hallucinatory underground. Before waking consciousness proved sufficiently consolidated to pass on, from generation to generation, not only rituals but also words, and in words something as difficult as dreams, it had to fight a border war with its own underground that persisted for thousands of years. It only gained the upper hand when it no longer had to mark the boundary defensively but was strong enough to blur it on its own, to interfere in the inner working of its underground, and to erect an outpost, as it were, on the territory of hallucination, which had already been forced back. This outpost is Freud's dream censor—another entity that causes us much too little astonishment. Waking consciousness pauses and yet remains present in the shape of its outpost. Compared with the censoring power of waking consciousness, the dream censor is admittedly a weakling. It has no chance against Gilgamesh's Humbaba dreams. But where an outpost of this kind exists, waking consciousness has literally grown beyond itself, has almost reached its maximum extension and solidity—and the dream world has shrunk down so far that it is experienced as bone-shattering force only in exceptional cases. But for smaller and medium-sized outbreaks of the hallucinatory underground, which the relatively calm, ordinary experience of the dream world brings with it, the weak force of the dream censor is relatively well armed. It is able to absorb, or at least cushion, many of them. Others have become so unthreatening to a solidified waking consciousness that it allows them in without further ado.

The easiest way to imagine dream censorship is to remind ourselves how it emerged—not as an anxious oversight body but as a cushion meant to assuage fear.[130] The two foremen of the dream began as upholsterers. Their task was to come up with costumes, disguises, cushions for the unmollified, tormenting motifs from the mental underground—cushions that would make the dream more bearable. Once this has been accomplished, condensation and displacement, the elementary mechanisms that had once constituted the hallucinations, can enfold and soften them as they rise up at night from the psychic underground. Thus, they become the guardians of sleep. And, just as mental space once became two-dimensional, when hallucination turned against itself, now, after waking consciousness has established an outpost on the territory of hallucination, dreams become two-dimensional. The moment a dream contains something unpleasant, the outpost pushes it back down into itself, turns it against itself—and gives it a false bottom. Hallucination that has been steered back to the underground gets an underground of its own. It is separated into a manifest content and a latent motif underneath it. The latter, the site of irritation that has generated the dream, is now expressed in a manifest dream content and is simultaneously pushed down, suppressed, covered over, and transformed into a cipher. Concrete dream images become riddles and enigmas. And where the dream reaches this two-dimensional, reflexive level, dream interpretation also enters its second—and for the moment final—great phase. It becomes decipherment.

This second phase left its mark on the Gilgamesh epic in an incredibly suggestive early form in which its origin is almost legible. The first tablet contains two additional dreams of Gilgamesh, dreams whose incomparably greater degree of complexity can already be seen in the fact that they are narrated around the corner, so to speak—in a situation that has only indirectly to do with them and that is nevertheless essential to their comprehension. The harlot Shamhat, representing the "love goddess" Ishtar, has been sent out into the countryside on Gilgamesh's orders, to bring Enkidu, who eats grass with the gazelles and gathers at the watering hole with the herd animals, under the spell of Uruk. Her companion, the "trapper," says:

"This is he, Shamhat! Uncradle your bosom,
    bare your sex, let him take in your charms!
Do not recoil, but take in his scent!
. . . .
Spread your clothing so he may lie on you, . . .
. . . .
his herd will spurn him, though he grew up amongst it."

And this is exactly what happens.

For six days and seven nights
    Enkidu was erect, as he coupled with Shamhat.

When with her delights he was fully sated,
    he turned his gaze to his herd.
The gazelles saw Enkidu, they started to run,
    the beasts of the field shied away from his presence.
. . . .
Enkidu was weakened, could not run as before,
    but now he had *reason*, and wise understanding.

He came back and sat at the feet of the harlot,
    watching the harlot, observing her features.
Then to the harlot's words he listened intently,
    [as Shamhat] talked to him, to Enkidu.[131]

Enkidu's sexual excess with Shamhat has made him a human being. It is not copulation itself that made this happen; after all, animals copulate all the time, without stopping. Rather, it is the circumstance that he has fallen under the spell of a divinity. The behavior of Shamhat (literally: "the voluptuous") reveals what a "love goddess" originally is—by no means a charming Aphrodite or Venus who turns the heads of young men and winks at the consequences, but a divinity whose "gentleness" consists, at first, only in the fact that she is paid part of what she is owed in a lesser currency—sexual excess instead of slaughter. Enkidu is consecrated to the goddess Ishtar, but only metaphorically, in such a way that he survives the consecration. He is dragged not into her yawning abyss but into the open womb of her representative. Sexual union with the latter is no longer a mere natural event but an excess to be celebrated. *Excedere* means "to go beyond," and in a very literal sense sexuality, when it falls under the spell of the cult, goes beyond its own naturalness and begins to represent something that it is not: sacrifice. With this, it becomes specifically human. The spiritual dimension opens up in it. In the words of the epic, after "six days and seven nights," Enkidu has been transformed from a hominid into a human, who is admittedly "weakened" and alienated from the world of animals, but is full of "reason." Now he has become ready to perceive human language; in a word, he is ready for the capital of culture, Uruk. But before he enters the city, hand in hand with Shamhat, she tells him two dreams of Gilgamesh, which concern Enkidu but in a coded form. He is already expected in Uruk. . . .

> "Before you even came from the uplands,
>> Gilgamesh in Uruk was seeing you in dreams:
> Gilgamesh rose to relate a dream, saying to his mother:
>> 'O mother, this is the dream that I had in the night—
>
> " 'The stars of the heavens appeared above me,
>> like a rock from the sky one fell down before me.
> I lifted it up, but . . . I could not dislodge it,
>
> . . . .
>> " '[the land was gathered] about it.
> A crowd [*was milling about*] before it,
>
> . . . .
> " '[Like a babe-in]-arms they were kissing its feet,
>> like a wife [I loved it,] caressed and embraced it.
> [I lifted it up,] set it down at your feet,
>> [and you, O mother, you] made it my equal.' "

And Gilgamesh's mother, the divine "[Wild-Cow] Ninsun," solves the dream as follows:

> "My son, the axe you saw is a friend,
>> like a wife you'll love him, caress and embrace him,
>
> . . . .
>> " 'A mighty comrade will come to you, and be his friend's
> savior,

" 'Mightiest in the land, strength he possesses,
         his strength is as mighty as a rock from the sky.' "[132]

The rock of Anu[133] has the format of a meteor—a "star" that has fallen
from the heavens. The Kaaba in Mecca is also a "rock" of this kind.
Collectives that have experience with meteors surround them with shuddering, appeasing attention. The practice, still in force in Mecca today, of
seeming to kiss the feet of the meteor already occurs in Gilgamesh's
dream. In the dream, however, this practice is outdone by an image that
seems too bizarre to be considered as the straightforward repetition of a
ritual, but that for this very reason seems to us all the more like a dreamlike condensation of ritual processes: "like a wife [I loved it,] caressed and
embraced it." Judged by psychoanalytic criteria, this is perverse—a crass
example of fetishism.[134] Isn't Gilgamesh, with the rock, acting exactly like
some of Freud's patients who caressed handkerchiefs or women's shoes
instead of the woman they couldn't possess—except that in Gilgamesh's
case, he is denying himself a homosexual inclination, since the rock
stands for Enkidu?

To interpret it this way is to apply modern-day circumstances of
censorship creation to a text from the second millennium B.C.E., with its
(very different) mode of coming to terms with history. It is to be blind to
the very thing that makes this text so instructive for us today—its historical difference. Mesopotamian rulers could dispose of their underlings in
ways that we can scarcely imagine nowadays, while at the same time they
were subject to rigid ritual constraints that took little account of personal
preferences. We know much too little about the historical figure of
Gilgamesh to even speculate reasonably about his sexual orientation,
much less to assume that the creation of sexual identity took place
according to models from the recent European past.[135] Certainly, the
dream image of making love to the rock is a perverse enigma. But the
riddle is not that of bourgeois sexual fetishism, in which a shoe, stocking,
or handkerchief is a coded, forbidden sexual object. What is forbidden
here is of a different kind altogether. Meteors, namely, are stones thrown
by higher powers—and as such they are the godfathers of a human-all-
too-human practice that involved throwing stones: stoning. The way the
"crowd" gathers around the rock that Anu has caused to fall from heaven,
the collective once gathered around the chosen one—with the rock in

hand that consecrated him to the divinity. The rock around which all of Uruk assembles is a cipher for the human objects at which real rocks were thrown at an earlier time—a practice that by this time has been forbidden, since human sacrifice is subject to a censorship so strict that not even the memory of it is allowed to surface.

If this is true, then Gilgamesh's dream of copulating with the rock is, for its part, a hallucinatory piece of memory of the first order, which recalls, in an extremely condensed form, how sexuality once became part of the cult: as a practice designed to provide relief. That divinities can be placated by sexual excess means, in simple language, that sexual excess belongs to the means of moderating the horror of sacrifice, of reversing and ultimately preventing it. In this literal sense of the word, it entered into the cult as a "perversion," a ritual measure aimed at turnaround and reinterpretation. The sacrifice does not remain what it was if the act is accompanied and saturated by excessive, demonstrative sexual practices. In the words of the dream, if the stone is appeased, "weakened" by caresses, Gilgamesh can "lift" it and throw it at the feet of his wise, divine mother. In other words he can present it to her for interpretation. Her interpretation, then, does verbally what Gilgamesh has previously done quite pragmatically. It turns the stone that has fallen on him into a good thing: "A mighty comrade will come to you, and be his friend's savior."

This has a practically messianic tenor—and unintentionally points to the fact that the "stone" is the cipher for a chosen one who, at the acme of Mesopotamian high culture, no longer saved by being stoned, but instead by being consumed. The interpretation of the divine "Wild-Cow" reveals the multidimensionality of the entire dream scenario. What Gilgamesh does with the "rock" in his dream, Shamhat does with Enkidu in the "reality" of the epic. But just as, in the latter case, Gilgamesh was saved by the fact that Enkidu came to Uruk—only together with him is he able to kill Humbaba and the bull of heaven—so the entry of sexuality into the cult and its ritual excess saved humanity from human sacrifice. Human sacrifice does not stop reverberating through the hallucinatory underground of the high culture, and, in the process, serving as one of the great sources of imagery in the Gilgamesh epic.

There are, by the way, *two* dreams that Shamhat tells about Gilgamesh. The story is almost the same, except that in the first dream it is a "rock" that draws the attention of the awestruck crowd in the market square of

Uruk and with which Gilgamesh then copulates. In the second dream, it is an ax. The ax too has its multidimensional aspect. Two different historical phases of sacrifice are represented. Stoning, in which all members of the collective cast stones at the chosen victim until he can no longer defend himself and they fall on him, is the earlier one. The later, much more cultivated phase is the one in which the chosen one is joined by a counterpart in the form of a shaman, priest, or ruler who is no less chosen, whose destiny it is to wield the sacrificial ax, and who, in doing so, represents the entire collective as much as the victim who gives his life for it.

The evolution of human culture includes the development of a culture of dreaming. The Gilgamesh epic is a great witness to this fact. In sketching the crudeness of the dreams that once brought about the breakthrough to the word, and the effort it must have cost to turn dreams against themselves in such a way that they began a double life as (1) latent motif and (2) manifest content, it provides the first cultural history of dreams. It can give us a sense of the historicity of dreams in a way no other written work can. In collectives that are constituted by human sacrifice, dreams are different than in collectives where ritual sexual practices are beginning to play the main role in the creation of community. Yet another situation prevails once the sexual rituals have become sedimented into fixed family and kinship relations that are, at best, consecrated in the sanctuary, but are no longer carried out there. The relations that create censorship may change more slowly than social relations, but they are by no means ahistorical. Anyone who thinks of the primitive thought activity in dreams as an unchanging basic stratum, and of the activity of waking, conscious thought as taking place above it, will have little intuitive sense of the changes that occurred in the structure of censorship and dreams in a market-centered society, one that relies less and less on firmly established sexual relations and all the more on the impact of dreamlike sequences of images.[136]

WILD INTERPRETATION

This is not the place to rehearse and continue the cultural history of dreams that began with Gilgamesh, nor to describe how the social integration of dreams about shamans and rulers gradually led to established institutions and models for their interpretation, which were reproduced and varied, layered, and popularized until dream interpretation was even offered for sale in ancient marketplaces, and finally, in the second century C.E., Artemidorus of Daldis wrote his *Interpretation of Dreams*—a comprehensive compendium of all possible dreams and interpretations, thematically organized and divided according to more or less scientific criteria into more and less credible ones—and an involuntary proof of how difficult it sometimes is to tell the difference between reliable and unreliable, serious and unserious dream interpretation.

Nor is this the place to take a new stab at giving the interpretation of dreams a scientific basis. Just as Friedrich Engels's *Socialism: Utopian and Scientific*[137] led to the opposite movement from science to utopia (and its utopian impulses are still the best thing about socialism), so Freud's *The Interpretation of Dreams* is most dubious where it pretends to be most scientific, namely where it presents sexual symbols as "stable translations." Reference to the Gilgamesh epic has made it extremely likely that "sexual symbol" originally meant the exact opposite of what Freud thought: not a symbol for sexuality, but sexuality as a symbol for something else, something more closely allied with drives than sexuality is, namely traumatic stimulus. If this is true, however, then Freud's "stable translations" are far less stable than he thought. In this case, the interpretation of dreams is significantly context-dependent and is far more dependent than the psychoanalytic setting would have us believe on the cultural standards, semantic schemata, and undecidable questions that arise in the concrete relationship between dreamers and dream interpreters. In short, the interpretation of dreams moves quite some distance from science toward the "wild psychoanalysis"[138] that Freud wanted to see strictly banned from his scientific method. But as soon as Freud himself was faced not with his sexually neurotic patients but with works of visual art, literary texts, ethnological materials, mass psychological phenomena, or entire social processes, he was warmly attracted to it. As soon as he was not forced to evaluate the particulars of an individual's personal associations, since fortunately they were no longer accessible, he proceeded to analyze and interpret as if freed from all inhibitions. In the face of this challenge, how intently he followed the scent! Without their speculative exorbitance, their unproven suppositions and risky conclusions, his works would not be half so interesting. To forbid all psychoanalytic "wildness" is the surest means of sterilizing it. Interdictions are of no use here.

We must set limits to "wild" interpretation—limits in two directions, like those Kant established in the case of exaggerated reason—to prevent interpretation from slipping over into uncontrolled association and to protect it from the illusion that it could ever become strictly scientific.

In this chapter, however, we have been concerned only with understanding dreams as the tip of the iceberg of primitive thought activity. As we have seen, our initial suspicion has been roundly confirmed: The foremen of dreams are far more than mere constructors of dreams. They are nothing less than elementary shapers of the intellect and of culture: driving forces of human becoming. But after having given these forces the names condensation, displacement, *and reversal*, and described their function as "imagination," we have still only touched on their exterior. What they themselves *are* has barely been mentioned. Yes, they are events created by nervous energy, although not of a kind that could be measured neurologically. They are translations, but not translations that we can simply reduce to "language." The opposite is true: Language itself, no less than imagination, first emerged from the interplay of these forces. Language always requires a physical substratum. It is a late product of natural history, a mental veneer applied to previous energetic forms, not their foundation—certainly not a foundation that would be self-explanatory. For this reason, the path taken by Jacques Lacan leads us astray. Does it become any more clear what the unconscious is, if we are told that it is "structured like a language"?[139] No, all that has happened is that one thing in need of an explanation has been defined in terms of another, like a mathematics that tries to solve for an unknown by introducing another unknown. Has anything been gained when we replace the Freudian terms by others drawn from linguistics, and instead of *condensation* say "metaphor," instead of *displacement,* "metonymy"?[140] On the contrary, physiological-energetic processes are merely being distilled into purely semiotic ones—into complex references and language structures that are supposedly autarkic and that prestructure all desire and all actions.[141] If we really want to know what language is, we must first set out in the opposite direction and to try to understand how the energetic work of the nerves has been able to *drive* the direction of human development—with which we inevitably are confronted with the question of what a drive is.

CHAPTER TWO

Drives

THE PRINCIPLE OF CONSTANCY

ORDINARILY, MODERN EUROPEAN LANGUAGES conjugate their verbs in either the active or the passive voice. Someone carries out an action, or an action is carried out by someone. But there is something in between: An action is carried out; it happens. For this, ancient Greek had a special form of conjugation that existed alongside the active and passive voices. It was called the "middle" voice. It has not survived, but it lives on, in a way, in intransitive verbs, which are spoken by a subject but do not refer to any object. For example: "The child grows." Here the child is the grammatical subject. But is the growing something the child does or something that happens to the child? Both. At the same time, the child is both object and subject of his growing; consequently he is neither. The situation that obtains for growing is similar, in German, to the situation when we consider drives, and driving. The German verb *treiben*, in one of its common usages, can mean "float." When a boat *treibt* on the water, it is both driving and being driven—and neither one nor the other. Here, the German word *treiben* has a mediate sense, which also characterizes the corresponding noun: *Trieb*,[1] or "drive." *Trieb* is a German idiom. Words like *instinct, impulse, wish,* or *desire* are imperfect replications; the closest German word may be *Drang;* in English, "urge." German *Trieb* has a wide range of meanings. The first fresh

85

green sprouts that appear in the spring on bushes and trees are called
Triebe, "shoots."

Where there are *Triebe*, there is movement. But not everything that
moves has a drive. Flying projectiles, for example, or leaves that have been
kicked up have no drive, nor do waves. All these are merely driven. Only
where a bounded form *moves itself* can we speak of a drive. A stone also
moves as long as it is falling; it even moves of its own force, namely its
weight, which causes it to fall. But we only speak of a drive when an object
is moved by something other than its own weight, something that coun-
teracts gravity. All organisms, including plants, have this drive when their
bulbs or roots put forth stems, trunks, branches, blossoms, and fruits.
Growth is an elementary form of drive. Plants are self-moving; they move
themselves while remaining in one place. Animals are the first beings
that are capable of moving themselves from place to place. A few especially clever animals have even been able to pass their self-movement on
to certain tools they call automobiles.

Self-movement is one of nature's mysteries. To this day, we do not
know how material acquired the capacity to do this. But the enormous
advantage of mobility, which humans learn to value increasingly as they
grow older, surely did not come into existence voluntarily. Certain constel-
lations of material learned to move because they lacked something. Stones
lack nothing, but this is evidently not true of bacteria. Like all organisms,
bacteria contain fluid and are at risk of drying out. The result is that they
must absorb nourishment. Drive is the urge to offset a lack. If membranes,
organs, and mucus membranes do not have a minimum amount of liquid,
death results, and the more highly developed the organism, the more
powerfully it experiences this drying out. It feels bodily stress, which can
cause unbearable pain in the form of hunger and thirst. The lack of nourishment is thus also an excess. Drive is the urgent need to reduce excessive
stress, an attempt to achieve a maximally stress-free state. To put it another
way, a drive is the tendency of an organic being toward inertia. It differs
from merely physical inertia to the extent that it works to counteract gravity.
At the same time, it extends the principle of inertia, giving it a sublimated,
looser form as a *tendency* toward inertia. The organism moves in order not
to have to move again. It tends toward rest. Its drive is a desire for rest. All
the excitement on earth comes from the obstacles that hold back this desire
to rest, that dam it up and drive it along detours and down false paths.

Drives appear to be a purely physiological-psychological matter. But a glance at the origins of Western philosophy suffices to show us how powerful this desire for rest is. Why did Thales of Miletus stumble upon the bold idea that all of nature should be reduced to a single element—water? Because he felt an urge to discover, among the multiplicity and agitation of appearances and movements, something absolutely reliable, something purely and simply existent, in which it would be possible to locate coherence, stability, reliability, orientation, and rest. Naturally, the ancient ontologists only longed for and made up this source of rest; they were never able to prove that it really exists. But that their need for the fiction was so strong that they spared no pains in imagining a world-ground (Thales), an invariant and unchanging essence (Parmenides), or eternal ideas (Plato) shows the extent of the lack they sought to compensate.

All of ancient ontology can be read as the expression and cipher of the desire for rest.[2] It serves the drives, about which it is silent and about which its silence is more eloquent than the neurological "principle of constancy" that Freud, following Gustav Theodor Fechner, formulated as follows: "The nervous system is an apparatus dedicated to eliminating the stimuli that reach it, or to reducing them to the lowest possible level; or an apparatus that, if it were only feasible, would aim to remain free from stimulation altogether."[3] Indeed: "if it were only feasible" . . . in other words, the nervous system desires something impossible, namely "to remain free from stimulation altogether." This it finds impossible, since it lives to process stimuli and is only alive as long as it does so. But processing and responding to stimuli means wanting to get rid of the excitation—and not just a few stimuli, but all of them. The work of the nervous system, therefore, aims at nothing less than a complete lack of excitation. As Freud correctly notes, it wants to "*remain* free from stimulation." It wishes to rid itself of the stimuli but by no means to get rid of itself. Its state should be a state of freedom from stimulation. In this, it cannot be successful, for where something is experienced, there is excitation, and where there is no excitation, there is death. Precisely this urge to achieve the impossible reveals the drive's utopian dimension. Greek ontology gives expression to what it ultimately lacks, namely the achievement of a state of rest within pure existence—the polar opposite of rest in death, since death is not actually a state of rest, but rupture, dissolution, nonexistence. The Buddhist word *nirvana* already transfigures the concept by making death into a utopia—a self-consciously resigned death, humbled by life and plastered like a steamy, comforting adhesive over the pulsing life of the drives as a way of preventing life's utopian excess, the impossibility of ever fulfilling its urge to enjoy the complete absence of excitation.[4]

By no means is the "principle of constancy" a "Nirvana principle,"[5] as Freud would have had us believe in his later years, following his discovery of traumatic repetition compulsion. The principle of constancy is a valid formula for the physiological dynamic of drives, although it lacks awareness of their paradoxical urge to attain the impossible. It lives up to its name, however, to the extent that it provides the consistent neurophysiological basis of all of Freudian theory and can be counted among the midwives of psychoanalysis. The term already appears in Freud's early, unpublished *Project for a Scientific Psychology* (1895), as "the principle of neuronal inertia," which means "that neurons tend to divest themselves of Q [the quantity of their neuronal excitation]." The nervous system seeks to give this quantity off "through a connecting path to the muscular mechanisms, and in that way to keep itself free from stimulus." The organism seeks to deal with external stimuli by means of reflex movements or, if it is sufficiently mobile, to avoid them altogether by a "flight from the stimulus." But there are also "endogenous stimuli—which have equally to be discharged. These have their origin in the cells of the body and give rise to the major needs: hunger, respiration, sexuality. From these the organism cannot withdraw as it does from external stimuli; it cannot employ their Q [quantity] for flight from the stimulus." Here, where he is forced to imagine something other than a flight from stimuli, is where, for Freud, "the psychic" begins. It occurs in response to internal stimuli, more specifically as a result of the detour that their discharge is forced to take. This detour requires considerably more than reflex or flight responses do; it requires costly movements, like the search for nourishment or sexual partners. In order to be able to carry these movements out at all, the organism must set aside a "store of quantity"; in other words, it must store excitation (energy) before it can discharge it. The internal stimuli resist the principle of inertia, but only in order to serve it better. It is "modified into an endeavor at least to keep the Q [quantity] as low as possible and to guard against any increase of it—that is, to keep it constant,"[6] but it is not leveraged out of existence.

Not until two decades later, long after he has developed the basic characteristics of psychoanalysis, does Freud return to undertake a systematic review of these ideas. Instead of "endogenous stimuli," he now says "drives." In the later lectures, he even says: "The theory of the drives is so to say our mythology. Drives are mythical entities, magnificent in their indefiniteness. In our work, we cannot for a moment disregard them, yet we are never sure that we are seeing them clearly."[7] In considering this famous passage, people are wont to forget that in the early years of psychoanalysis there was a lot of talk about excitation, excitation generated by wishes, affective representation, and stimuli, but little mention of drives. The word first comes to the fore in the *Three Essays on the History of Sexuality* (1905). Another decade goes by before Freud, in "Drives and their Fates,"[8] considers it necessary to explain what he means by drives. Drives, he now says, are a special sort of stimulus, namely "a stimulus to the psyche." "A drive stimulus emanates not from the outside world, but from inside the organism itself." And, "for example, when a strong light hits the eye, this is not a drive stimulus, but it is when we sense dryness in the mucous membrane of the throat, or irritation in the mucous membrane of the stomach. ... Furthermore, we remain true to the essence of the stimulus if we assume it has the effect of a single impact. ... The effect of a drive . . . is never that of a *momentary* impact, but always that of a *constant* force. And because it impinges not from outside, but from inside the body, flight is of no avail against it. It is better to call the drive stimulus a 'need'; what removes this need is its 'satisfaction.' This can be achieved only by making a sufficient (adequate) alteration to the internal source of stimulation."[9]

The thing that is special about internal stimuli is that their processing has an effect on them, either by causing their "source" to dry up or by diverting it. Through this reflexive relationship, an interplay develops between the source and the processing of the internal stimuli, and as it comes into balance, something is created that Freud rather grandiloquently terms "the psyche"—and that he occasionally imagines as having a substance of its own. This is true, for example, of the following passage, where he distills his reflections on the subject of "drive stimulus" into the well-known definition that many psychoanalysts still consider definitive:

"The 'drive' emerges as a concept on the borderline between the mental and the physical—the psychic representative of stimuli flowing into the psyche from inside the body."[10] In this passage, it is not just that mental and physical elements are imagined almost geographically, like two regions separated by a border to ensure that each remains autonomous with regard to the other. The "drive stimulus" also breaks down: into a drive, which is reduced to representing the stimulus mentally, without making at all clear what this representation accomplishes; and a stimulus that comes "from inside the body," without our having any sense of how it is still related to the source of the stimulus. Is it identical with the source, or is it different? Is it itself somatic, or merely a kind of emanation from the body? Besides, it is not actually the stimulus that is being advertised as being "on the borderline between the mental and the physical," but rather the drive. This brings yet another difficulty with it. Representation is a dual structure. A representative represents *something*; for example, an ambassador represents his country. But in this case he cannot also be some kind of an intermediary being between the country and himself. He is either a representative or something in between. As an in-between thing or "borderline concept," the representative rings hollow.

Freud himself, obviously dissatisfied with this mangled definition, made a second attempt within the year. "A drive can never be an object of consciousness, only the idea representing it. . . . If drives were not attached to ideas and did not manifest themselves as emotional states, we could know nothing of them."[11] This, to be sure, is a 180-degree turn. Here, the drive is no longer a psychic representative, it *is represented* psychically.[12] Now it is once again defined as a stimulus that "flows from within the body." What we are able to grasp, however, are only its psychosomatic effects. Its representatives are now called imagined ideas, or representations (*Vorstellungen*), and the notion that representations represent something needs no further explanation; this is how they are defined. And since it is a stimulus that is made manifest in them, they also always have an energetic aspect. They are "invested with a certain quantity of energy (libido, interest) from the drive,"[13] the so-called quantity of affect, which can be wholly or partially detached from the notion in which it is invested, or cathected, and displaced onto something else. This results in the very discrepancy between representations and emotional states whose resolution is the task of psychoanalytic work.

From their inception, Freud's several attempts to define drives are all anthropocentric, indeed therapy-focused. He takes it completely for granted that "the psychic" should be understood as the human psyche, even the neurotic one that is laid out on the analyst's couch. Nevertheless, it is only the last-mentioned definition that brings drive and representation into a plausible relationship. On one hand, it makes clear that drives, the organic tendency to inertia that the simplest organisms have in common with the most complicated ones, is only graspable in its manifestations, never in itself, immediately. On the other hand, it emphasizes that drives cannot help manifesting themselves: this is what they *consist* of. This is something Freud's drives have in common with Hegel's "essence." "Essence must appear," Hegel wrote in a famous passage.[14] It is conceived as pure dynamism, as a world drive inflated into a world spirit that saturates all physical and mental forms, manifests itself in all of them, and is identical with none of them. But for Freud this is much too windy. He is satisfied with a drive that is active in all organisms: the organic, natural basis of representation. It is on this basis, then, that every serious study of representation must begin—and, as its first step, must take a step backward to the neurophysiology from which psychoanalysis first emerged.

EXPERIENCE

We are all familiar with states of excitation and tension. Not that we have understood them or that we have known precisely what they are or where they come from; but we are familiar with them as something that we feel every day. And as long as there has been neuroscience, it has also been possible to tell what occurs in an organism when it experiences tensions. Physical stimuli, brought about by the effects of pressure, light rays, sound waves, smells, or inner organs affect the organism's nervous system, are translated into electrical impulses, and are discharged via innumerable nerve cells by means of complicated chemical reactions. We are justified in speaking of neuronal digestion. The organism experiences this process passively, by having a wealth of external impressions and inner sensations, and actively, by constantly reacting to them. After all, its nervous system, following the "principle of constancy," is doing nothing but processing, digesting, and discharging stimuli.

Since brain science began to investigate the reasons why this is so, an abyss has opened up. No human being experiences what he is doing neurologically. Who could ever count the billions of nerve cells that make up his own brain? We are aware of none of their dizzyingly large numbers or the innumerable intertwined paths that electrical impulses create as they find their way, via chemical microprocesses, through this labyrinth. True, that we experience anything at all is due entirely to these microprocesses. But the converse is also true: We only experience something because we do not experience these microprocesses. To put it another way, only because we are insensitive to the details of our own response to stimuli are we even capable of having an experience. Individual sensations are already concentration centers, already have a relatively crude shape, and fulfill, on an elementary physiological level, a criterion that René Descartes was only prepared to apply to incontrovertible truths: They appear *clear and distinct*. A truth, according to Descartes, must be so clear and distinct that there can be no doubt about it. A sensation—this would be the physiological response—must be so clear and distinct that it can be articulated, at least once there are words for it.

In this sense, even sensations are not primary. There is something underneath and behind them: life. What that is, we do not know. Metabolism is something that, while it can accurately be said to describe life's processes, is also rather extrinsic; it does not really get at the mystery of how something like life became possible. Life includes experience, at least for all higher organisms—and perhaps for the most primitive as well? They too already exist "in reciprocal exchange with the environment," and normally "the necessities—energy and matter—are available in sufficient quantity in their immediate surroundings."[15] Yet there are also, in the environment, "things that the living organism does not need or that can harm it. Its membranes must therefore be selective and can only allow certain materials in, and others out. This is the primal form of living beings' selective interaction with their environment, and hence the primal form of perception." This is how Gerhard Roth puts it. Certainly, where something is perceived, there is selectivity. But is the opposite necessarily and unqualifiedly true, that is, where there is selectivity, there is perception? At a minimum, the "primal form" of perception, if we are even prepared to use this term, does not occur through the medium of differentiated senses. It is a pre-sensual behavior of metabolism itself. "An example of this are plants, which take carbon dioxide from the air, and water (and some minerals) from the earth, and, with the help of sunlight, use them to make sugar in the process called photosynthesis. In other words, they produce metabolic energy. To do this, they do not need to have a nervous system. But still, it is hard to deny them perception. They have a light-driven diurnal rhythm and exhibit phototropism and geotropism, i.e., they clearly adapt their behavior to external stimuli such as light and gravity." But while it may be difficult to deny that these organisms have perception, it is at least as difficult to ascribe experience to them. They are borderline cases. But at least as soon as we see the first rudiments of nerves, the beginning of experience is present. Perception and experience become one.

Experience is a continuum of intensity. Its maximum is shock. If the intensity falls below a certain level, it vanishes into imperceptibility, without our being able to say that it has completely ceased. It is not true that during anesthesia and comas nothing at all is experienced, even if the patient swears afterward that she has not been aware of anything. Experience exists at and beneath the threshold of sensation—something that is also true, by the way, in regard to external objects. Some objects are no longer identifiable from a certain distance; if they move even farther away, we become unsure whether we sense them at all, and finally they may be so far away that it is possible to be certain that they definitively exert no stimulus on the nervous system. When it comes to inner stimuli, however, we do not have this certainty. Inner stimuli affect our own body even when the impact is so slight that we are unable to perceive it. "Imperceptible experience"—this sounds paradoxical, but it is actually the rule according to which the entire incalculable microprocessing of stimuli in the animal world takes place. Sense impressions are already highlights[16] of experience—sufficiently coarse, strong, and distinct to pass the regulatory threshold. And what is sensed is not experienced as the processing of the stimuli as such; instead, the latter is manifested as agreeable or disagreeable feelings of cold, warmth, color, form, sound, smell, taste, pressure, hunger, thirst, sexual urges, and so on.

In this process, something occurs that we can hardly marvel at sufficiently. Light and sound waves, temperature, odors, pressure, tension, pain can only be processed by the nervous system if it transforms them into electrical impulses. The nervous system equalizes all these stimuli, without any concern for where they come from. It dissolves all the qualitative differences among them and leaves only quantitative ones: varying degrees of intensity. "This is the principle of the *neutrality of the neural code*. This neutrality is necessary in order for different sensual systems and processing pathways to communicate with each other within a system of senses, and ultimately to transform the results of this processing into excitation of the motor system, and thus into behavior."[17] These are the words of a neurological specialist. He squelches our amazement by immediately conceiving of the process in a purposeful language. The electrical impulses must be neutralized *in order that* coordinated behavior can function. But this "in order that" is theory after the fact, not the motive of a nervous system *in statu nascendi*. The nervous system does not have the "purpose" of optimizing coordination between its innumerable cells. If we can ascribe any motive at all to it, then only this one: to rid itself of excitation as quickly and completely as possible. In the process, as a quasi-secondary product, coordinated behavior develops. What merits our amazement is not merely the fact that our nervous system succeeds in neutralizing the most diverse qualities of stimuli, turning them into electrical impulses, but even more the fact that these stimuli are still experienced as a qualitative fullness. The equalization of quality into quantity is linked to a re-differentiation of quantity into quality. The second move is the more mysterious. The processing of qualitative stimuli into quantitative excitation seems to appear to us in reverse, namely as qualities of experience that correspond in striking fashion to the qualitative stimuli— comparable to the way the external world does a headstand in the retina and is set back on its feet by actual experience. We know something about the processing of stimuli only because it is manifested in experience; only as human beings who experience can we become brain scientists. But we don't know how the processing of stimuli is manifested in experience. Here we encounter the enigma of representation. That life represents itself in experience remains utterly mysterious, even for the neuroscientist.

PATHWAYS

Freud set his course straight for this enigma when he associated drives with representation. He was also not wrong when he characterized what enters the nervous system, coming from stimuli, as "quantity," even if, somewhat simplemindedly, he imagined it as flowing energy and was not sufficiently knowledgeable about the neurons it traverses. At that time, little was known about the complicated neurochemical process that allows electrical energy, at the ends of the nerves, to jump across to others. Despite this, the concept Freud introduced, in the *Project* to characterize processing of stimuli—creating pathways, or paths (*Bahnung*)[18]—has proven to be especially serviceable at more-advanced levels of neuroscience. Through the billions of cells that an organism creates in just a few years, electrical impulses lay down their pathways. If, in this process, they are following any lawful procedure, it is that of inertia. They take the path of least resistance. And once a path like this has been created, it is already easier to create it the next time around. This is evidently true not just when humans hack their way through the jungle with machetes but already in the microscopic process that takes place at the tiny extremities of nerve cells.

There are various types of nerve cells. As described by psychoanalysts François Ansermet and Pierre Magistretti:

> Their names are expressive of their forms: double pyramidal cell, bipolar cell, spindle-shaped cell, granular cell, and Purkinje cell (named for the Czech histologist who described these cells in the nineteenth century), to mention only a few examples. Despite their differences in form and size—some neurons, such as the motor neurons that control the muscles of the big toe, have axons more than a meter long, which reach from the spinal cord to the foot, while others project only a couple of millimeters—their function is relatively uniform. This is fortunate for the neuroscientist, for how could he hope to research the brain if all of its 100 billion nerve cells followed individual rules for their function? . . . Functionally, each neuron has three parts: a receptor zone, the dentrites, which receive information from other neurons; a zone that integrates the information that has been received, the cell body; and a part that passes signals on to the other neurons, the axon. What is decisive are the contacts between the neurons, . . . the sites where the exchange of information takes place. This contact zone between the neurons is called the synapse. It includes a large, presynaptic part found at the end of the axon, and a postsynaptic part, which generally corresponds to a specialized

zone of the dendrites and is called the dendritic spine. . . .
Each neuron creates ca. 10,000 synapses with other neurons.
The result is a quadrillion contact points at which the
information can be transmitted between the neurons. . . . The
presynaptic part of the synapse contains a kind of small sack
that is called the vesicle and in which thousands of molecules
collect: the neurotransmitters . . . by means of which the
neurons transmit their signals. They are released when the end
of the axon is activated and the vesicles empty the
neurotransmitters they contain into the synaptic gap. . . . The
synaptic gap is a tiny space only a couple of millionths of a
millimeter wide, which separates the pre- and postsynaptic
sides from each other.[19]

Neuroscience deals with unimaginably large numbers and unimaginably small spaces. As tiny as the gap may be that we are talking about here, it is empty space. The transmitter molecules have to leap across it the way mountain climbers leap across crevasses in a glacier. When the electrical impulse arrives at the presynaptic side and drives the transmitters out of their vesicles like a swarm of pigeons out of their cote, it gives each of them a miniscule electrical charge, and it is this electrical charge that makes possible the leap across the gap. On the postsynaptic side sit molecules that carry the opposite charge. They are lying in wait for the newly released molecules, which dock there. Thus an electrical tension is created between the two nerve cells, just like the positive and negative poles of a battery, a sort of "current" or "line" of electrical impulses crossing from the pre- to the post-synaptic side. They can be received there only thanks to the fact that the post-synaptic membrane is not impenetrable but open, at certain places, for milliseconds. Here it lets the impulses in, turning the cell into a channel that conducts them through. And wherever a cell has opened a cell membrane once, it opens more easily the next time—the way a bottle can be opened more easily the second time than the first.

The so-called neural pathways are electrically created nerve channels. And just as a dried-out river leaves behind a riverbed that is already prepared to fill up with water after the next rainfall and, in the process, depending on the strength of the current, to become broader or deeper, create new channels, or be modified in other ways, so the nerve current immediately prepares the cells that have been opened for it to pass through, thanks to the electrical charges and chemical effects, to open again. It creates in them a state of heightened readiness for the next burst of electrical impulses that seeks to find its way through the nervous system. In other words, the neural river prepares the area it flows through for the next stream, for its repetition, with modifications.

Research on the complex neurochemical process that makes this passage possible has made enormous progress. There is, however, one thing it cannot do, namely, predict the exact path that the processing of stimuli will take through the nervous system. The reason for this is the enormous number of nerve cells. The processing of stimuli has a prodigious number of choices. It faces an excess of offerings that it cannot come close to exhausting. A brain leaves innumerable possible pathways unused. Here we see a crass disproportion between supply and demand— a drastic case of waste. But precisely this wasteful surplus of possibilities is the brain's fund of intelligence. It loosens neural determinations. Because of the surplus of possibilities, it is no longer possible to make an unambiguous decision as to which order of synapses is optimal for the electrical impulses' trip through the brain. Here, it is not only brain researchers who come up against the limits of complexity, but the stimulus itself, in its processing. How, in its urge for discharge, faced with ten thousand synapses per neuron and given the innumerable, nearly equally permeable sites that are on offer, should it always, without error, choose the most permeable one—especially since, in the brain, resistance to the current is part of the same process and is undergoing continuous movement and modification? In this case, it must not only respond to external conditions, like the river. As certainly as the processing of stimuli follows neurochemical laws, it is equally certain that the specific pathway chosen by electrical impulses, as they seek their passage through thousands of nerve cells, is not the only one that is possible. In many, many cases the impulse could also have made its way through neighboring cells and taken a slightly different route. In the concrete process of energy discharge, there is an element of spontaneity, something not determined, a degree of freedom. This, then, represents a specific potential for intelligence.

To create a pathway is an activity. Someone breaks a new path. The results are pathways. In the jungle this is, in principle, no different than in the brain, except that the jungle in which animals and people create paths has been there for a long time. An organism, on the contrary, must begin laying down pathways while its own brain is still in the process of being created. It cannot wait to discharge stimuli until it has been completely constructed. The construction occurs along fixed natural parameters. Tiny combinations of nucleic acids, also known as genes, are responsible for the fact that nerve cells, as a rule, always follow the same pattern as they grow into the complex structure of the brain. In one particular phase of growth, this happens with breathtaking speed. But while nerve cell follows nerve cell according to a genetic program, multiple stimulus pathways are also coming into being within and among these cells. Naturally, all these pathways remain within the genetic parameters, they are not some kind of wild detours or direct connections that don't follow from the brain's own substance and structure. The structure is genetically determined—but not only. Organisms acquire habits of development that cannot be reduced to their genetic nature but are continuously reproduced in a comparable fashion. These habits are called "epigenetic." The "basic organization of the brain, as it has evolved in human phylogeny, the fact that our brain is a typical vertebrate, mammalian, and primate brain is genetically predetermined. A corollary of this is the fact that in normal cases the sense organs of all members of this genus, species, and so on, are connected in the same *orderly* way to specific regions of the brain, and that these brain regions are then interconnected in an equally orderly fashion. All this occurs to some extent independent of experience, but not, in fact, as if there were genes that prescribed everything with precision. Rather, during the individual development of a brain there exists a specific genetic framework within which the structural order of the brain . . . develops in a self-organizing, *epigenetic* manner. Thus, the optic nerve finds its way to the regions it seeks in the diencephalon or midbrain, even if there is an attempt to force it make a 'detour,' or if it is bisected and then allowed to grow back."[20]

The word *epigenetic* is actually only shorthand for something that is not precisely localizable, that is not genetic but also not individually acquired. The prefix *epi-* means "after" or "following." An epilog is an afterword, an epiphenomenon something that "follows after" a phenomenon, an accessory; philosophically, we might describe it as accidental (from Latin: *accidens*)—a feature that is added to substance and without which the thing is not a concrete object. The genetic substance of an organism must also have accidental features like this, a sort of back office without whose participation it could not develop into an individual organism. Genetic parameters do not just develop on their own, but always in relation to something, in something, and thanks to something. At the same time, an organism is not able to modify or revise its epigenetically developed features later on. They are just as much part of its natural endowment as the genes. The boundary that separates an organism from its genetic precursors is as blurry as the one that distinguishes its separate individuality. It is never possible to point precisely to the spot where the no-longer-modifiable epigenetic precursors end and the region begins where an organism is still able to make changes over the course of its lifetime. And yet this blurry boundary is decisive, for the genetically/epigenetically structured bundles of nerve cells, already crisscrossed by numerous pathways, comprise the predetermined part of the organism. What the organism modifies within these nerve bundles, where it lays down its own individual paths—this is its self-determination.

STIMULUS FLIGHT

Thus, we see that self-determination does not happen the way an idealist philosophy imagines it, based on the presumption of a completely free subject that designs itself with purely individual gusto and creates its own laws and determinants. If this were so, the organism would be the sovereign master of its nerve pathways. But this is by no means the case. Instead, the pathways are flight paths, in the most literal sense of the term. "Stimulus flight" can mean something other than what Freud meant by it: namely, not only the flight of an organism attempting to get away from certain stimuli, but also the flight that it, in turn, inflicts on stimuli it has not been able to evade. If it cannot flee from them, it makes sure they flee from it. It creates pathways for them, flight paths. In doing so, it is the organism that acts and determines. But it acts out of necessity. It drives the stimuli through its nervous system because they drive it to it: it is both driver and driven. Neurologically, drives are a flight from stimulus, either as an outward movement, the flight from excitation or, when this avenue blocked, as an internal movement, which drives the excitation to flee and provides emergency exits for it.

Stimulus flight is something extremely non-self-directed. The paths that are created are neither intentional, nor are they even laid down with much care. Nevertheless, their creation is an action; it is at the same time no less a drive than something driven. The indeterminacy that characterizes stimulus flight in the instant of its creation deserves all the attention we can muster. Here, we observe the enormous surplus of possibilities for opening a route through the nervous system; we also see the need that drives the process. The two forces, acting in tandem, give the drive its never entirely predictable or graspable energetic shape[21]—down the path that is more or less that of least resistance. But the brain has many such paths. They represent a kind of constellation of variants around a never entirely determinate optimum. There is no way to predict which of them the brain will drive the irritating stimuli through. Here, what decides is a wee bit of spontaneity. The traces that are created during stimulus flight are also traces of spontaneity, trace elements of freedom in the organic.

Without spontaneity, no organism could determine its own path. Organic self-determination, however, consists solely in the fact that the organism determines its own stimulus flight paths. In the process of creating them, it also commits itself to them. It gives itself pathways by means of which it simultaneously defines and determines itself. Not, it must be said, absolutely. Just as the organism had various possibilities for creating pathways, so it can also act in various ways vis-à-vis the pathways it has just made. It cannot just cover them up again. But *how* it deepens, builds on, modifies, and varies them is not given in advance. And at one particularly remarkable site, which is often covered up terminologically, it accomplishes something astonishing, all on its own. This happens where, as we say, it also "prepares" the pathways it creates for later reuse. How can it do this? How are the nerve endings over which the stimuli are driven made "receptive" to accommodating still more of them, and, above all, how is it possible that this repetition occurs?

The comparison with the dry riverbed, which fills up with water again the next time it rains, may be helpful, but it is also crude. For the neuronal flight paths do not traverse the nervous system with the same consistency as a channel through the earth. At critical points, the synapses, gaps, open up, and the stimulus that is being discharged has to jump over them. Medieval scholasticism claimed that *Natura non facit saltus* (Nature makes no leaps). Neurophysiology proves the opposite: *Natura facit saltus.* At each synaptic gap that is reached by a stimulus in flight, an act of leaping across occurs. At the decisive point, the identifiable path is lacking. We may speak of pathways only in light of the prior assumption that a specific series of such leaps over synaptic gaps, once it has occurred during stimulus flight, creates in the pre- and post-synaptic areas beside those gaps a specific state of readiness to allow a new, similar stimulus flight to pass over them again. Our superhighways remain solidly asphalted and visible to all even when no one is driving on them. A nerve pathway, on the contrary, is only virtual. It only becomes manifest through the repeated use that recreates it as a pathway, and also modifies it. Neurophysiology has a lapidary term for what happens here: The previously formed pathway is "reactivated." But how does an organism accomplish this "reactivating"?

For reactivation to take place, innumerable tiny elevations that are ready to open, created by a previous stimulus flight through the nervous system, must suddenly be transformed from a state of readiness into one of actual opening, with all the microchemical processes that make this happen. It is a dizzying achievement of transformation and coordination, and we are no more able to say where the organism acquired the ability to do this than to predetermine the result. Only one thing is certain: An organism has the strong inclination to reestablish pathways that have already been created. But each reestablished pathway will also be one that has been modified in some way. The feat the organism accomplishes appears, on one hand, to be a logistical masterpiece. Creating paths for stimuli through the nervous system, constantly reproducing and modifying these pathways and their links to a network that is so complicated neuroscientists are far from being able to comprehend it—all this is well-nigh miraculous. Yet at the same time, this accomplishment is something that only happens to the organism; something that stimulus flight *does to it*, that seems to happen to it on the fly and as a result of this flight. The entirety of neurological logistics consists of running away, with no goal or plan in sight. The organism drives the logistics, but as something that is also driven. Blindly, by chance, it recreates flight paths through the nervous system.

The Nobel Prize–winning biologist Jacques Monod considered the creation of physical structures to have been a matter of conserving chance,[22] although he did not give serious thought to what this means.

After all, chance does not conserve itself. It can be conserved only by something that transcends it, something that "emerges" from it in a dual sense, both coming from it and going beyond it. Conserved chance has ceased to be merely accidental. An organism may be utterly committed to its first flight paths; but at the moment it recreates them, its actions are no longer the result of chance. Through repetition, it begins to establish structures. Nor is the capacity to recreate a neuronal flight path adequately explained by giving an account of all the neurochemical processes that took place the first time it was created. This is where we find the beginnings of the conservation of chance, and with it of organic intelligence. It is, in equal measure, both structurally productive and spontaneous. There is an aspect of it that is not predetermined—an impulse, a degree of freedom, however slight—or else it could not create a structure. For the structuring impulse cannot already *have* the structure it is constructing— the structure only emerges as a result. *Impulse* and *drive* are makeshift terms for what emerges by chance and is neither fully accidental nor fully prestructured. The organic intelligence that is generated in this process, however, is only another word for memory. As soon as an organism is able to reactivate the stimulus flight paths that crisscross it, it is able to draw on them for its behavioral repertoire. In the case of similar pressure from stimuli, it can behave the way it did before. The elementary form of organic memory is nothing but this capacity for repetition.

Our next step is to get a theoretical grip on this elementary memory. For the creation of pathways and the paths themselves, we can also say "drive," and the "fate of the drives." A drive cannot become effective without also assuming a fateful aspect, giving itself a structure and committing itself to it. In other words, a drive cannot express itself without becoming intelligent. In this case, the fate of the drives, or what in some translations is called their vicissitudes, is only another word for memory—the repertoire of behaviors that the organism has at its disposal, over which it also has disposition. The organism may be able to modify this faculty, but it cannot escape from it. On one hand, it has a basic fund of natural, inborn dispositions over which it has no sway. The physical structure of the brain does not allow stimulus flight to happen any which way. At the same time, the pathways are subject to modification in two directions. Ongoing consolidation of a previously traveled pathway is just as much a modification as is its ongoing correction. And the tendency of the previously traveled pathways to become second nature, from which the organism can no longer escape, normally increases with age. In the course of a lifetime, it tends to become more and more fated; in other words, the repertoire of behaviors tends to sink to the level of an inborn disposition and to merge with it.

For a nervous system—already at the most primitive animal level—three things are therefore decisive: its natural disposition, the creation of pathways (stimulus flight, discharge of excitation), and the pathways that result (repertoire of behaviors, memory). These three factors are so interwoven that none of them can exist without the other two. The natural disposition, that is, the bundles of nerve cells, cannot exist, indeed cannot even come into being, without stimuli passing through them—in other words without the process of creating pathways and its result, the paths themselves. Creating pathways, in turn, can only take place within a neural network, and not without leaving pathways behind. The pathways, finally, cannot exist without the nerve bundles through which they pass or the activity that has created the pathways. Here we are dealing not with three separate systems but with the elementary sort of symbiosis that always occurs when nerve cells discharge stimuli.

At this point, we are reminded of a concept that was constitutive for Hegel's dialectics, in German: *Moment*. Latin *momentum*, an abbreviation of *movimentum*, literally means "a thing that is moved," including the sense that it is moved by itself, or is self-moving. *Momentum*, as a concept, oscillates between active and passive voice in a fashion similar to "drive." By extension, it can also mean a movement that traverses such a brief distance or span of time that it is actually no longer even a movement but something that takes place in the blink of an eye. Finally, it can also be the decisive movement, which then takes on the meaning of weight, importance, validity, or meaning.[23] In Hegel, these nuances of meaning have slid together and have been intensified in a particular way. Everything that exists, that has reality, is concrete in the literal sense of having grown together. It owes its lasting quality to "moments," whereby each moment is both static (an aspect or component; the blink of an eye that can be perceived separately) and dynamic (a force that makes the components join and work together). Moments are not just parts; they are what brings the existing world—whether we are talking about a single object, a system, or an organism—together as a unity, without ceasing to be a multiplicity. Every mineral is already both multiplicity and unity, and this is even more true of a complex organ such as a brain. The bundles of nerve cells, the laying down of pathways, and the pathways that have emerged, as the three moments of living synergy, are by no means merely functions within a division of labor, or subsystems of a larger system. They not only work together but are interlocked in such a way as to make the possibility of each one contingent on the presence of the others. Nor is this all. They are so interwoven with each other that each of them only receives its individual identity through the others. The neural network consists in the fact that it is crisscrossed by the activity of creating pathways, leaving behind paths through the network. The specific character of the activity of laying down pathways consists in occurring within a neural network and in the process leaving behind pathways. The pathways, in turn, consist of the fact that they occur as the distillation of pathway-making activity within a neural network. My thesis is the following: This three-fold encapsulation is the physical preform of a constellation that Freud identified at the level of the human, and imagined as three "authorities": id (it), ego (I), and superego (over-I).[24] But how could stimulus flight have risen to the level of human beings?

MEMORY

If it is true that stimulus flight tends toward repetition, toward "conservation of chance" and the creation of pathways, and that these pathways are the elementary form of organic memory, organic intelligence, then this intelligence is an enormous advance in natural history. Organisms participate in creating the structures within which they absorb and discharge stimuli. Self-definition and self-determination start here—albeit on a very limited scale. Stimulus discharge through already existing pathways only occurs so that disturbing stimuli, which an organism has experienced and somehow survived thanks to stimulus flight, do not have to be reexperienced. Repetition occurs so that discomfort and pain are *not* necessarily repeated. Creating pathways and reactivating them are vital means of survival and protection—the more urgent, the more powerful and threatening the stimuli are that affect the organism. Thus, the elementary form of memory is fear. Fear cannot exist without the memory of something unpleasant, at the very moment when that thing presents a new threat. Only something that has already been experienced can be experienced as a threat. "Fear is a poor counselor," we occasionally say today. At the beginning of the animal kingdom, many millions of years ago, it was the only counselor there was—the survival mechanism par excellence.

True, fear started small, in every sense of the word, with minimal intelligence and limited to a single behavior. As soon as an organism starts becoming aware that stimuli it has previously experienced as life threatening are approaching, it mobilizes the pathways over which it has successfully discharged them in the past. If it worked once or more than once before, it should work now. "Never change a running system."[25] Only survivors can be afraid; fear is already a pattern of success. At the same time, the elementary forms of fear have a minimal degree of intensity. We may not have accurate information about what a kauri snail feels when it curls itself up to get out of the way of a threatening stimulus. But certainly it is far from experiencing the level of anxiety, agitation, and horror that is reserved for organisms with more highly developed nervous systems. The kauri snail's capacity for representation is extraordinarily modest. It is capable, at the moment of discharging relevant stimuli, of representing them on a limited, crude scale of sensations, which may possibly include, for example, agreeable and disagreeable, hard and soft, warm and cold, dry and wet, light and dark. It is also capable, as soon as the stimulus appears again, of converting the pathways it has created to discharge this kind of stimuli from a condition of virtuality to one of actuality. It makes these pathways once again present, and this and nothing else is the original sense of the Latin *representare*.

This representation, of course, is entirely under the spell of presence. A stimulus can only be experienced as long as it is in the process of being discharged—in some cases as something that was already experienced. To reexperience something and to rerepresent an already created pathway are one and the same thing. This is the truth content of Plato's famous saying that all learning is really recollection.[26] What are recollected are, naturally, not eternal, self-sufficient ideas that the soul supposedly already gazed on before birth, but stimuli that, the first time they strike an organism, force it to take stimulus flight and create flight paths. At the same time they are also too close and too powerful to be recognized as yet. The only stimuli that can be recognized are those for which a pathway already exists, so their energy can be captured and they attract attention as something that already has similar predecessors—even if this attention, this "cognition," consists of nothing but the dull, vague, and fleeting repetition of the feeling that "there was already something like this"—a feeling that goes away as soon as the stimulus stops. In other words, the recognition or recollection only lasts as long as the stimulus whose discharge is the reason it is occurring. It consists in nothing but the repeated feeling of similar experience, the repetition of similar action. Memory, here, is nothing but the process of repetition: it is what neuroscience calls "procedural" memory.

This, however, is where we have to begin if we want to find out what distinguishes that odd mammal, *Homo sapiens*, from the rest of the animal kingdom. In comparison to the kauri snail, mammals such as cats, dogs, or chimpanzees are already almost humanlike. Their register of feelings, perceptions, and behaviors is many times greater than that of the snail. Nor is their memory limited to "there was already something like that." On the contrary, the most varying degrees of hardness, smells, sounds, colors, forms, and even individuals are remembered. Dogs notice that their master is coming in through the door and occasionally accompany this individual recognition with movements and sounds that can hardly be interpreted otherwise than as signs of what we call joy or at least contentment. These acts of memory far surpass those of the kauri snail, but in one respect they have remained almost the same: They are still similarly under the spell of the present. Admittedly, the spell has loosened up a bit. When cats and dogs dream, they obviously repeat, in sleep, the processing of certain stimuli that have long since ceased to affect them. If they are put in a new environment or robbed of their familiar companions, if they then run around uneasily looking for something and refuse to eat, or if they hide, the word *sadness* is surely an all-too human word. But there can be no doubt that they are not only able to recognize what is there, but also to respond with discomfiture when something is missing that they are used to. They have a sense of things that are absent. But it doesn't go beyond the initial stages. "Out of sight, out of mind" still applies in principle. Their memory does not reach significantly beyond their real-time sensation and perception; not so far, anyway, as to reach a new stage in the history of memory.

Only *Homo sapiens* reached this stage—with unspeakable difficulty and in constant danger of backsliding. "Out of sight, out of mind" has not totally disappeared among people, after all. It remains widespread as a reproach to inconstant, unreliable contemporaries who don't keep their word. And for approximately a generation, it has had a new world power as its ally: the high-tech machinery of electronic images and sounds. It floods our eyes and ears with a wealth of stimuli that give us no chance to process them in a halfway proportionate fashion. The next burst of stimuli is already following close behind. If, for a moment, we look at the high-tech devices from a historical bird's-eye view, we can see that with their tendency toward the absolute Now, toward permanent epiphany; with their categorical imperative "Attention!" "Look at this," they are jarring a capacity that we may consider specific to humans: the capacity to keep in mind something that has disappeared from the senses. We can also call it "imagination." Naturally, this capacity does not disappear over-night. But even if the first undoubted symptoms of its loss only appear over the course of a few generations, this is breathtakingly fast compared to the time it took to acquire it. Let us not count the millions of years it took for a suitable brain to develop that could accommodate it. Let us confine ourselves to the brain of *Homo sapiens* himself. With a volume of ca. 67–110 cubic inches (1100–1800 ccm), it is not the biggest brain; even Neanderthals had a larger one, not to mention elephants and whales. It is disproportionately large in comparison to the size of the body, and it has an especially luxuriant cerebral cortex, but these are merely the physical prerequisite for imagination; they do not explain it. The decisive break-through occurred only in the last one hundred thousand years. Over this period, as far as we know, the structure and size of *Homo sapiens'* brain remained relatively constant. It is not physical expansion of the brain that led to imagination, but a changed utilization of already existing brain resources—a specific detour for stimulus flight.

LOOSENING THE DRIVES

Freud's concept of "stimulus flight" appeals to us because of its intelli-gent ambiguity. Its primary meaning is to flee from a stimulus, to escape from it by changing one's location. But what if that kind of flight doesn't work, either because it is too late and the external stimulus has already entered the organism, or because the stimulus is internal to begin with and a change of place is therefore pointless? Then, according to Freud, something other than stimulus flight has to take place. But if we examine it carefully, this "other" is only a different sort of stimulus flight. It turns inward to make the stimulus flee. What psychoanalysis calls "drive dynamics" consists in this movement of flight inside the organism. The continuation of flight by other means, its displacement from outside to inside, is altogether one of the most elementary things nerves accomplish—indeed it may be their essence. Among species that have survived until now, *Homo sapiens* stands out by virtue of the fact that in comparison to body size he has by far the most neurons. He is more fully penetrated by nerve cells and has more "bundles of nerves" than all other living things. He is more sensitive to stimuli, and as a result necessarily more inventive when it comes to their processing. There are also some species of animals for whom flight behavior has taken a peculiar turn, especially in situations when it is too late to run or swim away. In this circumstance, a hare will duck into the earth as if it itself were earth. An inchworm hangs motionless on the branch as if it were part of it. The flatfish (plaice), when it seeks shelter, takes on the muddy color of the ocean floor. This is called mimicry—becoming similar to the environment in order to avoid being seen. But this becoming invisible is a metamorphosis of flight. In its moment of greatest need, the organism attempts to flee without moving from the spot. It stifles its original flight impulse and remains motionless where it is. This kind of self-constraint marks a caesura in natural history whose importance can hardly be overestimated. One of the most powerful impulses in nature turns back upon itself, becoming unnatural, perverse. Mimicry is nature's first ruse against itself. Another way of saying this is that the nature of the drive turns back upon itself. It becomes reflexive.

Some millions of years were required before this first attempt at constraining the drives developed into a whole technique for turning drives around, and this only in a single species—the same one that is the greatest "bundle of nerves." Stimuli, as we mentioned above, create a continuum of intensity. Some are so weak that their impact is not even perceptible. Others are so powerful, shattering, and agonizing that an organism will never be able to create enough flight paths to discharge them. They continue to generate a terrible state of excitation within the organism even after they themselves have long since faded. Hominids are not the only creatures to have experienced such powerful attacks of stimuli; the entire animal kingdom has traumatic experiences. But hominids, as the most nervous animals, reacted to traumatic attacks with the greatest sensitivity, and in the process they gradually developed behaviors for which the most appropriate word may be *overreaction*.

In a high culture, overreaction has an unenviable reputation. The person who responds to a critical question with insult, ridicule, or a punch in the face, or who sounds a fire alarm when the milk boils over, lacks a sense of proportionality, judgment, and self-control. But these virtues have had to be developed, after all, and for this to occur the behavior of hominids first had to take on a certain disproportionality. In the attempt to create flight paths for the unbearable surplus of excitation left behind by traumatic stimuli, some surplus reactions must also have been created. How this happened, we don't know. But obviously the organism was no longer content to react to stimuli only while the latter were having a direct impact on it. Even after the fact, the organism found them so disturbing that it continued to attempt to discharge them again and again. Delayed work of this kind is reaction, but it is not completely consumed in it. The reworking assumes an air of self-sufficiency and becomes a driving force of another kind, namely by beginning a new process of driving the past out: a *representatio* that no longer consists only in the experience of a present stimulus, along the traces of a previously created flight path. *Representatio* steps outside the spell of presence. The memory that it achieves goes beyond the mere re-recognition of something present, whether as a dull "but once there was something like this" or a bright "there is that same figure again!" The experience of something present gives way to the presence of something absent, immediate experience becomes mediated experience, and recognition becomes memory. Something no longer present is, in a certain way, rendered once again present by a process of reenactment. Except that this reenactment now refers to something past, which itself is irretrievable and can only be made present in a mediated way—by being presented. Memory is the presentation of something absent. At first, this presentation occurs in an external, performative manner; it is acted out. The traumatic stimulus that drives an organism to rework something also drives it to seek helpers who make this reworking possible. The help is provided by stimuli that are in a position to represent the original stimulus (now in the past) so that it remains in the present in a mediated form. In other words, the reworking manifests itself in the urge to find replacement stimuli that stand in for the originals in a significant way—that mean it. They are similarly traumatic and agonizing, but with the decisive difference that they no longer jump out at the organism unexpectedly. Instead, it is the organism that causes them to happen. In the process, it makes sure all the previously created flight paths are maximally open—and creates inside itself the state that we call "fear." Organisms that move from naturally occurring stimuli to self-generated replacement stimuli are catching up with fear. In the process, they are doing a U-turn, a flight forward of a kind that, until they had done so, had never been seen before in nature. The mimicry of the flatfish, inchworms, and hares was only a first, hesitant step in this direction. Now a regular technique developed: *do something terrifying to yourself in order to get rid of terrible things*, namely the unbearable effect of the full power of traumatic shock. In the words of the poet: "I feel drawn to the very thing that terrifies me."[27] The psychoanalytic term of art for this is traumatic repetition compulsion.

Where this compulsion becomes habitual, the energy of the drive not only turns against itself to the point of self-denial, as in mimicry; it actively transcends this point. It is displaced from the original power of the natural stimulus, which attacks suddenly, diffusely, and unpredictably, onto replacement stimuli that can be specially generated, planned, and repeated. In this way the original force of the stimulus is condensed and assumes a graspable form. Here they are again: displacement and condensation, this time in a version derived from drive theory. Now we can see what was not yet clear in the first chapter—displacement and condensation were the result of a loosening of the drives. Where the reversal of stimulus flight was transformed into flight forward, past the point of self-constraint and fixation as mimicry, this loosening began. Heightened sensitivity and vulnerability to torment made this possible. Neurologically speaking, a disproportionally large brain led to disproportionate behavior: to overreaction, delayed action (*Nachträglichkeit*), and reworking. From this disposition, traumatic repetition compulsion made a manifest reality. With it, delayed action came to be in the world, as an unceasing pursuit, a kind of continuous homework. "In every century, humanity has to be kept in after school," remarked Walter Benjamin.[28] What he meant was that every century leaves behind a wealth of unfinished tasks. But this thought should be taken much more fundamentally. Culture is nature's homework—nature's homework on itself, a process

that has no end. Only in *Homo sapiens* did this process reach full development, giving the life of his drives flexibility beyond compare: the space of
representation, of mind, and of culture. Reversal, displacement, and
condensation are the loosened movements of drives. They constituted
this space. In them, the life of drives, the principle of constancy became
specifically human.

Where the trio of neural networks, pathway creation, and actual pathways attains a human level, it achieves a qualitatively new interiority, the
interiority of reversal, displacement, and condensation. These three are
not only linked in such a way that each acquires its identity through the
others; in addition, each is, in a certain respect, already the other two. The
displacement of original stimuli onto replacement stimuli cannot occur
without simultaneously condensing a sudden, ungraspable stimulus
force and performing a reversal that attempts to reduce the distress of the
original stimuli through continuous substitute repetition. Displacement
itself is already condensation and reversal; condensation itself is displacement and reversal; reversal itself is condensation and displacement. Here,
how can we help being reminded of the Christian notion of the Holy
Trinity? As is well known, it presumes an eternal, immeasurably powerful,
wise, and benevolent God, who has created the world and is guiding it—
despite the failures of humanity—toward a good end. How, then, was this
God capable of surrendering himself entirely to the world, even becoming
human to the extent of his death on the cross, while at the same time
remaining entirely self-contained? The answer, crystallized over three
centuries of Christian reflection: God is a trinity, as father absolute identity and indivisibility, as son eternal division in himself ("eternally
begotten"), and as Holy Ghost ("who proceeds from the father and the
son")[29] complete unity of the divided. One God, three persons, in precisely
such fashion that each person is both a "moment" of God, in the Hegelian
sense, and wholly God—and to this extent embraces the other two. We
are free to believe or disbelieve this, but as a dialectical idea it is brilliant.
It means that the divine whole does not merely consist of three moments.
Each of these moments is also the whole, still wholly condensed in itself.
The moment itself is already the whole from which, as a moment, it is
simultaneously separated.

This, however, is exactly how stimulus flight works once it has
reached the human level. It literally becomes a trinity. Reversal,

condensation, and displacement have become nothing but its various moments. But in each of these moments, stimulus flight is simultaneously the whole and undivided movement. Natural science is precisely incapable of coming to terms with this. With the aid of highly developed technological tools, it may be able to follow the flight of a stimulus very precisely on its path through the nervous system. But the specific loosening that *Homo sapiens* afforded his stimulus flight is precisely what does not become visible in the movement of its energy. No measurement of brain currents will ever be able to trace the trinity of displacement, condensation, and reversal. In a quite literal sense, they are exactly what confers meaning. The German verb *bedeuten*, meaning "to point at" as well as "to mean," gives a good sense of the way stimulus flight points beyond itself. And meaning, as Norbert Wiener, the founder of information science, already knew, is the aspect of the transfer of electrical impulses that cannot be measured. It is part of what is not measurable in this transfer, part of the "noise," as it were, which must be, if not eliminated, at least reduced to a minimum.[30] Only where there is meaning is there intelligence, and only organisms possessing intelligence can measure, weigh, and calculate—can ultimately, like the pioneers of information science, mobilize all of mathematics in the hopeless attempt to calculate meaning out of existence.

One doesn't "have" intelligence, admittedly, the way someone has a nose, or a computer. Intelligence is not a thing or a substance. It exists only in its activity, as the loosened movement of drives in which the activity of creating pathways has been united in the trinity of displacement, condensation, and reversal. Living intelligence—we may also call it mind—exists only in this movement of creating pathways, together with all their modifying and varying extensions. At the same time, the pathways that remain from this process are only leftovers, reminiscent of the way writing is never living intelligence but only one of its precipitates— an external one, in fact—that an organism, by coordinating its muscles and nerves, purposefully sets down on a prepared surface, while the inner, neural paths we are concerned with here flash hastily and involuntarily through a living nervous system that is far removed from the static condition of a writing surface. The metaphor of writing should be used for these pathways only with the greatest caution. All writing is a trace, it is true, but not every trace is writing.[31] Besides, the traces or pathways left by the nerves are pre-scriptural. They are internal. Indeed in a way they are only virtual. As long as they are not actualized by the creation of new pathways, they might as well be blown away: latent spirit. Here, what is true of the prehuman structure of drives is no different in humans. The pathways that are created in this process result from the self-determination of the organism. To the extent that a loosened movement of drives, one with the capacity for intelligence, has been created in the organism, the pathways are not just a remainder but also means of realizing intelligence. They are the reservoir and the repertoire on which the organism draws. As long as it does not draw on them, they are literally nothing, they quite simply do not exist. The organism mobilizes them. But it itself only *is* to the extent that it does draw on them. Repertoire and reservoir are nothing without the organism, and the organism is nothing without them. They are "above" it in a dual sense: On one hand, they are nothing but leftovers, on the other, they are its projection, a kind of self-made governing authority. This has consequences for our understanding of a prominent Freudian concept, the superego, or over-I.

THE PSYCHIC "APPARATUS"

Freud did not come up with the superego until relatively late in his life. For a long time, he distinguished primarily between two "systems": consciousness and the unconscious. The first seemed to be self-evident, the latter all the more in need of explanation. How, in the psyche, can something be not conscious and yet still be "there," indeed not just "there," but present as a special, wayward force that irritates, plagues, and paralyzes consciousness? Dreams provided the key. In sleep, where waking consciousness pauses and its control function is absent, the waywardness of the unconscious can find room to breathe and emerge. In the process, the unconscious reveals itself as something multilayered. It has a layer of sediment that is emotional and drive-related and that is almost inaccessible to consciousness. Above it is a layer that not only has the stuff to reach consciousness, but virtually presses toward it. But it is not permitted to emerge; it is kept unconscious, *repressed*—something that entails a large expenditure of energy. The upper layer is preconscious. It is capable, at any time, of becoming conscious. Not separated from consciousness by any threshold of inhibition, it merely happens not to belong to the contents of current consciousness. If we look more closely, however, it appears that the barrier separating consciousness and repression is not clearly demarcated. After all, in dreams repressed contents can easily rise to the level of consciousness, even though this happens in a way that leaves them alien and inaccessible.[32] It follows that the line of demarcation does not run cleanly between conscious and unconscious material, but orthogonal to it.

With this, however, Freud's beloved notion of two systems, or occasionally three systems—depending on whether preconscious awareness is presented as a separate system or is reckoned as being on the side of consciousness or the unconscious—starts to become wobbly. It was his growing insight into repression that gave it the final push. He realized that not only does repression *keep* certain contents unconscious it also *occurs* unconsciously.[33] It has a greater reach than consciousness, as we can see from dreams, where waking consciousness is lacking, but consciousness's protector, the dream censor, remains active. So it is not just "consciousness" that prevents unconscious contents from gaining access to its realm. Consequently, Freud saw himself forced to abandon the trinity of conscious, unconscious, and preconscious. He replaced it with another one, which achieved greater fame: ego (I), id (it), and superego (over-I). It is not difficult to see the advantage of the new scheme. Instead of a more mechanical systems model, we have a dynamic model of authorities. Occasionally, the way they work together is imagined as if they were people. On one hand, this makes them more "human." On the other, it threatens to make their contours blurry. The most clear among them is perhaps the id, "which contains the passions."[34] This nominalized pronoun, which in German simply means "it," and which Freud borrowed from Georg Groddeck, seemed to him to be especially suitable for the animal foundation of human life, its archaic, impersonal, drive-controlled base. The id's opposite number is the ego. The ego, as Freud says drily, sits on the surface of the id "like a man on horseback,"[35] and "represents what may be called reason and common sense,"[36] although it also includes other capacities, for example "control over the approaches to motility."[37] Thus, Freud speaks of the ego as the "coherent organization of mental processes" in an individual.[38]

We could turn this into a nicely rounded definition, for example: "The ego is the entirety of forces that carry out repression and control motor abilities and that govern relations—both conscious and unconscious—with the external world." Except that there is a third authority that also makes its presence known, and that contests the accomplishments of the centralized ego: the superego. In his earlier writings, at first, Freud talks about an "ideal ego," or "ideal I,"[39] because he has discovered that human narcissism is directed not at the real, very inadequate ego, but at an idealized one. An ego cannot come into being without giving itself a more elevated sense of self, by means of an ideal. But the ideal ego is not constituted in a vacuum, it always forms *on something*, a model. In his essay "On Narcissism. An Introduction," Freud is still thinking primarily of the mother.[40] Later on, when he replaces the ideal ego or ego ideal with the superego, or over-I, and integrates the process of ideal-formation into his three-authorities model, it takes on the sharper features of the father. The child (initially always thought of as male) grows up in the shadow of commands and prohibitions; primarily we are talking about the prohibition of erotic desires. Laws, institutions, and authorities are actually nothing but a universalized father who has become anonymous. Where these things have become sufficiently internalized, they involuntarily take on the function of keeping unconscious wishes down—a function that, it is true, is also carried out by the ego when it "represents what may be called reason and thoughtfulness" and exercises "control of the approaches to motility." The superego acts as the ego's adversary while simultaneously serving as its managing director. Or does the ego manage the business of the superego? The apportionment of responsibilities between the two is as fuzzy as the way they came into being. Which one derives from which?

The situation is made even more complicated by a significant failure of reflection. For Freud, the creation of ideals is limited to wanting and needing to resemble the model, and he knows of no more powerful model than the father. Thus, the illusion is created that idealization and internalization are actually naturally occurring consequences of paternal power. This, of course, is far from being the case. Other primates also have powerful fathers, without our being able to prove the existence of anything like an ideal. At one point Freud, in an aside, assumes that a kind of superego exists "as well [for] the higher animals which resemble man mentally . . . wherever, as is the case with man, there is a long period of dependence in childhood."[41] No mammal is as unindependent and defenseless at birth as a human baby. But these shortcomings do not, as yet, constitute an ideal. The creation of ideals is something other than imitative dependence on parental animals—namely internalization of a model, an admirable achievement of imagination and representation. Freud passes this by with sovereign disregard. Occasionally, he does call the superego "conscience," but without stopping to notice that there is no conscience without knowledge. There is, in Freud's "psychic apparatus," no one in charge of the imaginative and logical structures, so to speak. Neither the ego nor the superego is exclusively responsible for them— certainly not the id—and yet they do not give the impression, either, that they could be completely cordoned off from any one of the three authorities. So where do they belong?

This is an unanswered question—both for psychoanalysis and for philosophy. In Freud's "psychic apparatus," there is room neither for imagination nor for conceptuality. In philosophical logic, there is no room for the unconscious, repression, or dreams. Kant, it is true, said in one of his early writings that he saw no reason to believe that in a waking state our mind follows different laws than when it is asleep. But in the Critique of Pure Reason he only addressed those laws that the mind reveals when it is awake. What is relevant are only "pure concepts of the understanding" or "categories," in other words those structures that a waking human consciousness must always have at its disposal if it is to bring the multiplicity of sensual impressions under the sway of rules. Sleep and dream, imagination and the unconscious, to the extent that they appear at all, are subordinated to the logic of pure categories of the understanding. Their hierarchy has remained determinative for philosophical discourse. This is true even of the young Theodor W. Adorno, who took Freud so seriously, philosophically, that he experienced the blind spot of philosophy and the blind spot of psychoanalysis as glaring shortcomings. His early essay, "The Concept of the Unconscious in the Transcendental Theory of Mind,"[42] which he conceived but never submitted as his postdoctoral thesis, and which remained unpublished during his lifetime (though it was intended for inclusion in his collected works), is a pioneering work. It attempts to think Kant's categories together with Freud's "psychic apparatus." The attempt, admittedly, has its own particular slant. Freud appears merely as an especially rigorous and consequential Kantian, who brings not only external sense impressions under the regulated sway of the understanding, but also all psychic phenomena, including dreams, compulsions, neuroses, and hysterias, however bizarre and senseless they may appear. To the extent that these phenomena manifest repressed, forbidden, and split or dissociated thoughts that are pressing toward consciousness, they do have some sense. Instead of denouncing them as a priori senseless, as contemporary psychiatry overwhelmingly did, and suppressing them with medication, what is needed is to interpret them and make the patient as conscious of them as possible, so he can recall them cathartically and free himself from them. This comprehensive process of making conscious, which Freud—years after Adorno's piece was written, by the way—summarized in the famous formula, "Where id was, there ego shall be,"[43] is interpreted by the young Adorno as a contribution to the unity of consciousness in a Kantian sense: "Everything unconscious is without exception and necessarily related to conscious things, in such a way that it incorporates contexts of conscious thought . . . in abbreviated form and can be identified, as to its contents, only by recourse to consciousness."[44]

Here, psychoanalysis is interpreted as the demystification of the unconscious by means of its incorporation under the categories of reason, toward which the unconscious, to the extent that it makes any "sense," is always already oriented and whose principled precedence, "transcendentality," is thus proven. This naturally amounts to a precipitous capture of Freud for transcendental philosophy.[45] As surely as it is incorrect to speak of the unconscious without relating it to consciousness, it is equally wrong to draw from this fact the conclusion that the structure of consciousness in fully developed *Homo sapiens* is prior in some principled way, as something that has always existed—and that the unconscious is nothing but the scum it has left behind. This is not how Freud thought. His attentiveness to regressive states, particularly in dreams, always has a genealogical aspect. It tries to shed light on the "primitive thought activity" that returns in dreams and that is characterized precisely by its lack of the consequential quality that in waking consciousness distinguishes between unity and multiplicity, affirmation and negation, before and after, possibility and impossibility—with which this consequential kind of thinking is shown to be a relatively late achievement of *Homo sapiens*. Freud senses in it a kind of mental armor that *Homo sapiens* has acquired over the course of its history. In his late work, at any rate, he refers to with a term, *Rindenschicht*, that literally means a "layer of bark."[46] This has its physiological significance, for in German the word for "bark,' *Rinde*, also means "cortex." The same way the cerebral cortex, which is the primary seat of consciousness, was formed as a kind of "rind" surrounding the brain stem, so the mental structures that govern our interaction with the external world have grown up gradually around the inner source of wishes and excitations, like a kind of protective accretion.

Admittedly, this comparison has its limits. A rind, or bark, is an external accretion; mental structures are internal accretions. To understand how accretion and internalization are connected, the concept of the rind is not helpful. That of the superego, however, is quite helpful, if we grasp it in a more elementary sense than Freud did, namely as a leftover and projection of human stimulus flight that has taken shape in a species-specific ensemble of flight paths, or, to put it slightly differently, in a species-specific repertoire of means of perception and behavior. Means of perception are basic sensibilities that have worn paths within organisms in such a fashion that all further channeling takes place along their traces. Means of perception—our senses—have only been able to develop through the reactivation, reiterated millions of times, of stimulus flight paths that the organism originally laid down spontaneously for the discharge of powerful stimuli, and then gradually built upon. Means of perception are consolidated stimulus flight paths. In the same way as they were created, they have also grown more acute and differentiated—through repetition. The simplest living organisms already have consolidated means of perception, otherwise they could not survive as species. Moving or at rest, hard or soft, dry or wet, cold or warm, light or dark, one or many: the capacity to distinguish these things, however vague and unstable it may be in the beginning, constitutes the basic content of animal means of perception. "Means of perception" is only another way of referring to the drives and their fates, and to repertoire or memory. When memory became specifically human, as it loosened the spell of presence and no longer only recognized things that were immediately available to it; when it opened a flexible space for retrospection, something new was created along the pathways of animal modes of perception: means of representation. And just as memory is not created by anything except active remembering, so the means of representation could only emerge as a consequence of representing.

We now know what drove certain hominid collectives to representation: the discharge of traumatic stimuli through targeted, shared repetition. But to learn to represent something to oneself also means to represent something *differently* from the way it is. Representation transforms—initially, to the point of excess. In this case, representation is not only something external and performative but also a complete change of direction. It consists in taking something for its opposite: present for past, graspable for ungraspable, near for far, little for much, and . . . death for salvation. The ways in which this act of representation left its mark can be identified with remarkable precision—they are the forms that shape the process of ritual killing. The collective cannot bear it without, in a certain rhythm, selecting one or a few who should stand "for many" ungraspable terrors and bring an unmastered past to present awareness. Their proper preparation for sacrifice, always following the same schema and in the same place, makes its consequential character a measure of collective protection and makes *theoria*, literally the exact implementation of divine rules, into a virtue.

However different the ways may be in which ritual killing developed in different parts of the world, the basic pattern of traumatic repetition compulsion always shone through all its variants. Means of representation, after all, are the specific pathways that traumatic repetition compulsion has left behind in its gradual consolidation as sacrificial ritual. Neurologically speaking, these are specific stimulus flight paths; in terms of a theory of experience, they are ritual structures. "Mind," at first, is nothing but stimulus flight that has been loosened by displacement, condensation, and reversal and gradually, as a result of continuous repetition, has taken on the form that we retrospectively term "sacrifice." The paths that this stimulus flight creates are the precipitates of this spirit.

THE GENESIS OF IDEALS

The creation of mind, or spirit (*Geist*),[47] coincides with the creation of ideals. Ideals are much older than ego-ideals. They had already been in existence for a long time before humans were in a position to experience their organism as the separate, independent entity that we call "ego," or "I." The beginning of the creation of ideals can already be found where mental space opened up. What, other than an ideal, is the "genius" that filled this space, the spectral and frightening, purportedly collective power that cast its protective aura over the ritual process, protected the mental space, and gave it a purpose, a sense? Over the centuries, ideals have continued to be something imaginary and elevated, providing orientation and meaning. But the original form of their imagination and elevation was reversal, turning something into its opposite. It meant taking horror itself as the thing that could preserve us from horror. Traumatic repetition compulsion is the creator of ideals par excellence. No other attack has impact of traumatic fright. Repeating it, in order to be freed from its power—this is the elementary form of what in psychoanalysis is called "identification with the aggressor." All imaginable natural forces can be considered potential aggressors: wild animals, storms, earthquakes, volcanic eruptions, landslides, and so on. The fathers of the collective are as vulnerable to these forces as its other members; compared with nature, their own strength is relatively modest. Only under culturally highly developed, advanced patriarchal conditions can a father's violence come to epitomize children's experience of violence, can identification with the (male) assailant turn into a desire to resemble the father. Under these conditions, internalization of the father as an ego-ideal can appear as a way to escape the oppressive sense of his overweening power. This, however, is a very late, limited aspect of the creation of ideals, at a point when the question of how there can even be something as astonishing as internalization is not being asked. The reversal that is accomplished by representation, which in the course of a desperate stimulus flight has learned how to take presence for absence, the present for the past, an individual for the multitude, and—above all—salvation for horror, is not seriously considered at that point.

The world of representation and imagination opened up only as the result of an effort of extreme resistance. It began as something completely nonsensical. But only with it did sense enter the world. Sense began as antisense. And, just as traumatic repetition compulsion consists in working on itself in order to be divested of itself, or, in the terminology of the principle of constancy, "reducing [the incoming stimuli] to the lowest possible level," where they approach zero, so the "sense of the world" consists in reducing its antisense to the point where it very nearly disappears. According to the theory of representation, this means bridging the gulfs between graspable and ungraspable, past and present, individual and multitude, horror and salvation. And sure enough, the ungraspable becomes more graspable, unmastered experiences become more manageable, horror more bearable when it is better represented, when the primary representatives of horror, as horrible as they indeed are, are cushioned by a congeries of additional representations. The history of sacrifice, in its basic characteristics, appears as a history of this kind of representation. The emotional images of ritual killing, the primary images, are represented in turn by a "genius," who floats above the ritual action as an imagined sheltering power, making the action significantly more tolerable by giving it a purpose, an addressee, a higher meaning, and, in this way, first raising it to the rank of a sacrificial act.

Representation continued to develop according to this pattern. Human sacrifice was represented by offering up large mammals, then smaller animals, harvest fruits, precious metals, and finally less-choice materials. Inside the interior mental space, representation itself was also becoming more differentiated, according to its own internal logic. The spectral "genius" is less torturous if it, in turn, is represented by images that are less troubling, less hallucinatory, more graspable, objectifiable, and susceptible to distancing—images whose similarity to natural objects gradually increases until they form a collection of copies of external reality and ultimately camouflage the "genius" as whose attributes they began. The images must already have been assembled into a collection of this kind before they could be represented acoustically. Only when there was a relatively fixed arsenal of images could sounds be attached to them in a way that was regular and repeatable enough for a verbal system to result. Like the history of sacrifice, the cultural history of the human brain can be read as a history of layered images. Only where a highly differentiated network existed could images create their pathways. Only where relatively fixed means of image representation existed could the creation of sounds develop into a corresponding, rule-governed language. Perception, representation, and language have different centers of activity in the brain, it is true, and yet they are synthetic achievements of the whole brain. They mutually construct each other, forming intermeshed layers, in such a way that images and language are capable both of representing perception and of representing each other. However, the relationship is not symmetrical. Only after sounds have come to represent images, in other words after they have become words, can images also represent words, like an echo.

The point here has been to understand these achievements of representation in line with drive theory, and with Freud's insight that representation is an essential aspect of drive dynamics—at least in the case of humans. We have shown the capacities for representation and language to be precipitates of a loosened movement of drives. They are something that is "left over" from it and are thus, in a very literal sense, an "over-I," or superego, that is considerably more broad than the internalization of paternal authority. This is nothing less than the specifically human repertoire, a kind of cultural fund supporting all activity that in any way deserves the appellation "mental" or "spiritual." Assuming that this is true, what, then, should we think of the powers that Freud calls the ego and the id? Do we assign the ego to the specifically human movement of stimulus flight, and the id to the neuronal network? Of course, it is not that simple. The neural network cannot be established without already being involved in the discharge of stimuli. To this extent, the movement of stimulus discharge is always already part of it. At the same time, it is also distinct from it—as the riverbed is distinct from the river. But even among animals, stimulus discharge became remarkably coordinated. Already in snails and worms, not just dogs and cats, there is something that exercises control over the approaches to motility, that is, that guides the movements of the muscles in the service of self-preservation, without our being in a position to say that this something is an ego. In animals, we prefer to speak of an "instinct," which would thus be defined as the coordinated movement of drives in an unloosened state of nature. In this state, everything is id—the neural network, the creation of the pathways, and the pathways themselves. Only after the movement of creating pathways has been loosened by condensation, displacement, and reversal does a space open up for deferred actions—the space of the mental. To the extent that this space opens up in each individual we may speak of the dimension of the ego, even if, in the early life of *Homo sapiens*, individuals were by no means able to experience themselves as "I." The ego, however, is not something absolutely other than the movement of the drive as it creates pathways—it is merely its modification. In this movement, it is both id and ego. To the extent that it is a movement of the drive, it is id; to the extent that it has been loosened, it is ego. And what applies to the movement of drives is also true of their results. Sedimented ego, which is called superego, and sedimented id are merely two aspects of the same

process of sedimentation. The sedimentation is cultural and simultaneously natural. Culture is nothing but nature that has been loosened, not
something that exists alongside it. Freud turns this interconnectedness
into a separation. Id, ego, and superego become three authorities within
an "apparatus." But they can only be three moments of one and the same
movement of stimulus flight—a flight that has, out of profound need,
learned the trick of becoming dialectical, in other words, of turning
against itself, differentiating itself from itself, and at the same time
remaining identical with itself.

"Soul is only the name for something in the body," says Nietzsche.[48]
Accordingly, "ego" and "superego" are only names for something within
the drives—for the breathtaking loosening of drives that instantiated the
trinity of reversal, condensation, and displacement. It caused an ego to
spring up in the animal id and precipitate itself into a superego. "Mind" is
only the name for the loosened movement of drives to which we owe id,
ego, and superego, as three moments. They are not defensible as "authorities." It is no accident that they occasionally slip from Freud's grasp, for
example when he thinks he sees, in sublimation, the case in which the
"ego deals with the first object-cathexes of the id . . . by taking over the
libido from them into itself and binding it to the alteration of the ego
produced by means of identification. . . . By thus getting hold of the libido
from the object-cathexes, setting itself up as sole love-object, and desexu-
alizing or sublimating the libido of the id, the ego is working in opposition to the purposes of Eros. . . .[49] Unwittingly, here, "authorities" have
become separate individuals who spy and play tricks on each other—
actors in a psychological farce. If, on the other hand, id, ego, and superego
are subjected to the discipline of reflection and conceived as moments of
a dialectical movement of drives, they are perfectly up-to-date and in no
way rendered obsolete by neuroscience.

EXCESS

The life of the drives became loosened, meaningful—in a word, specifically human—only in *Homo sapiens*, as a result of traumatic repetition
compulsion. The latter is the human drive par excellence, and, as it
happens, precedes the erotic drive. In Freud's words, it is "more primitive, more original, more instinctual than the pleasure principle," to
whose prehistory it belongs. In other words, its origin is not to be found

in sexuality. But how was it able to gain access to the process of loosening of the drives, of deferred action (*Nachträglichkeit*) and representation, so that a process that originally consisted in the purely hormonal discharge of tensions and reproductive function could gradually become transformed into something meaningful, something that absorbed the erotic dimension? Once again, history is hopelessly inadequate here. We do not have a single authentic witness to this development throughout the entire long period of the evolution of *Homo sapiens*. The oldest verbal and visual documents we have are already very late, distant echoes of the process. Many details will forever have to remain unclear. And yet, drive dynamics always also imply a logic of drives and thus a logic of their development as well. We can reconstruct its basic characteristics based on two fundamental physiological facts. Nietzsche expressed one of them in the famous lines,

> "Woe saith: Hence! Go!
> "But joys all want eternity—
> "Want deep profound eternity!"[50]

This is unrivaled as a philosophical expression of the formula for the principle of constancy, for getting rid of torturous stimuli while turning the brief space of time—the mere blink of an eye, during which successful stimulus discharge becomes pleasure and a feeling of satisfaction—into a permanent state. The momentary joy is switched to a permanent state, "where time does not snatch away the lovely sound, where no breeze disperses the sweet fragrance,"[51] and so on—Augustine's words are the model that would later provide Christianity with its image of eternity, the "standing Now." It is literally utopian, that is, it has no place in this world; it is the very state of rest that the tension of the drives seeks to attain.

The same is true if we look at pleasure and eternity in their earlier, animal forms. Every pleasure and feeling of comfort is complete in itself: it has no desire to become anything other than what it is. Pain or "woe," on the other hand, cannot exist without wanting to stop. The special case of human masochism is no exception. Pain can be enjoyed only when it stands in for an absent or anticipated pleasure, that is, only as attenuated enjoyment that is at the point of turning into its opposite. But pleasure in pain has relatively narrow boundaries; where torture begins, masochism ends. There are much greater "woes" than sexual woe. The unease that accompanies hormonally induced sexual tension comes nowhere near the torment that hunger and thirst can produce, not to mention traumatic attack. Only when sexual privation is combined with the feeling of a lack of fulfillment can it become unbearable. But for this to happen, sexuality must first have become meaningful. Now we must show how this could come about.

This brings us to the second set of basic physiological facts. The specifically human capacity that in this chapter we have called the loosening of drives means, in physiological terms, that certain stimulus flight pathways have strayed from their habitual track. There is a vivid Latin verb for this: *delirare*. The man who, while plowing his field, jumps out of the furrow is doing this. He is "delirious." From this perspective, the loosening of drives is a very drastic, foundational sort of delirium. Because there is nothing drives can do except manifest themselves, their loosening took a rather congenial ritual form: excess. Sacrificial rituals require preparation. A collective that senses the urge for sacrifice feels, at the same time, that it is letting itself in for something monstrous. Psychologically, it begins to rehearse the fear that failed to protect it during the traumatic attack. As the theory of ritual prescribes, the collective starts to enter a special state in which it will be capable of its own ritual act—a state characterized by reeling, trance, ecstasy, and intoxication. Only in this state can it bear the ritual killing. Thus, anything that serves as a means of reaching this "heightened" state is welcome, whether it be the performance of continuous, identical collective movements, which will later come to be called "dance"; the regular sounds that accompany these movements as elementary forms of rhythm and song; the ingestion of intoxicating substances; or intentional self-wounding, the "marks of Cain" that not only point to the sparing of the collective and its active and passive participation in the fate of the chosen victim, but also represent rather elementary attempts to distract from and anesthetize pain as a means of blunting the collective's double-sided participation in the act of sacrifice. *Excedere* means "to go or step beyond," and excess, initially, is no less than a stepping outside of nature to enter a state of culture—an accomplishment that demands enormous effort and that only succeeds thanks to a shared, patient process of intensification—a collective self-disciplining of the first order. This is the strict opposite of what, in high cultures, is regarded as excess: a partial "flipping out"[52] of the rules of social behavior. Excesses had to be learned. In the beginning, their development must have been a very arduous work of ritual creation. Loosening drives and creating ritual structures are two sides of the same process.

It is striking that sexuality, which we nowadays associate preferentially with the word *excess*, has few excessive characteristics in the animal kingdom, including primates. Among animals, mating with several partners instead of only one has nothing to do with excess, but initially only with a poorly developed ability to choose. Even mating seasons, with their manifold types of display and courtship behavior, while they may be periods of heightened hormonal tension that seek discharge through copulation, are not periods of excess. Animals don't "go wild." They remain within the fixed parameters of their habitual mechanisms for stimulus flight. We cannot speak of a loosening of drives. And the sexual tension that periodically increases and decreases does not, by any means, reach such torturous intensity that it would need to be discharged by means of constant repetition. Nevertheless, the pioneers of psychoanalysis were united in their attempts to derive culture from sexual tension. C. G. Jung imagines the process in such a fashion that the sexual act, somehow, "was thrust out of its own sphere," first to "the analogous oral zone," which was both "retained as erotically important" and prepared for "the production of mating calls" and hence also language; and second to the hands, which became active both onanistically and in the rubbing of fire sticks, which is also seen as an ersatz sexual action that mutates into a cultural activity, to become "the first art." But because "secondary sexual activity (displaced coitus) never was or will be in a position to achieve the natural satisfaction comparable to activity at the proper location," it also, supposedly, represented "the first step toward the characteristic dissatisfaction that drove human beings, later, from discovery to discovery, without ever allowing them to achieve satisfaction."[53]

This is an old wives' tale of human development. A completely nebulous process that causes sexuality to be "thrust out of its own sphere" (who or what caused this thrust?) is supposed to have ensured that the sexual activity of hominids was translated into ersatz behavior—courtship displays into dancing and making fire, mating calls into language. Freud, for his part, may not have been convinced that it was so easy for hominids to glide over into a state of culture, but his version of human evolution is a fairy tale, too. It is the story of the primal horde, and of "a violent and jealous father who keeps all the females for himself and drives away his sons as they grow up. . . . The violent primal father had doubt-less been the feared and envied model of each one of the company of brothers." Hence, "the brothers who had been driven out came together, killed and devoured their father and so made an end of the patriarchal horde."[54] This history is clairvoyant to the extent that it has human culture begin with the collective murder of an individual, but it is anachronistic and unpsychological in its belief that sexual jealousy was the driving force behind this deed. There is sexual jealousy in nature; but natural sexuality is not burdened with so much tension and such unbearable intensity that, all by itself, it necessitated the movement toward culture. On the contrary: it was culture that first accounted for the specific tension we call "erotic." Sadism and masochism are also cultural phenomena. Animals may be cruel. They are not sadists.

If it is true that traumatic repetition compulsion, when it first began to be historically identifiable in the sacrificial cult, already had a long history behind it, then it is equally true that the development of sexuality into eroticism only became identifiable at a later phase of its develop-ment. The Aurignacian period (35,000–28,000 years ago), which is the era of the oldest known cave paintings and of very ancient sculptures, is already an early high culture. Nonetheless, some earlier developments can be deduced from the impressive visual documents that have come down to us. A long time must have passed during which early human collectives performed and created the models of moving images in which they themselves represented the terrors of nature. The process must have become so routine and distanced that they were even capable of making individual copies that could be preserved in ivory or stone. Where this occurred, the copies took the form of animals. The relief sculpture of an enormous snake that was recently discovered in a cave in the Kalahari Desert (South Africa) may be 70,000 years old—twice as old as the oldest documented images from the Aurignacian. It is one more piece of evidence for the fact that the creation of still images can have had no other motive, in the beginning, than to banish fear. The sudden, lightning-quick appearance of the snake, its difficult-to-distinguish, quasi-formless slithering movements, which even before the snake's mortal bite call forth "certain typically intuitive, irrational, phobic reactions . . . of the vegetative nervous system . . . in humans and also in primates"[55]—all this literally seems to cry out to be captured in the form of the image. We cannot prove that the oldest standing images are those of snakes, but the snake does provide an incomparable image of the fright that drove the invention of still imagery—and was meant to be forgotten in it. The snake uniquely represents the ungraspable quality of nature's terrors and, at the same time, allows it to be grasped. It is the creature that makes it easiest for us to understand why only wild animals could ignite the powers of image-making. Nothing concretizes fright better than a snake. Unfathomable lightning bolts become palpable in the snake's lightning-quick strike. The rumble of thunder or earthquakes takes shape in the lion, whose roars penetrate the marrow of our bones. And once humans have learned to banish fear in the form of animal images, they can banish them even further—can surround, overlay, and replace them with images of less-fear-inducing animals. The logic of cushioning, which we saw earlier in the development of representation, is at work here too. The paintings in the famous caves of southern France, in this context, offer an entire system of animal representation. Its genealogy is uncertain. Horses are the animals that appear most frequently but are certainly not the most fearful ones. They are followed by bison, aurochs, ibex, stag, mammoth, reindeer, bear, lion, and rhinoceros, without our being able to relate their order to a level of dangerousness or frequency. Certainly, all these images refer to the hunt, at which the humans inhabiting the region had become adept both technically, in their weaponry, and organizationally. To this extent, it is not wrong to speak of hunting magic. But modern-day humans have a tendency to conceive of the hunt instrumentally, as if our Stone Age ancestors, by banishing animals in the form of images, were only seeking to turn them into defenseless targets. But taming the violence of animals meant much more. Individuals were fully armed for the hunt only by rituals that sought to make the fearful power of animals their own—to turn the overweening power of nature into a force that could protect. This is magic's original figure. It is embodied in the reverse logic of traumatic repetition compulsion. The cave paintings set the scene for its ritual performance by banishing animal power to the walls.

The "genius" was the first "wherefor" of the cult, its first addressee. When its spectral power took the concrete form of animal power, and its ghostly shape assumed the shape of the animals, the "wherefor" also passed over to them. Animals became the addressees of the cult. They became "sacred": totems. The first animal images were totem images, a kind of larger-then-life talismans. Their variety on the walls of the caves gives evidence of a multiply ramified totemic system whose details are no longer clear to us.[56] Nevertheless, it conveys an evolutionary logic. The logic does not emerge directly from the paintings themselves. But there is a myth that reveals it in a relatively straightforward fashion. It is the Australian story I cited in the first chapter, where it says, "Then the Great Snake transformed the beings who obeyed the laws into human beings, and she gave each of them his totem, from which the human was descended. Thus, the tribes and clans knew themselves by their totem. They were the descendants of the emus, the kangaroos, the black-headed python, and many other ancestors from the dreamtime." The "dream-time" was the time of the snake cult, and it was not only constitutive for the Aborigines. The discovery in the Kalahari Desert and the widespread currency of snakes in the ancient history of Indian, Mesopotamian, Mediterranean, and American mythologies—preferentially, there, in the form of an entity that has been vanquished, slain, and forced under-ground—speak for the fact that the snake was, if not the first, at least one of the first addressees of the cult in animal form, and hence a key point of origin for totemism. Primal totems are too fear-inspiring for us to focus on them for long. We begin to represent them by less-fearful, more-familiar ones. The ramification of collective hordes into organized tribes, clans, and subclans also enhanced this process of representation. To distinguish itself from others, a clan needs its own identity, that is, its own cult addressee. That the snake "gave each of them his totem" is an atavistic memory both of the process by which human collectives became differentiated and of the process of representing fear itself. The more branches the totemic system developed, the more the initial shock of totemic fear got lost in them. In the Australian myth, it has been preserved. In the cave paintings in the European southwest, it is already so attenuated that we can no longer identify primal totems—a further hint of the high degree of development this culture had achieved.

Compared to the images that represent animals, those of humans are only secondary. They are definitely not what came first, but were only gradually added to the animal images, and at first not even sharply differ-entiated from them. To the extent that they have heads at all, they tend to be blurred and still largely animal-like, while something else is quite pronounced—their sex organs. The oldest surviving image of a human being, a small female torso of ivory known as the "Venus" of Willendorf, ca. 25,000 years old, has disproportionately prominent breasts and vulva. We may be certain that this statuette was part of a ritual in which the importance of the female sex was celebrated; we do not know to what extent or for what purpose. Five more millennia were to elapse before a human image showed up in the context of animals. It was in the famous cave in Lascaux, as part of a story told in images. A powerful aurochs—its abdomen has been pierced by a spear so that its entrails are hanging out—has lowered its head for attack. Right next to it, a figure resembling a human being, strikingly primitive and unrealistically portrayed, a kind of stick figure, is shown leaning diagonally backward, its arms outstretched, with a birdlike head and an erect penis. Is this male figure shown at the moment it falls down after being butted by the aurochs? Or in the excited state of a cultic dance, particularly in view of the fact that a direct line leads from the figure's birdlike head, above the right arm, to a separate bird figure pointing to the wall beneath it—a figure that likely also has ritual significance? The two interpretations are not necessarily mutually exclusive. We should not be so anachronistic as to read the butting of an aurochs, which upends a man, as a snapshot from an actual hunting scene. If, on the other hand, we interpret the scene as the condensation of a ritual, then the two apparently incompatible elements come together. The aurochs *as a totem* fells a man, thus signifying that a human being is offered to it. The offering is accompanied by an excited dance, whose visible sign is sexual arousal. It announces itself as a component of the "elevated," intoxication- and trance-inducing state in which the collective finds itself during the performance of the ritual. What if the cave painting in Lascaux unveils the origin of a motif that retains its power even today, as one of the great motivating forces of the dramatic form? I refer to the *Liebestod*—death inspired by love.

EROS

Copulating animals do not make "love." Neither do they engage in excess. Together, they discharge their shared hormonal tension. Entirely in conformity with the principle of constancy, this has something agreeable, comforting, and calming about it that aims to be lasting. On its own, sexuality has absolutely no cause to remove itself from this state of nature. If this did happen, then it was not voluntarily. The development of traumatic repetition compulsion affected the entire organism, including its sexuality. As the hominids engaged in the rhythmic movements, the ingestion of intoxicating drugs, and the self-wounding practices that initiated them into the heightened state of ritual performance; as they pressed against each other in fear in order to cross together the threshold of ritual killing of the "chosen" victim, they must have noticed that bodily contact helps reduce fear, that sexual movements have their own rhythm, that sexual arousal can also be collectively heightened and driven to excess, and in the process can have an effect that in its own way is intoxicating, pain reducing, and distracting. We need only conceive displacement and condensation somewhat more broadly and elementarily than Freud did for it to become evident that the inclusion of sexuality in ritual, along with its related intensification and exaltation, was one of early humanity's great achievements of displacement and condensation. Displacement and condensation appear here as elementary forces contributing to the loosening of drives. Here, we also perceive an additional aspect of this loosening, namely, that it transcends the discharge of traumatic excitation to the point that it discharges sexual excitation as well.

Humans, who for millennia have been born into a situation of loosened drives, as if this has always been the case, will find it difficult to imagine how this loosening was experienced at the beginning. But we can comfortably assume that it did not feel like being relieved of a burden. Nothing suggests that the discharge of natural hormonal tension was experienced as anything but well-being and relief. Conversely, it is likely that as the drives began to be loosened, this sense of well-being gave way to delirium, in which the habitual natural processes and signals that typically led to the discharge of heterosexual tensions literally ran off the tracks and led to a situation that was experienced more as a disturbance of the sense of balance than as sexual liberation. We must not talk here of an exuberance of desire. The loosening of drives may only have been able to begin collectively, but it has nothing at all to do with what modern humans imagine as "group sex." We do not know what sexual excess looked like in the beginning, how it surrounded the ritual of killing, to what extent it prepared, coincided with, or reworked it, or whether the collective, as its members pressed against and into each other, engaged in sexual contact with all those involved or might even have required it. In any case, the loosening of drives that took place must also have loosened the natural predisposition to heterosexuality. And as sexuality, in the force field of the ritual killing, assumed an intensity that was intoxicating and/or numbing, one of the ritual's fundamental characteristics passed over into it: its quality as an image. Sexual excess became part of the sacrificial performance—and simultaneously also an image of the sacrifice itself. The desperate attempt of the latter, after all, was to bring the collective into harmony with the terrible and superior power of nature. Where sexuality is drawn into this evocation of harmony, it ceases to be merely a natural process. Copulation no longer serves only as a means of discharging tension. It is celebrated. It begins to represent, in a nonsanguinary way, the harmony with the powers of nature that the ritual sacrifice was only able to perform by bloodletting. And only sexuality that, in this way, has been charged with meaning, that points beyond itself and has become image, deserves the name of Eros, the erotic.

Only where there is eroticism do we find what psychoanalysis calls "cathexis." Cathexis, meaning a libidinous attachment to an object,[57] is not the same thing as the discharge of hormonal tension. At best, it is what happens during such discharge if it takes place repeatedly in the same context. Cathexis requires repetition and continuity— well-established stimulus flight paths. It is an achievement of memory. To create a libidinous attachment means to associate a meaning with something, and the primary meanings, as this book has shown, are reinterpretations. If collective sexual excess becomes libidinously attached to the ritual of killing, "cathects" with it, then it imagines the ritual as the opposite of this killing. It attempts to cushion it. Cathexis begins as appeasement and mitigation. However brutal the process may have been in the beginning—not very different from an indiscriminate attack—it nevertheless aims at something more than this brutality. The individuals who carry out the sacrifice commit a bloody act in order that they themselves may be spared. In sexual excess, however, they actually spare each other. And the protective, shielding behavior toward each other is nothing other than the primal form of love. All respect, all tenderness and compassion come from the original act of sparing the other. To care about protecting the other from hurt—what is love, if not this?

Love did not develop voluntarily. It was literally driven out of nature. It is completely anachronistic to imagine that a naturally loving and tender sexual drive occasionally became linked to an unrelated aggressive or destructive drive and then brought forth the perverse phenomenon of sadomasochism. The loosening or eroticization of the natural sexual drive is itself already perverse. Generally, culture is perverted nature—after all, it originates in the mechanism of reversal—and the same is true of all the tenderness and love of which humanity has ever been capable. They germinated in the force field of sacrificial horror. Their early stage, we should note, had little to do with what is practiced as sadomasochism in the context of a high culture, where the violence is done and suffered as a sexual stimulant. Originally, the opposite was the case: What was at stake was the de-escalation of violence and horror by means of sexuality. This, precisely, is the context in which we emerged, and the original meaning of *Liebestod*: the first crude forms of love were ignited by the death of the sacrificial victim. Sacrificial death allowed the dimension of protection, of sparing the other, to blossom within sexuality. It eroticized sexuality.

Eros began with the cult. It is no accident that the ancient Greeks called it a god. This is much more than an empty phrase, as is most magnificently documented in Plato's *Symposium*—that group of enco-miums to Eros whose most imaginative expression is laid in the mouth of Aristophanes, the comedic playwright. It is the history of primitive humans, who are supposed to have existed in three types—male, female, and man-woman. And "each of these beings was globular in shape, with rounded back and sides, four arms and four legs, and two faces, both the same, on a cylindrical back, and one head, with one face one side and one the other, and four ears, and two lots of privates, and all the other parts to match."[58] And since these beings were so strong and fast that they "actually tried . . . to scale the heights of heaven and set upon the gods," Zeus "cut them all in half, just as you or I might chop up . . . apples for pickling," and let them run around on two legs. Only with this did they turn into the beings that since then have been reproducing themselves as the species we call human.

The tale of the origin of this species as hybrid double beings whom Zeus first made into humans by cutting them in two is one of the most graphic condensations of the genealogy of human drives. The fiction of the hybrid double being allows Plato to articulate one of humanity's most deadly serious memories in comedic fashion. Only when a god cuts humans in two, "just as you or I might chop up . . . apples for pickling"—in other words, only when humans are slaughtered for the sake of the gods—does the human creation occur. What Plato is saying here is the same as the Greek verb *rezein*, which means both "to make a sacrifice" and, generally, "to act," and thus expresses the fact that sacrifice is the very essence of human action: it is *the* specifically human act, bar none. But the real point is where the story goes from there. It is nothing other than the sacrificial "bisection" of humans, at the instigation of Zeus, that unleashes Eros. "Now, when the work of bisection was complete it left each half with a desperate yearning for the other, and they ran together and flung their arms around each other's necks, and asked for nothing better than to be rolled into one."[59] This attempt to reintegrate our former nature, to make two into one, and to bridge the gulf between one human being and another is called love (Eros). Eros is "a relic of that original state, when we were whole."[60] The reintegration never succeeds fully, but it does not cease being a vanishing point of human striving. It always points beyond itself. Where a human being is "bisected," in other words has become human, he is, in Plato's word, *symbolon*: a fragment that refers to its opposite member, from which it has been broken off. It means an integral unity that it does not achieve.

DEATH DRIVE

What Aristophanes recounts in the *Symposium*, with a kind of wink, is an artistic myth that was specially invented by Plato, not an atavistic mythological legacy. And yet it is a great trace of the memory of Eros's origin in human sacrifice. For Freud, remarkably, this same passage becomes the star witness for his theory of the death drive, which he happened upon in *Beyond the Pleasure Principle* and which continued to pursue him during the last two decades of his life. Freud takes the fantasy of the bisection of primitive man as a "hint" of the "poet-philosopher" for "the hypothesis that living substance at the time of its coming to life was torn apart into small particles, which have ever since endeavored to reunite."[61] This supposition ignores both the cultic dimension of the Platonic myth and the difference between Eros and sex. The sexual drive is watered down to a general life force that is designed to hold the body's cells together, and the question of how nonliving substance was called into life precisely by being "torn apart," where tearing apart, after all, means killing, is not even asked. Here we have a living example of fixation. Freud is at the point of confirming his commitment to the death drive and grasps at anything that seems to support its existence.

For a quarter of a century, the principle of constancy had served as the physiological foundation of Freud's theory. Up to then, it had made it possible for him to understand the masked wish fulfillments that he uncovered in his patients' dreams as the secret discharge of especially urgent, because forbidden, impulses—specifically sexual-incestuous ones.[62] Then, with the First World War came the increasing numbers of soldiers' dreams, which night after night repeated the "steel thunder" of the front and which, even with the best intentions, could no longer be interpreted as manifestations of the forbidden sexual impulses that Freud had until then assumed to be the motor of all dreams. He discovered the full force of traumatic repetition compulsion, which he had previously only perceived in a tempered form, as sexually traumatic. Now, in one of his most insightful moments, he called it "more primitive, more original, and more instinctual than the pleasure principle" it pushed aside—its "prehistory." In plain language: Sexuality is not the primary force in human drives. This insight shook the foundations of Freud's dogma of sexuality as the constitutive force in dreams, as well as his treatment of cultural theory: the fairy tale that culture is a consequence of sexual envy. Traumatic repetition compulsion threatened the entire structure of Freud's previous work of psychoanalysis. It must not be admitted. The title *Beyond the Pleasure Principle* can definitely be read as a surreptitious command aimed at traumatic repetition compulsion: Stay away from the pleasure principle, don't interfere with its sexuality-centered circles. The goal was to disarm traumatic repetition compulsion, to discharge it like a bothersome stimulus. The hypothesis of the death drive was Freud's specially created stimulus flight path, in response to this need. He allowed himself to be carried along it into a "Beyond" that left the pre-psychological sphere of pure biology and the realm of psychological therapy, where psychoanalysis has its concrete impact, far behind. How did Freud justify this? With nothing less than the principle of constancy. For decades, Freud had seen the principle of constancy as one of life's principles. Now, he believed he had discovered a new side to it. Does the urge to work off traumatizing stimuli, over and over again, not demonstrate the fact that it is urging the organism toward a complete lack of stimuli—in other words, toward death? Is the principle of constancy not, in the final analysis, a "Nirvana principle"?

Freud actually tried to prove this, by hook or by crook. In the process, the principle of constancy was made to play the same role that the oedipal family situation had played when it came to the fairy tale about the slain father. "The attributes of life were at some time evoked in inanimate matter by the action of a force of whose nature we can form no conception. . . . The tension which then arose in what had hitherto been an inanimate substance endeavored to cancel itself out. In this way the first drive came into being: the drive to return to the inanimate state."[63] It is, admittedly, utterly impossible to conceive how, in the face of an urge of this kind, evolving life could ever have survived past the momentary existence of single-celled organisms. Instead, the opposite is supposed to have happened: "External influences . . . obliged the still surviving substance to diverge ever more widely from its original life path and to make ever more complicated detours before reaching its aim of death."[64] Single-celled animals became multicelled, extremely complex organisms, until the death drive finally brought forth its own opponents in the form of germ cells: "the group of the sexual drives. . . . They are the true life drives."[65]

If only the emergence of the sexual drives from the death drive were at least conceived as a reflexive movement; but no, it is imagined as the division of a cell. One divides into two, and in the process it generates its own opposite. For one cell, this may hold. But how is a drive supposed to divide, particularly when it is a drive toward death, with no opponents and equally little reason to divide in two and generate an opposing drive? The division of drives into a death drive and a life drive also implies, *nolens volens*, a divided principle of constancy. On one hand, this principle is supposed to drive toward its satisfaction; on the other, toward death, without anyone being able to give a plausible explanation as to how the two are simultaneously at work in a single organism and how they are also supposed to make it last. And what about repression, displacement, and condensation in the case of the death drive? What is the nature of the suffering, what are the illnesses that result from inhibiting its discharge? Are its neuroses . . . life itself? Is libidinous satisfaction its frustration, and libidinous frustration its satisfaction? There is not even a partial attempt to sketch out a psycho-thanatoid counterpart to the psychosexual development that is the entire object of psychoanalytic attention. If the death drive were a real drive, there would have to be such a counterpart. But where speculation about it begins, every serious energetic reflection stops. There remains only the vague reference to the "inertia inherent in organic life,"[66] and the consequence that is drawn from this, namely that "all the organic drives are conservative, are acquired historically and tend toward the restoration of an earlier state of things."[67]

This last is a weak attempt at covering over of the division of the principle of constancy by mixing up two concepts: conservative and regressive. To be conservative means to want to sustain oneself, to stay the way one is. To be regressive means to want to go back to an earlier state. Freud acts as if both amount to the same thing, as if wanting to discharge stimuli is equivalent to not wanting to go on living. Now, it is true that there are phenomena that aim at their own end. If a thunderstorm aims at its own discharge, it "wants" to stop. It has a death drive, as it were—but only because it is already dead. The discharge of energy occurs on a purely physical level, in a constellation that is without life. But as soon as the discharge takes place in a living body, it does this in accordance with the conditions of that body—the conditions of life. Thunderstorms may be regressive. Organisms are primarily conservative: they aim at a comfortable minimum of stimuli, with the goal of optimal *survival*. Some of them do develop regressive tendencies, for example when they assume a fetal position during sleep. But this too serves to reduce stimuli as part of a survival strategy and is not in the slightest a sign of life having an "instinct' or "urge" that drives it toward death. Other living things develop traumatic repetition compulsion. Its repetitions also have the goal of making themselves superfluous. In other words, they seek their own end, but naturally they do this in the service of a life without frightening shocks. Metaphorically, we can declare every expression of a drive to be a death drive, for every one of them wants the end of a lack. But Freud precisely did not mean anything this nonspecific. Certainly, he is right when he says, "inanimate things existed before living ones."[68] But a state of nonlife is not the original condition of any living body, as if it had first existed and only then had life breathed into it, as the dust of the ground in the Garden of Eden received the breath of life. A living body is a cellular structure from the moment it begins; it is an organic organization, and it wants both to be stimulus free and to experience freedom from stimuli. It wants the impossible—not an inorganic original state, but something that has never existed. It is not regressive, but utopian.

INCEST

Plato's myth, with its theory of drives, has precisely this utopian drift. Eros may be conceived as a longing to return to a primal state, but it is an imaginary one—utopia in reverse. Restored nature does not mean dead nature; it means a nature that has been healed, that is unbroken and alive. Eros wants more than just "satisfaction" or "life." It wants nature healed, reconciled, unharmed. Plato understood this better than Freud, because he continued to recall Eros's origin in the cult. Certainly, the Greek god Eros is already an allegory, not an ancient cult divinity. The notion that archaic collectives would have worshipped "love as such" is already amiss. They did not do that even on the altars of Ishtar, Aphrodite, or Venus, whose status as "love goddesses" merely suggests that the sexual privation of the victims who were brought to them was really impressive. The brutal early forms of delirious human sexuality will continue to be dark spots in our understanding of early humankind, particularly given the fact that there was no pleasurable reason to remember them. Nonetheless, there seems to be a kind of fundamental fact that lies so deeply buried in human memory that it can be neither forgotten nor brought to light. Mythology mentions it only sporadically and obliquely, and yet it has an uncanny, unspoken presence and is considered absolutely forbidden. I am talking about incest. Even today, the incest taboo continues to be an enigma. Nature knows no incest barrier. Mice and rabbits copulate without paying any attention to their relation to each other, and something of this lack of concern even reaches as far as the primates. Incest does not hurt. It is close at hand—for who is closer than one's own relatives? That in the long term its impact is degenerative is only apparent at a relatively high cultural level and does not directly threaten individuals. We are not allowed to do this, it makes our descendants dumb—this is an ex post facto consideration, not the kind of elementary reaction that leads to taboo. So what made incest into a taboo? The fact that it makes a confusing mess of family relationships or can cause emotional pain and trauma? It does this only where these family relationships already exist. But the question we are asking here is why human collectives felt the urgent need to put an end to incest by making relations of descent and consanguinity into strict regulators of sexual behavior. In other words, why did they find incest unbearable? Certainly not because the "brothers" in the primal horde, out of bad conscience over the murder of the primal father, decided that from then on they would not copulate with female members of their own clan, the way their randy old father had, and would look for their women in other hordes.

But Freud's fairy tale does start more or less in the right place. Something must have *made* incest unbearable. After everything that has already been said, can the reason be anything but its inclusion in ritual killing? With it, incest stopped being natural. It became specifically human: excessive, charged with meaning—and drawn into the collective drive aimed at feeling unanimity in regard to the victim. The ritual slaughter of a member of the clan could, after all, only be borne if all the clan members participated as one, if they came together without animosity to make collective rhythmic movements and sounds and to use intoxicating drugs while carrying out narcotic self-wounding—all in order to achieve the shared ecstatic state that was the necessary precondition for their capacity to perform the deed. And where, in this process, unavoidable bodily contact led to sexual acts and made them, as well, part of the communal excess, incest also took on a new quality and intensity. The collective, as it were, pulled itself together intentionally to achieve this end, and performed it ritually in order to alleviate the horror of the sacrifice. On the other hand, precisely as a result of this, incest became the representative of this horror—and so closely associated with it that one thing could no longer be recalled without the other. But if this is true, then Freud's fundamental suspicion is shown to be completely justified, namely, that archaic incest is inseparable from collective human killing, and that for this reason all culture rests on a strict prohibition of both—a double taboo. Except that Freud did not realize *how* incest and killing belong together or to what extent incest itself was already an attempt to gain control of the seemingly endless killing; that culture, in the form of these two primal taboos, turns its own primal state into a taboo; and that cultural development is the product of a flight from its own origins—its attempt at repression. He did not see that the saga of King Oedipus, who kills his father and marries his mother, is already a highly cultivated screen memory that conceals the real state of affairs more than it reveals it. By individualizing its memory within the patriarchal family structure, it also covers it up. The explanation flees the true origins of culture the way Oedipus flees the oracle's prediction, while Freud, for his part, read the story as a candid revelation, as if the triadic family constellation were the original schema of culture as a whole, and as if Oedipus's double act were a nonmetaphorical expression of "the two primal wishes of children,"[69]—whereas Oedipus actually commits his crimes unknowingly and against his will, in a desperate attempt to escape from them.[70]

Once we are clear about the fact that early humanity had good reason to flee incestuous sexual excess, because no matter how much it sought to alleviate the horror of sacrifice it was horrible itself, then the concept of stimulus flight, whose first meaning was related to drive theory, takes on a philosophical and historical dimension. The overcoming of collective incest must have been a stimulus flight of this kind. How it occurred, what kinds of behavior led to it, we will scarcely be able to discern. But there is one thing that cannot have been lacking here either: the mitigating effect of representation. The same way ritual killing could be represented by sexual excess, this excess could also be represented by its opposite, collective sexual abstention. It too is an *excedere*, a going beyond the natural way of handling one's own sexual instincts, a kind of negative excess—the opposite of collective incest and to this extent a particularly apt means of being liberated from it. Besides this, it also reaches a new level of representation of the sacrifice. The collective temporarily makes an offering of its own sexual needs. In this way, it lends emphasis to the sacrificial slaughter and simultaneously represents it in a nonbloody and nonincestuous manner. To practice sexual renunciation for a lifetime was not by any means something that early humans, given the level of their sexual self-control, could contemplate. Hermits and monks are virtuosos of renunciation—phenomena that belong to high cultures. In comparison, renunciatory excess is crude and sporadic—not something that could be made permanent. Thus, the flight of early humankind from its own incestuous sexual practices could lead to nothing other than strict observance of degrees of relatedness. As regulators of sexual behavior, family relationships are sedimented ritual structures that have become profane. The loosened movement of sexual drives took shelter there. Just as the incestuous coming together of the collective had once been a part of ritual practice, its negation also had to have had its inception in ritual. At first, it took the form of collective renunciatory excess, before turning to a more targeted form that made certain groups of people—for example, members of different generations or of the same nuclear family—renounce the possibility of having sex with each other. Ultimately, this compulsion would also become a separate phenomenon in the form of celibacy as a generalized stance in life.

The flight of early humans from their own incest also includes flight from the excitation center of ritual, toward profane relations in which the loosened, delirious, eroticized sexual drive can be de-escalated and become lasting. The "ancient society" that Lewis H. Morgan explored in his pathbreaking ethnographic work of the same title,[71] is, in any case, anything but the primal state of humanity. Instead, it depicts an already highly developed complex of lineage and clan relations in which the incest taboo has already become so cooled off, ramified, and refined, so ordinary and sedimented as a collective stance, that the excess to which it was once opposed is scarcely recognizable as such. At best, the excess can be surmised from the rigor of the rules forbidding it. If, on the other hand, we open the Gilgamesh epic, that most ancient survivor of humanity's great narratives and memory books, we find a high culture that is at once urbane and despotically patriarchal, but in which a glowing core of sexual excess is nevertheless not yet extinguished. "For six days and seven nights / Enkidu was erect, as he mated with Shamhat." Only complete sexual exhaustion, which so "weakened" Enkidu that his legs "stood still" and became incapable of running with the herd, give him "reason" and "wide understanding,"[72] even though the excess itself has long since become embedded in a strict work of ritual. The incident has the fixed temporality of a week, quite possibly a very special week, such as that preceding the solstice or equinox. The urge to continue repeatedly bringing to mind the unmastered past of human sexual relations, based on murderous excess, is projected onto representatives who perform it on behalf of the entire collective—most likely at precisely determined times of the year and in the framework of specific sacrificial celebrations. "Religious prostitution" is a rather warped expression for this; where it does occur, it has nothing to do with love for sale. "Shamhat the harlot" is not some kind of street-walker, but a cultic official, a priestess—possibly the high priestess—because she stands for the fact that the unmastered cultic history of Eros, completely in keeping with the principle of constancy, is rendered harm-less for the community through the ritual discharge of stimuli. From this perspective, Gilgamesh is practically the male equivalent of Shamhat. When he exercises the *ius primae noctis*,[73] it is as if he were giving the brides the seal of divinity that releases them to marriage. He also reenacts, in fast-forward, the passage from the cult's collective excess to well-tempered, profane family relationships, which has cost humanity such immense time and trouble.

The profanation of Eros was also its gradual naturalization. The unnatural loosening of drives that had once set traumatic repetition compulsion in motion finally became the nature of *Homo sapiens*. Whether the history of this sedimentation can ever be written according to the strict criteria of modern historicity remains to be seen. Nevertheless, its course has a logic that I would like to call "erogenetic." Freud calls those zones of the body "erogenetic" that "may act as substitutes for the genitals and behave analogously to them."[74] But the human body had to acquire the capacity for this kind of representation. Erogenous zones have a long erogenetic prehistory. When especially sensitive and excitable parts of the body begin to become erogenous, they begin to stand in for each other—to mean each other. In a sense, they become semantically charged and take on a sensitivity that is significant in the literal sense—a quality that they did not naturally have but that gradually becomes part of their nature—and that enters into the complex of meanings associated with eroticized sexuality. At first, after all, collective incestuous excess was meaningful only to the extent that it signified the ritual of killing. But meaning could be displaced. It could shift from the ritual itself to the ritual's representation, so that individuals, separately from the whole, performed the excess in lieu of the collective, and in this process also became meaningful for each other. That sexual partners "mean the world" to each other began not as a spontaneous, private wave of feeling, but in the cult—in the solemn union of priestly representatives, whose copulation conjured up the well-being of the collective and the stability of its social order.

For something to be libidinously cathected always also means to have meaning conferred upon it. You can only love what means something to you, and this always signifies that it means more to you than what it is. Only this "more" allows the physical well-being of hormonal relaxation to be transformed into to the experience of happiness. This transformation is a decisive step in the profanation of Eros. Its moderating, protective meaning, which was learned nowhere else but in the force field of ritual horror, moves beyond the charmed circle. It becomes humanized. Many millennia were required before Eros became sublimated in the form of the joyful love of two people who don't want to let go of each other their whole life long, before it became so profoundly sunk in human nature that it could begin its individual history on the lips of a newborn. But as surely as only profane Eros can seem human, the opposite is just as certain: it can never become wholly profane. As long as it means something, it has not completely shaken off its origins in the cult, and never ceases to point beyond itself, toward the reconciled and safeguarded nature that the ritual once suggested—and that even the most loving act can only point toward but not bring about.

MYSTICISM OF THE NEWBORN

With this, we turn again to Plato's beautiful myth. For the cult-driven bisection of humans has a natural prehistory. At every birth, one double being becomes two individuals. And the newborn, at first, doesn't want to be an individual at all. It wants the flood of stimuli to which its birth exposes it—light, noises, changes in temperature, touch, and so on—to stop. Fully in line with the principle of constancy, it wants to return to the prenatal state, in which it was free of stimuli and fully taken care of. Thus, every mammal, not just the human one, wants to return to the womb from which it has just emerged. It does not actually seek the mother. It finds her in its search for maximal stimulus discharge. The sucking reflex, which it brings with it as a disposition and which leads it directly to the mother's breasts, does make it possible for the newborn to nourish itself with its mother's milk. But the primary intent of sucking is a different one: to reverse the division into two individual creatures. The newborn attempts to suck itself back into the womb and to suck the womb into itself. Its sucking is no less than a mystical act, and the feeling it derives in performing it is no different than the one theological mystics experience later on. The *unio mystica* is always a failure; it goes no further than a felt and partial unity. In point of fact, the newborn no more becomes one with its mother than Meister Eckhart with God.[75] Still, the sucking achieves something that it did not intend and that is a rich recompense for the failure of reunification: the enjoyment of nourishment. Sucking proves to be strenuous, nourishing, and pleasurable, and only when these three characteristics work together does the newborn enter the state of satisfied exhaustion that represents the archetype of happiness.

For cats, dogs, and apes, sucking on the maternal teats is already a mystical act, as well, but one in which the mysticism is latent; it remains in its natural state, so to speak. It does not burst forth or become cultural or meaningful. This surely has to do with the fact—apart from the brain volume of the affected species—that the shock of birth that every living creature experiences when it is expelled from the mother's body is normally not sufficient, on its own, to elicit the culture-creating power of traumatic repetition compulsion. It follows that the natural process of birth, which divides one living being into two, is, on its own, also not yet Eros. In order for the dimension of the erotic to enter the picture, a further, specifically human division has to occur. It is this division that Plato, with a sure aim, associates with Zeus. Only when hominids have become human, as the result of their violent cultic division into two, can the division that results from birth also assume specifically human traits. Only then can the mother learn to perceive her child as meaningful—as an object of education and not just instinctual nurturing. The child can experience something far more astonishing. In the act of sucking that gives the newborn its German name (*Säugling*), the dimension of meaning begins to unfold. This is only possible if the erogenous capacity, that is, the capacity of Eros to be displaced from one body part onto another and to create relations of representation between them, also has a historical, "erogenetic" developmental thrust.[76] Eros was not learned in the symbiosis between mother and child, as all those psychologists take to be self-evident who have never bothered to ask why it is that young dogs, horses, or chimpanzees do not arrive at eroticism despite all their sucking. Eros *injected itself* into the mother-child symbiosis during the unimaginably long journey on which it was transformed from a center of cultic excitation into a natural disposition of the human species. During this process, it also became displaced, to the extent that its physical source wandered from one end of the human body to the other—from the genitalia to the mouth. As a matter of species history, Eros began in the cult. If we are talking about individual history, it began in the head. The human newborn is an apt symbol for the fact that Eros is sexuality that has gone to the head. Here once again, as with its origins of human history, Eros did not undertake this voluntarily. The laborious sucking at the mother's breast may be pleasurable but it is not yet erotic. It becomes this only when the newborn experiences denial, when he must become aware that the maternal breast is not *his* breast, that it isn't *he himself* but something different, something all its own, which contradicts him. Only then does it become an object for him; *obicere* means "to place or throw against," or "to oppose." The child thus becomes a subject in a very literal sense: *subicere* means "to place under," or "to subject." To experience the mother as an object and oneself as a subject means, in other words, to become aware of her resistance, to know oneself to be subjected to her and to feel rejected. This in turn entails nothing less than starting to feel one's own insignificance. The experience of self begins as the experience of insignificance. The newborn must transcend this experience. To do this, he needs a lot of help from outside, but he must do the decisive part himself. He must learn to accept denial, not only by allowing it to happen again and again but by beginning to provoke it intentionally, to cause it to happen and start to direct it himself. In this process, he recapitulates something, on a small scale and in a more moderate form, that humanity once demonstrated collectively when it mastered collective shocks: the affirmation of the unbearable.

The affirmation of the unbearable with which every newborn struggles has already been going on for some time when he begins to stimulate his lips, from which the maternal nipple has been removed, with the hem of a blanket or similar object, and in this way creates for himself a certain ersatz for the pleasure of sucking that has been denied him. To the observer, this shows that the newborn is affirming himself. He is turning his primary self-experience, which is one of insignificance, into self-approval. Self-affirmation only happens through its opposite. In philosophical terms, it is always the negation of a negation—like its philosophical opposite, the affirmation of the other. When the mother refuses to make herself available to her newborn, the maternal breast becomes genuinely other to him, and he must learn to negate this external negativity as well as his own insignificance. In affirming himself, he also affirms the other—and in doing so he gains awareness that the maternal breast, for him, no longer consists in disparate states of awareness of denial and availability, but begins to grow together into a single object. Only when he has the experience that the breast that is denied is none other than the one that is available does it actually become a breast for him. To become aware of it as an object means to become aware of a resistance that repels him as well as a source of stability that invites—and to realize that the two belong together. With this, the source of stability acquires a new quality. It not only helps make denial bearable; it also makes its availability into something other than what it was before it was denied, namely the overcoming of a resistance, the negation of a negation. No longer does it exude simple pleasure. It is a pleasure that means more than it is: it means the end of denial.[77]

In newborns, the sucking instinct is by no means already a "partial drive," as Freud would have us believe. It only *becomes* partial to the extent that the erogenous process involves other body parts, and the genitalia gradually become centers of excitement and desire. At the beginning, the sucking drive is *the* drive par excellence. There is no other. Hunger and love, which Freud, for a time, arbitrarily split into the two contrary fundamental drives of self-preservation and sexuality, are still undivided in the sucking drive. And Eros, then, actually does emerge in the organs of sucking, the lips. They are the—pre-sexual—place where the urge for stimulus discharge becomes meaningful, out of opposition to denial. The newborn's playing with his lips means the locus of pleasure that has been withdrawn from him; and when he once again "has" this locus, it means something other than what it is. It becomes an ideal. The newborn is only capable of creating an ideal because the loosening of drives, which humanity acquired under the most terrible circumstances, is already part of his birthright. To put it in drastic terms: Only because in the Early Stone Age grown-ups, in reaction to fear, learned to hallucinate a "genius" who offered salvation from it, was the way prepared for newborns to hallucinate salvation in response to an organ that rejects them. Phylogenetically and ontogenetically, mental representation, or the creation of ideals, begins as hallucination. The newborn's example is especially well suited to demonstrate how little the production of an ideal is fixed on a particular object. The ideal is not simply identical to the "security blanket" or the breast, indeed it is not even identical to the mother, which is why in a later phase it can be transferred without difficulty to the father and other individuals and objects. All of these *are* less the ideal than they are representations of it. They themselves stand for something else: for the end of denial. But this, precisely, is not an object at all but a state—the one that sucking intends.

We have every reason to take the mysticism of sucking seriously. Instead of splitting it in two—into the drive for "self-preservation" and a "sexual" drive that is "attached to" it[78]—it is a good idea to be aware of its peculiar sense. When the newborn mammal tries to suck itself into the mother, and the mother into itself, it is trying to reverse its birth. It wants to return to the stimulus-free, carefree womb. But it wants to go back under new conditions. For birth has not only surrounded it with unpleasant new stimuli that it wants to get rid of, but in the process also made it, for the first time, fully capable of experiencing stimuli. Not that nothing at all was experienced in the womb. Once it reaches a certain stage of development, the fetus is quite sensitive to temperature and above all to shocks. The mother's movements, her metabolism, her voice—all this is penetratingly communicated to the life that is developing. It would not even survive the shocks if it were not surrounded by a protective amniotic sac. But the fetus is blind, for all practical purposes; whether its perception of sound is already hearing is unclear, and the extent to which it already smells or tastes anything is questionable. Birth first makes sense organs fully functional. With this, it is as if a new deck has been dealt. The processing of stimuli, on one hand, makes the infant want to return to the prenatal stimulus-free state. But it wants this state differently from what it was, for it is now a fully evolved, sensate being with the capacity to experience things, and this being wants something that prenatal life could not quite do and postnatal life no longer can: it wants to experience this state.

Once again, the paradoxical dynamic of the principle of constancy makes itself felt here. In doing what is necessary for life, it also wants the impossible. It is in equal measures a realist and a theologian—something, by the way, that is already implicit at a prehuman level. The nonhuman mammal also wants to suck its way into the impossible. It too, with the nourishment it enjoys at the mother's teats, partakes of only second-best, while seeking the best. And yet this search is pre-erotic—it has no overarching hallucinations. The human newborn also starts out pre-erotically. As it fills its belly with the mother's milk, it feels a penetratingly intensive enjoyment, in which satiation and union come together in a way that it will never experience later in life. And yet this enjoyment is deceptive. It is experienced as a union with the mother's breast that is nonexistent. The primary mystical experience is also a primary deception.

Disappointment follows close behind. And only the working through of this experience, the negation of its negation, leads to a second-degree enjoyment above which, as a kind of *genius infantis*, the ideal begins to float: the end of denial, the unbroken, reunited nature for which Plato's bisected beings long. Only this kind of enjoyment, accompanied by the arc of something that means and hallucinates more than it is, is erotic. Eros is characterized by both insatiability and a pointing beyond it: transcendence. Eros always gives something less than full satisfaction and at the same time more than mere satisfaction: happiness. True happiness contains the spice of imperfection.

MYTHS OF ORIGIN

We can learn more about this from Plato than from Freud. Freud simply did not perceive the utopian dimension of drives. Why not? Was he afraid of giving the theologians his little finger, thinking they would take the whole hand? In any case, his failure to perceive this tarnishes his entire analysis of childhood, as is demonstrated in an exemplary way by the key passage in *The Interpretation of Dreams* where he wants to explain the origins of infant hallucination and links it to an experience of satisfaction. With this, he does not mean any kind of experience, but satisfying experience of a whole—the authentic first experience, which he considers to be so profound that it inevitably leaves behind a "mnemonic image" or "memory trace." Whenever, thereafter, the need that was so impressively satisfied reoccurs, he conjectures that it also awakens its remembered image. Every new satisfaction actually "wants to reestablish the situation of the original satisfaction," to achieve a "perceptual identity" with it,[79] and because this does not succeed, this identity is hallucinated by means of the mnemonic image. Even though Freud tries to cover it up by using especially prosaic language, what he constructs here is a complete, not repeatable primal satisfaction that an individual, in his entire wishing life, can never recuperate, that he never again reaches in reality, but only in hallucination. The fact that the very first satisfaction that results from sucking, however intensive and comprehensive its pleasure may be, does not provide the things that sucking intends; that the attempts to repeat it always make the infant want more than mere repetition, is no more to be found here than the question why, of all things, complete satisfaction should be the primary creator of memory, whereas we know, after all, that memory arose in the attempt to get rid of unmastered, tormenting stimuli.

The fiction of a blessed state of origin, which Freud starts to sketch out in *The Interpretation of Dreams*, continued to exercise such fascination that Freud's later years he started to surround it with a protective cocoon—"autoerotism." He uses this word for the early phase when the newborn begins to be involved with his own lips. But what he means by this is not that eroticism begins where the sucking instinct is thrown back upon itself by denial and becomes self-related; he means exactly the opposite. "The sexual drives initially behave auto-erotically, finding their satisfaction in the subject's own body and therefore never experiencing the state of frustration that necessitated the introduction of the reality principle."[80] The newborn, he writes, is initially "autistic," like "the bird embryo with its food supply enclosed within the eggshell, maternal care being restricted to the provision of warmth." Here, "autistic" does not stand for the severe psychic handicap of being incapable of contact, as it does in psychiatry. It means the self-sufficient, undamaged state that has not yet been battered by any denials but is "a psychic system cut off from the stimuli of the outside world," when "the state of equilibrium in the psyche was originally disrupted by the urgent demands of inner needs. At this stage, whatever was thought of (wished for) was simply hallucinated, as still happens every night in our dream thoughts."[81]

But when is the helpless little human child ever supposed to have found itself in this birds-egg-like state? As soon as it is born, it is all over with the bird's egg. Freud can only suggest this early state of self-sufficiency by making hallucination into a primary behavior. Here he once again turns into a philosophical idealist. Hallucinatory satisfaction is supposed to come before the real kind, thinking before being. Perhaps he means something else, namely that the newborn's intensive primary enjoyment has something deceptive about it. But this deception is prehallucinatory. A child does not start hallucinating on the first day of his life. Hallucination also has to be learned. After all, as Freud himself recognizes, it is primitive thought activity. Which does not get started voluntarily, but only as a result of denial. The story about the state prior to all denial, in which the child already achieves full satisfaction before it is tossed out of this unity with himself by the "reality principle," is the third great fairy tale that Freud tells—the fairy tale of the newborn's paradise.

He can only tell this story by making an apparently casual but telling terminological change. In *The Interpretation of Dreams*, he still spoke of an "unpleasure principle,"[82] and emphasized that where there is a wish there is also deprivation. In "Two Principles," the same principle is called "the pleasure-unpleasure principle (or the pleasure principle for short),"[83] as if it were nothing but a practical abbreviation, when "unpleasure" falls away and only "pleasure" remains. Actually, it is a 180-degree turn into its opposite. Now, Freud suggests that before the search for pleasure has begun, it is already found. And the lifelong search consists in wanting to re-find this original pleasure. "Pleasure principle" is a cipher for the paradise of the newborn, and "reality principle" is shorthand for the expulsion from paradise. The theological model of biblical prehistory has had such an impact on the Jew Freud that in his conception of child development he could not escape it.

Thus, he was also never ever able to make a plausible distinction between autoeroticism and narcissism. Narcissism, "in which a person treats his own body in the same way in which the body of a sexual object is ordinarily treated,"[84] is only supposed to arise when the child turns his externally directed wish to be loved inward toward himself, while the "autoerotic drives" are said to be present "from the very first."[85] But all the signs of autoerotism we actually observe are already phenomena that involve a turning back upon themselves. The child touches his lips with his own fingers, and then with the hem of a blanket or a cuddly toy, because he has already met with the experience of being rejected by an external resistance. "Autoerotic" cannot be strictly separated from "narcissism"—it is a tautology: only after it has been turned back upon itself *is* the sexual drive actually erotic. But Freud himself did occasionally intuit that it was not the sexual drive that taught humanity how to turn a drive back upon itself. It is no accident that narcissism makes him think "that the person who suffers from organic pain and unpleasant feelings gives up interest in the things of the external world, insofar as they are not related to his suffering." What leads Freud to translate this fact "into terms of the libido theory" is the following: "The sick man withdraws his libidinal cathexes back upon his own ego, and sends them out again when he recovers. 'Concentrated is his soul,' says Wilhelm Busch of the poet suffering from toothache, 'in his molar's narrow hole.'"[86]

Freud goes almost so far as to claim that the behavior of the sufferer is narcissistic. In doing so, he mixes up two things: the pain itself, which trumps all other experience as long as the organism cannot rid itself of certain intolerable stimuli, and the measures that the sufferer takes to reduce the pain, whether by bending over the place that hurts, placing his hands on it, shaking himself—or doing something that causes still more pain. To call these measures narcissistic would perhaps have been crudely cynical, but there is no doubt that the sufferer means to do "something good" with them. In a certain way, they prefigure narcissism. To remove something that is unpleasant, they turn against the person himself, and this turn, if it is accompanied by an increase in pleasure, is called narcissism. Decreasing unpleasantness is the negative of increasing pleasure. On one hand, it is its strict opposite; on the other, it is a necessary preparation for it. Only when a certain degree of freedom from pain has been achieved is it even possible to feel pleasure. The point at which pain reduction turns into pleasure will never be able to be precisely located. Neurophysiologically, both are nothing but the discharge of tension or stimuli, and the principle of constancy does not tell us at what point the discharge of stimuli is followed by the particular aftertaste of sweetness that we experience as pleasure.

Freud's attempt to give the phenomena of pain a translation "into terms of the libido theory" is unacceptable. It invites us—surely unintentionally—to see the torture victim as a Narcissus. But a translation of the struggle against pain into libido—this actually did occur in human history. We need only read Freud's "translation" in reverse—not interpreting pain as narcissism, but seeing narcissism as a cultivated offshoot of the struggle against pain. If the newborn, in the context of a developed culture, begins to work on the denial of his own insignificance—and "primary narcissism," in Freud's sense, is nothing other than this—he is recreating a behavior that traumatic repetition compulsion once modeled, in a process that *nolens volens* recalls the origin of Eros in ritual sacrifice.

Freud's need to understand even tormenting pain in terms of libido theory shows us how deep his belief in the pleasure principle is. For him, it is not just a metaphor for the ceaseless striving after pleasure; rather, it is a *principium* in the literal sense: origin, source, the "first" thing from which everything else is to be understood. Theologically speaking, in the beginning was desire. Ontogenetically speaking, this means: In the beginning, the newborn, however briefly and ineffably, found himself in a state of unadulterated wish fulfillment, until the "bitter experience of life,"[87] in other words the reality principle, burst the bubble of paradise. But if we look closely at Freud's fairy tale of the newborn's paradise, we can see how wonderfully it harmonizes with the fairy tale of the murdered primal father. Before the primal father met his fate, didn't he live in a state of unadulterated wish fulfillment? Couldn't he take any women he wanted from the horde in his embrace? Wasn't his rule the unadulterated rule of the pleasure principle, his murder the intrusion of the reality principle that marked the beginning of human culture? Indeed, the autoerotic newborn and the primal father are cut from the same cloth. The latter represents, in terms of human history, what the former embodies as an individual—that in the beginning there was desire and its pleasurable fulfillment, whereby the distinction between desire, on one hand, and sexual desire and Eros, on the other, is blurred to the point of complete obscurity. And Freud's third fairy tale, the one about the death drive, is the narrative that supports the other two. It is meant to hold a space open for them, to ensure that they can continue to be told without interruption, and that traumatic repetition compulsion, which seemed "more primitive, more elementary, more instinctual than the pleasure principle which it overrides," remains nicely outside it: "beyond the pleasure principle."[88]

Not all members of the psychoanalytic "community" still believe today in all three fairy tales. Melanie Klein already did a thorough job of undermining the one about the newborn's paradise. At the same time, belief in the death drive is especially deeply anchored among Klein's followers. The fairy tale of the murder of the primal father, on the other hand, continues to be halfheartedly maintained by the various schools, since it has no practical significance for treatment and there is no better one to be had. It is scarcely remarked that the three fairy tales interconnect in such a way that each one is influenced by the other two—and that together they are part of the founding history of psychoanalysis. In general, people are not yet aware that *all three* fairy tales need to be rejected if we want to get to the bottom of primitive thought activity. The place to start is where drives became human, where their elementary physiological form, stimulus flight, was loosened in the process of working through fright and became representation. This interaction of reversal, condensation, and displacement made possible the miracle of the drives' loosening.

Their interplay brought imagination into the world. It is admittedly not easy, in the original, hallucinatory phase of representation, to see primitive *thought* activity, since it still lacks almost everything we associate with thinking. And its diffuse images would never have become abstract, logical, conceptual thought if something else had not been added to it, had not penetrated and purified it; something that must now take center stage: modulated sound, or *the word.*

CHAPTER THREE

Words

THE OATH

WHAT IS A WORD, anyway? Nothing but a voiced breath, it is barely spoken before it has already flown away, to go under in many other words that layer and undermine each other, disappear in a general murmur, and—since the mass media are also ceaselessly multiplying—have become a constant background noise of high-tech culture. Language is more than a piling up of words; it is a grammatical-syntactic structure that founds an order and an orientation. The single word, by comparison, is just an inconstant, disappearing element within it.

All the more remarkable are those moments when the word absolutely counts: when someone gives his word, whether before a judge or an altar, or in a situation where it is bitterly necessary for someone to believe what he says. "To give one's word" means to vouch for the fact that something is one way and not another—to stand for it with one's entire self. Here, the word is not empty, but "full," not just a vanishing part of language but its extract. In the word that we give, language contracts into its essence. To give one's word is always a solemn act. Even when it happens informally, it has something of the ritual about it. It differentiates itself from ordinary speech and gives the word special status, an emphasis that it ordinarily lacks. If you are present during an act of this kind, you may mistrust the speaker—after all, he may be lying. But then the word would be false because he is misusing it, not because giving one's word is false. On the contrary, everyone involved assumes that nothing more dignified can happen to the word than for it to be solemnly given—that indeed it is only in this way that it fully comes into its own. It is all the more unworthy to misuse the word in a situation of this kind.

The primal form of giving one's word is the oath. In swearing an oath, the speaker pledges his life for what he says. If his words are not full to overflowing with what they say, if they do not already carry within themselves the reality of which they treat, if they prove to be empty, to be null in any respect, then they are supposed to turn against the speaker and make him, himself, null and void—to destroy him. Perjury is the empty word in a state of emergency; for a long time it was punishable by death. And an oath is the fulfilled word in a similarly critical state; only in oaths is the word fulfilled in its full sense. And even if we don't know anything else about the origins of the word, we can already aver: Certainly the word did not come into the world empty and then gradually become full. To the contrary: where first words are formed, they are extremely meaningful. When small children, gradually, out of their babbling, learn to model the syllables "mama" and "papa," these two combinations of sounds mean the whole world.

Words *start out* "full"; they only *become* empty through continuing use. The person who says the word "table" usually means an object with four legs supporting a flat surface. But if you say this word two hundred times in a row, you will notice how the meaning disappears. All that remains of the word is a sound or noise. It is the dual sense of repetition that is responsible for this. Only the fact that a specific sequence of sounds can be repeated as often as one wants makes it into a word. Only repetition picks a word out of the current of sound and gives it emphasis. Repetition reinforces. But after a certain point, it does just the opposite. It uses words up, and worn out words become empty. Empty words are words that have become empty through constant use. Once upon a time they were full. The solemn act of someone giving one's word involuntarily recalls this. Here, the word, without the speaker necessarily having to be aware of this, returns to its origins, to the sphere of ritual. This is where it started. It does not necessarily follow from this that the oath itself was the primal form of the word, but it is a good signpost in that direction.

If it is not the primal form of the word, the oath is at least ancient. But even our modern jurisprudence can't do without it. And it remains a ritual. The witness is solemnly sworn. He is told in no uncertain terms that he must describe a specific state of affairs exactly as he experienced it. But the court can do no more than appeal to the truthfulness of the witness and threaten to punish him if he makes a false statement. The archaic ritual has taken on a highly rationalized form. It no longer belongs to any specific religion, and it no longer entails an appeal to any higher powers, although it has inherited their aura. It generates a vague solemnity. It is supposed to somehow purify the witness and impel him to be truthful—to use words that to the best of his knowledge and belief reproduce what he has experienced. The archaic oath claimed to be much more. Its words did not just want to state what was unalterably the case; it wanted to be itself the thing that it stated. To give one's word did not mean simply to impart some words, but through words to impart the thing itself. To swear was to conjure up—not merely to emphasize that the thing being spoken about was true, but to speak words that embodied, indeed *were* that thing itself.

The archaic oath has a certain childishness about it. For children, what they perceive *is* the way the perceive it; what they say *is* the way they say it. They do not make a distinction between their teddy bear and the word they use for it. For them, Teddy is not just a name, it is the teddy bear itself. They do not yet know that one can say something with complete honesty and yet be fundamentally mistaken. The archaic oath does not know this yet, either. It does not yet distinguish between truth and truthfulness; for it, everything truthfully spoken is also true.

To represent oaths not just as inalterably true but as the thing itself could not be done without invoking higher powers. It was necessary to swear "by" something—a divinity who made sure that in the oath the thing that was sworn to was also present, and who would kill the person swearing the oath on the spot if his word was empty. The ancient Greek word *horkos*, whose root meaning is "an oath," or "sworn statement," can also stand for the divine power by which one swears, and ultimately even for the pledge—the sacrifice that was made as a means of confirming the oath. *Horkon temnein*, literally "to cut an oath," means the same thing as "to make a covenant." Two parties, for example two tribes, swear to make peace and confirm their oath by "cutting" cattle or sheep in half, that is, by slaughtering and offering them up. The conclusion of a binding—or bonded—covenant or agreement is the key moment in the swearing of the oath, among other things because it makes the interlocking nature of word and thing especially evident. When the parties swear to each other that they will make peace, they are, at that moment, already practicing something of the peace to which they mutually agree. The sworn word can appear even more suggestively as if it were already the thing itself.

The oath is one of the great moral achievements of humanity—the bringing about of a situation in which all participants commit themselves to tell the absolute truth. This is admittedly not yet a guarantee, as commitments by industry to add so-and-so-many jobs prove to us with every passing year. Truthfulness can never be guaranteed or forced; one can only create optimal conditions for it: witnesses, something offered up as a pledge, as a behind-the-scenes threat. But in the case when an oath is given with utter honesty, it is an absolutely full word.

And yet it is still not a word in the primal sense. Before words condensed into the formulas of the oath, they already had a long history. The archaic oath is already a phenomenon of high culture. And "full" is not the same as "pure." Even when the oath is truthful, we can by no means be sure that it is also true. Worse yet: the high moral achievement of the oath is paid for by the fact that it purports to be the actual thing that is sworn to. The ritual staging of truthfulness actually gives us the clue that this is so. The higher powers that are invoked as witnesses and the pledge that the person giving his word brings as his sacrifice to them support the oath. They are meant to bear witness to the fact that the individual's word is more than just a word—that it is the thing itself. But they bear witness to the exact opposite. If the oath needs this kind of support, it involuntarily confesses that as a mere spoken word it is not the thing it purports to be.

This shows that all talk of a "full" or "fulfilled" word is paradoxical. The truthful oath may represent the absolutely full word—there is nothing more full—and yet it is less full than it pretends to be. For it only simulates the thing without actually being it. If it was as full as it would like us to think it is, it would no longer even be a word. The word, if it were to be completely fulfilled, would *be* the thing itself. That the full word, precisely, remains unfulfilled is reflected in a stock phrase from the New Testament: "that it might be fulfilled which was spoken . . . by the prophet."[1] As is well known, the early Christians had the bold notion that their Jesus of Nazareth was the culmination of the whole of ancient Israeli prophecy, and that all its visions of the future had been coined for him. True to this assumption, they brutally tore out of context everything in the writings of Isaiah, Jeremiah, Hosea, and so on that seemed to fit in somehow with Jesus, and presented it as the annunciation of his acts. And yet this forcing of prophetic texts is not uninteresting from a linguistic perspective. Every word of a prophet was considered to be "full," in other words filled with divine inspiration and hence inalterably true. Prophecies, however, are promissory truths. However full, or "fulfilled" they may be as words, what they say is still unfulfilled. They are like oaths on the future, or bonded agreements. Precisely the word that knows itself to be "full" also knows about its insufficiency. It is like a wish. Precisely when we are most deeply filled with a wish, that wish is *un*fulfilled, and this involuntarily leads us to wonder: What if the word has the structure of a wish, if words are something like wishes that have cooled off?

The most famous vote of mistrust in oaths is found, of all things, in the New Testament, in Jesus's Sermon on the Mount: "Again, ye have heard that it hath been said by them of old time, Thou shalt not forswear thyself, but shalt perform unto the Lord thine oaths: But I say unto you, Swear not at all. . . . But let your communication be, Yea, yea; Nay, nay: for whatsoever is more than these cometh of evil."[2] It is very unlikely that Jesus, as he said this, was aware of the entire scope of the oath's ambiguity—the circumstance that it owes its seriousness to its character as a stimulant; that it was only able to become the great moral achievement of truthfulness, for which it stands, by living above its means;[3] and that precisely where the word is full to the brim it reveals its own lack of fulfillment. Jesus thought a tad more simply: Oaths are in order to the extent that they demand true speech; they are not in order to the extent that they require a state of emergency. Why should we only occasionally speak truly? Thus, "Never swear" means the same thing as "Always swear." Only when every single thing you say, every "Yea" and "Nay," has the full truth of an oath without needing the oath's ritual backing will we have achieved what the oath demands. An oath that has been fulfilled no longer needs ritual, it has become everyday speech—and to this extent no longer an oath, but merely the profane word, although a "full" one, a word in the full sense.

The commandments of the Sermon on the Mount were probably spoken without much hemming and hawing, with an abruptness that, on first hearing, must have been as fascinating as it was disturbing. What the audience heard needed to be reworked before it could be grasped. Consequently, the early oral transmission already softened it in many places, including the uncompromising "Swear not at all." The good intention to speak nothing but the truth from now on is not enforceable. Words and their speakers are caught up in relations of power, oppression, need, error, and lies in such a way that no one is strong enough to remain completely innocent of them. Every true word already exists in a context of half-truths, errors, and lies, which threaten to tarnish it. It would be possible to keep the commandment to speak the truth everywhere and at all times only if we lived in a true world—where it would be superfluous. The reason the commandment is so urgent is because the world as it exists is contaminated with falsehood. This dichotomy shows up in the oath. It is dishonest to the extent that it remains in an exceptional status. But it is honest to the extent that it admits the sheer impossibility of making all speech, by decree and intent, into true speech. For, as Bertolt Brecht famously intoned in *The Threepenny Opera*, "But this is not the way things are" (*Doch die Verhältnisse, die sind nicht so*).[4] Jesus's prohibition against the swearing of oaths skips lightly over this second aspect. The prohibition is one-sided, exaggerated—only understandable if we take account of something else that circulated, viruslike, in the Judaic culture of the time, with its desolate position as a little Roman province: the obsession that the world as it existed was at an end and a new "true" world, the "kingdom of God," would soon descend upon it. In Jesus, this obsession assumed a singularly acute form. Obviously, what he had in mind was to make the "kingdom" that God was about to bring about descend immediately, by means of suggestive rhetoric, beatitudes, and parables. While the words of the prophets are oaths against the future, Jesus's words suggest that the longed-for future is at hand. They want to do more than just announce; they already want to be the overture for the "kingdom of God." In doing so, they perform their conjuring function even more urgently than all the traditional prophetic words. As a conjuring up of the true world, the injunction "Swear not at all" is profoundly implicated in simulating an archaic oath.

TRANSLATING NATURE'S CONVULSIONS

Jesus is not the only one who failed to do away with oaths; the whole modern world is still carrying them in its baggage. Oaths, in turn, have not ceased having the effects of the things they conjure up. In general, this seems to be a property of the word in its early phase. It appears wherever ancient languages came up with a word for "words." Let us take the Hebrew word *dabar*, for example. The Egyptian-Aramaic root from which it is derived is associated with driving forth, leading, guiding, in other words with shepherding. *Dobar* means "drove" (as in a herd of cattle), or "drift"; *dabar* is also a driving, guiding force. If it is translated as "word," it means a word that is spoken aloud, a call; whispering won't do when you are calling a herd together. But at the same time, the word *dabar* (plural *debarim*) also means "a matter," "event," or "coming to pass," and there is a Bible passage where the two meanings play into each other in a revealing way. The patriarch Abraham has left Mesopotamia and Canaan for Egypt, and after recounting everything that has happened to him in the process, the text says: "After these things [*debarim*] the word [*dabar*] of the Lord came unto Abraham in a vision."[5] Here it would not be appropriate to translate the Hebrew with "After these words": what is meant are the events that have just been recounted. The King James Version translates the phrase as "After these things," and Luther, even more cleverly, translated it as "After these stories." This can stand either for the events themselves or for the words in which they were retold. It lends the word, which in Luther's word *geschah*, "came to pass" for Abraham, the emphasis of a great event—one that, as modern colloquial German has it, "wrote history."

When the inhabitants of the ancient world started to reproduce the spoken word, it was in the form of concise statements that were full to the brim. Only then were they worthy of being quoted, and quoting them came close to recitation. The Hebrew verb *hajah*, which we translate as "event" or "coming to pass," is preferably used for natural phenomena, such as when a storm comes up,[6] a rainbow appears,[7] or "there is light."[8] But *hajah* can also introduce great quotations, for example (in Luther's German) *das Wort geschah*, "the word came to pass"—a stock phrase that returns in an almost monotonous fashion when the God of Israel turns to his chosen people, Abraham, Moses, and the prophets. This suggests two things: first, that the absolutely full word is the word of God; and second, that it overcomes and shatters its addressees like an elementary force of nature. They are scarcely able to bear it.

The association of the word of God with the forces of nature brings us close to the origin of the word, but only if we don't take the "word of God" at face value, as if God were actually to have spoken. Rather, we should construe it as follows: Where the word emerged, it was full to the brim of what would later be called "God" and was closely linked to natural events—not everyday occurrences like hiccups or sore muscles, but events of the sort that break in upon us so overwhelmingly that they make an unforgettable impression. And there is one passage in the Old Testament in which a natural phenomenon, God, and the word are tied together in a knot that is nothing less than a maximally concise and condensed genealogy of the word. We easily pass over this passage only because it is so well known. The people of Israel have left Egypt, arrived at Mount Sinai, and been ordered by Moses to prepare for the "third day":

> And it came to pass (*hajah*) on the third day in the morning, that there were thunders and lightnings, and a thick cloud upon the mount, and the voice of the trumpet exceeding loud; so that all the people that was in the camp trembled. And Moses brought forth the people out of the camp to meet with God; and they stood at the nether part of the mount. And mount Sinai was altogether on a smoke, because the Lord descended upon it in fire: and the smoke thereof ascended as the smoke of a furnace, and the whole mount smoked greatly. And when the voice of the trumpet sounded long, and waxed louder and louder, Moses spake, and God answered him by a voice. . . . And God spake all these words, saying, I am the Lord thy God, which have brought thee out of the land of Egypt, out of the house of bondage. Thou shalt have no other gods before me.[9]

As everyone knows, this last sentence contains the words of the first commandment. The other nine follow: make no graven images; don't take the name of the Lord in vain; keep the Sabbath; honor your father and your mother; do not kill; do not commit adultery; do not steal; do not bear false witness; do not covet the belongings of others. And then it says: "And all the people saw the thunderings, and the lightnings, and the noise of the trumpet, and the mountain smoking: and . . . stood afar off.

And they said unto Moses, Speak thou with us, and we will hear: but let not God speak with us, lest we die."[10]

Normally, the passage from which the above quotation is taken is only looked at as the source of the Ten Commandments. But how interestingly they are framed! Naturally, this frame, for everyone who would like to see the Ten Commandments understood as God's permanent ethics program for all humankind, is nothing but trouble. It lets us see that the various components out of which the Old Testament Yahweh emerged include not only the Egyptian and Mesopotamian high-culture attributes of sublimity and majesty, but also a strand that was specific to the Sinai, in which Yahweh is surrounded by the insignia of an archaic volcano god: thunder and lightning, fire, smoke, and trembling. Biblical exegesis has its churchly hands full trying to play down these reminders of a terrifying origin and to emphasize the elevated spirituality with which God then speaks the well-formed words of his commandments. The point remains: the people of Israel perceive nothing of God's expressed words except thunder and lightning, smoke, and trumpet calls. It is as if during the Sunday sermon you were to hear only grunting and burping. Except that at the same time the comedy of the Sinai scene also entails the entire serious business of a genealogy of the word. In fact, we approach the origins of the word only when we count thunder and lightning, smoke and trumpet calls among the things that first ignited it.

In more general terms: the word emerged from the experience of being shattered by nature's convulsions. Volcanic eruptions and thunderstorms are its maximum. They make the earth tremble, and the trembling of the people is only an aspect of an all-embracing quaking of nature.[11] A bit of culture is then projected back onto this natural earthquake: the sound of a wind instrument, which in Hebrew is called a shofar, meaning "a horn," especially a ram's horn. The horn is not only one of the oldest drinking vessels; its use as a loudspeaker (megaphone) is one of the first attempts not just to suffer through an earthquake, but to cause one—to subsume it under human intention. The first sounds brought forth from horns must have caused in humans a profound shudder that was not dissimilar to thunder and the bellowing of animals. But they were self-made thunder and bellowing, and to this extent were already an archaic response to the quaking of nature, its antidote, the anti-quake that, by the way, would later become an obligatory part of war making, as the story of the fall of Jericho describes in incomparably drastic terms. The people of Israel, so the story goes, had arrived in the Promised Land after forty years in the desert, but the city of Jericho refused to open its doors to them. Whereupon the Israelites circled the city for six days, and on the seventh day Joshua told the people: "Shout; for the Lord hath given you the city. . . . So the people shouted when the priests blew with the trumpets: and it came to pass, when the people heard the sound of the trumpet, and the people shouted with a great shout, that the wall fell down flat, so that the people went up into the city, every man straight before him, and they took the city."[12] War cries and trumpet blasts call each other forth; one strengthens the other. That the two together should have flattened Jericho's walls is naturally a fairy-tale-like exaggeration. But it speaks truly of the shattering potential of the megaphone and the war cries that assemble around it. The sudden outbreak of sound decomposes the enemy the way an earthquake breaks down walls.

The shofar is an assembly point, not just strategically, as a people at war gathers around the horn blowers, but also acoustically, as the many voices of war are collected in the sound of the shofar to produce a single penetrating noise. It is their distillate, the concentrated echo of a natural quaking that is not just an echo of nature, like the shout a rocky mountainside sends back to the shouter's ear in attenuated form. A concentrated echo is an echo that has been shaped and formed. It requires know-how. A ram's horn would have had to be worked to make the small hole in its tip through which a loud sound can be produced, and someone would have had to be skilled enough to blow through this hole in just the right way so that the sound took on a shattering force. This is art, albeit in its most primitive form. It doesn't have much to do with what we call music, but it is music's beginning. If music grips and shatters us, then it is because its primal form was a shaped and formed echo of nature's shattering convulsion. This echo still trembles in the most subtle art, music. But a shaped and formed echo is two different things. On one hand, it is the echo as confirmation. "Once again": *da capo*. On the other hand, it is the echo as contradiction, as softening: *diminuendo*.[13] Once again, we are face-to-face with traumatic repetition compulsion—only now from its acoustic side. The only possible way to get rid of shattering experiences is by repeatedly reworking them. This happens out of need. People don't start turning a ram's horn into a wind instrument because it is fun, but rather because they are seeking an emergency exit from a shattering natural experience that they have not yet learned to deal with. The little hole in the ram's horn, in its readiness to receive the mouth, is an emergency exit. Unprocessed excitation can breathe through it and be reduced. The sound of the shofar is the continuation of nature's shattering convulsion in a different form. However, with this, it is also something other than mere shattering of nature—it is the cultural forming of that shattering.

RITUAL ACOUSTICS

If it is true, as we said in the first chapter, that early humankind condensed and displaced a diffuse natural horror into a ritual space, in order, within that space, to perform it as ritual killing, this cannot have happened soundlessly. The "chosen ones" had ample cause to cry out, and the collectives, as they prepared to slaughter their own members, also had grounds for outshouting the chosen ones—to drown them out and scream themselves free, so to speak, of the horror of their own deed. And if collective screaming was an ineluctable part of the ritual, it was also inevitable that it too would assume ritual form—that it would become quasi-choral. In the late Greek sacrifice of a bull, the fundamental structure of which Walter Burkert distilled from Homer's epics and the tragedies, the choral moment was still the high point at which the entire ceremony aims.

After the bull has been led to the sacrificial rock, or altar, "next a circle is drawn, the sacrificial basket and water jug are borne around the gathered crowd. . . . The first collective act is the washing of hands. . . . The bull is also sprinkled with water." People shout "shake yourself" and "convince themselves that the movement of the animal means a 'voluntary nod,' a yes to the act of sacrifice. . . . From the basket, the participants take the unground grains of barley" and throw them at the bull. "Shared, simultaneous throwing from all sides is an aggressive gesture, even when what is thrown are the most harmless objects imaginable; in some archaic rituals, instead of this, people actually threw stones." Here, if not earlier, it has become incontestable that the barley throwing is a cipher for ritual stoning, which was originally aimed not at a bull but at a member of the tribe. "Under the grains in the basket, the knife was concealed that is now revealed." The priest grasps it, cuts a few hairs from the animal's brow, and then "the mortal blow follows. The women who are present cry out, shrilly and loudly. Whether fright, triumph, or both simultaneously, the 'Greek custom of the sacrificial cry' marks the emotional climax of the process, by drowning out the death rattle."[14]

This was not only a Greek ritual. The Greek word for the sacrificial cry, *ololygé*, with its two prominent *l*'s introduced by dark vowels, is both acoustically and semantically closely related to Hebrew *jalal* (to howl) and *halal* (to rejoice). They too circled around the choric site where fright and triumph were as indistinguishable as the howling and rejoicing that originally had a lot more to drown out than the death rattle of a bull, namely the hair-raising screams of a human struggling against being killed. In its communal drowning out of the victim and his screams, the sacrificing collective constituted itself as a chorus. Archaic jubilation was characterized by sudden bursts that forced their way out as cries of triumph—something it could not have accomplished if it did not still reverberate with the horror it joyfully vanquished.[15] The solemn blowing of the horn still forms part of Jewish celebrations and is, for its part, a concentrate of the chorus. It condenses and displaces the chorus's many voices with the penetrating sound of a solo instrument—and is a triumph in yet another sense, which is more anchored in cultural history. The blowing of horns is a signature of the Neolithic revolution, the epoch approximately twelve millennia ago when animals were domesticated in the Middle East and new forms of agriculture, wood-, stone-, and metalworking, along with new technologies of war making, settlement, and storage, became widespread. With this, the possibility also opened up of replacing human sacrifice with the slaughter of animals. Only animals that had been tamed could be ritually slaughtered—not the wild animals that were hunted. If, then, people blew on the horn of an animal whose ritual slaughter had rendered human killing unnecessary, it lent acoustic expression to the victory of animal over human sacrifice. At the same time, this changed nothing in the fact that the sacrificial chorus continued to reverberate in the sounds of the horn—like the aftershocks of an earthquake.[16]

Exodus 19 is the condensed memory of all this. The sound of the horn, which represents a still uncanny but already rather highly cultivated echo of shattering nature, is reconnected with its elementary form. Thunderstorms, volcanic eruption, and the sound of the shofar create a virtual trinity. They present themselves as the media by which God announces himself in Sinai—as the underground, if not the very earth of his word. From its convulsive power, there emerge words with the validity of the absolute word: the Ten Commandments. They serve as the model for high cultures' imposition of law. The spirit of the people of Israel labored for a long time before assuming the polished form in which it now burst forth, booming, from Sinai. The people, it is true, perceived nothing but erupting fire, quaking earth, and bursts of sound from the horn. "Moses spake, and God answered him by a sound."[17] It is not clear what "sound" is meant here—the sound of thunder, or that of the shofar? In any case, the people perceive the combination of the two as a mortal threat. They "said unto Moses, Speak thou with us, and we will hear: but let not God speak with us, lest we die."[18] Moses is supposed to act as an interpreter of God's word and to translate the manifestations of God's word, that is, thunder, lightning, smoke, and sound, into words that are bearable. What kind of interpreting is this? Does it translate divine words into human ones, or does it transform something that announces itself as a violent natural phenomenon into words for the first time?

Either way, the elemental words of the law are presented as a translation of nature. The sound of the horn has a mediating function. It is neither thunder nor word, but it underlines both the thunder's resemblance to language and the authentic word's similarity to thunder. The word cannot have begun as a whisper. The "full" word is the word *fortissimo*. Like the sound of the shofar, it is loud to the point of reaching the pain threshold, for, like it, it is a formed echo of a natural convulsion.[19] Translation is not only something internal to language. It does not just begin where one word or language is translated into another. The word itself is something translated—carried across. A species of hominid carried itself across into the word in order to escape from unbearably shattering natural events. This is a process that must have taken several tens of thousands, if not hundreds of thousands of years. Its difficulty is easy to underestimate in retrospect. Whole collectives, together, had to regulate their vocal sounds. This, naturally, did not occur as a result of their sitting down together and deciding on the rules for their vocal potential. For this, the rules in question would already have had to exist, but they only emerged during the process. Nor was the process one by which certain specific sounds, for example those associated with courtship, broadened over the course of time and more or less automatically turned into the first love songs and verbal expressions, becoming music and language out of pure, exuberant desire and pleasure. No organism comes up with the idea, out of pleasure or desire, of imposing rules on its vocal potential. Rather, the emergence of vocal regulation required the collective's extremely persistent work on the nature of its own drives. It was gaining mastery over the collective's own voice—without a trainer, without any encouraging teachers, without aural models toward which people might have oriented themselves in the process. This is an unheard-of effort, in the exact sense of the word. Specific sound combinations had to be practiced in such a way that they were capable of being reproduced at any time, and that on the basis of these sounds others could be practiced and made reproducible. The linguistic apparatus of an entire collective had to be trained toward this end. Only when the regulation of this linguistic apparatus functions effortlessly, that is, on a relatively high cultural level, can speaking and singing themselves become enjoyable.

Repetition is an inalienable part of the word. Only a combination of sounds that can be repeated at will in a given collective has the status of a word. But how does something become repeatable? Through repetition. The pianist can only repeat her virtuoso pieces so brilliantly because she has repeated them innumerable times before. And if this kind of repetition has gone over into her flesh and blood and has become a great pleasure, it is because the awkwardness and mistakes of her first practice sessions are now far in the past. She has had the experience that all the musical material's resistance to her dexterity was able to overcome. In every performance she celebrates a victory. Practiced repetition is a source of pleasure; beginning repetition is an arduous process of trying, failing, trying again, and failing again, until finally, through persistence and patience, certain modes of behavior have become repeatable. The persistence that a new generation requires in order to train itself in already existing cultural capacities is, however, much less than the persistence required to establish these capacities initially. Yes, it costs small children considerable effort to find their place in the words that are spoken in their surroundings. But this is child's play compared to the effort involved in forming natural sounds into the first words. To create words where no words yet exist, to coordinate throat, vocal chords, tongue, gums, teeth, and lips to generate unheard-of sounds, and to do this in such a way that these sounds, which after all are very fleeting, nevertheless take the solid form of specific sound sequences—this is a work of repetition that takes millennia. Only someone who has no choice will undertake this work, someone who can do nothing else, who is driven to it by unbearable force of necessity and has the feeling that in this way she can reduce or get rid of something unbearable. If repetition is part of the nature of the word, then its emergence includes forced repetition, which finds no other way to get rid of shattering natural events than by attempting to work them off through constant repetition.

PRIMAL WORDS

This does not yet tell us anything about the nature of the first words, much less how they sounded or what they stood for. For a long time, ethnology was on a hunting expedition for primal words (*Urworte*), which they believed they could find among primitive peoples. But the question What was the first word? is like the question Who was the first philosopher? Just as Thales' thought did not emerge from the void, but had plenty of predecessors, so the key words that are discovered in primitive cultures all have forms that preceded them. Historical research and ethnological fieldwork will never be able to come up with the definitive first word. However, we can name a few that are definitively *not* possibilities. Conjunctions, pronouns, and verbs are certainly not candidates for primal words. Children ordinarily name their mother first. But this only means that in orderly family relations, which have long had the benefit of developed language, the mother is a strong candidate for the first word. It does not mean that she was the object of humanity's primal word. Psychologists who claim this are imagining humanity's linguistic break-through as identical to the language learning of small children under moderate cultural conditions. They are ignoring the difference between ontogenesis and phylogenesis.

Certainly, human children, on their way to becoming grown-ups, have to pass through many things, once again, that humanity already passed through collectively. But the process is vastly shortened and modified, along pathways that human history has long since predesigned and smoothed out. As a result, modern children are spared many of the child-hood diseases of *Homo sapiens*. By no means can we draw conclusions about species history based on individual history. There is, though, one point in regard to which ontogenesis is a reliable indicator. While present-day children must still overcome considerable resistance in learning to walk, speak, read, or write, the species faced considerably greater resistance when it began to practice these skills. That the first words are not just first sounds but first sounds that are formed in a specific way—in this respect ontogenesis is remarkably revealing. When a baby's babbling produces the first phonemes that have the character of words, he literally pulls himself together. His sound register narrows. "The phonetic richness of babbling is replaced by the phonemic austerity of the first language levels," whereby "the acquisition of vocabulary and the dying off of prelinguistic inventory are parallel processes."[20] The first words are phonemic units that stake out objective entities within a diffuse context. A child must already have achieved a considerable degree of concentration before he is capable of phonemes like "mama." But his efforts ordinarily take place in relatively well protected spaces and are supported and guided by a well-disposed being who repeats "mama" to him innumerable times. He is not required to go through the entire passion story of primary word-creation that the species Homo sapiens had to endure in its effort to work off shattering natural convulsions with the help of constantly repeated sequences of sounds. Even if we don't know how these sounded—when the first words were formed, they can hardly have been anything but expressions of fright. The Old Testament has the advantage that it provides an insight into this process that is like no other. Not that it tells us what the first word was. But Exodus 19 offers a text that can be read as a time-lapse version of the word's emergence. In addition, it contains a large number of episodes in which the word overcomes selected individuals, as it if were a natural event, and profoundly shatters them. Finally, what the Old Testament has to say about the word finds an echo in the way it itself creates words. Here we find a prominent example that brings us very close to the secret of the genesis of the word.

There is a one-syllable Hebrew word that, at first glance, seems quite ordinary and straightforward: šm, pronounced sham, and literally translated as "there." Usually, this "there" has a spatial meaning. "And the Lord God planted a garden eastward in Eden; and there he put the man whom he had formed."[21] But occasionally sham also appears in a temporal sense. Yahweh looks critically at humankind, and: "There were they in great fear."[22] We are consequently inclined to see sham as an adverb, which can have both a spatial and a temporal sense. But there is one striking passage where this categorization does not apply. The prophet Ezekiel, who is famous for the powerful and violent visions that overcame him in Babylonian captivity after the destruction of Jerusalem, is pitiless in his reckoning with his people. He blames them, not Yahweh, for their fate, and is finally seized, despite everything, by hope. The "desolate and ruined city" of Jerusalem rises up, restored, before his inner eye. He constructs a utopian city plan, measures out in the most minute detail a place for each of the twelve tribes of Israel, and closes his book with the words: "And the name of the city from that day shall be, the Lord is there (*Yahweh šmh*, pronounced 'Yahweh shamah')."[23] *Šmh* is actually the same as *šm*, but with the addition of an *h* for emphasis. The breath of the *h* adds an element of remoteness; the spatial and temporal aspects of the word can no longer be distinguished. *Yahweh shamah* can mean both "Yahweh here" and "Yahweh now." It means both: "Here, in the holy city, is Yahweh's place" and also: "Only now, when his city has been appropriately prepared, is his rule the untroubled presence that he promised his people when they left Egypt."

Yahweh shamah gives the impression that it could be an archaic ritual formula. At the same time, it evidently comes from Ezekiel. But it reveals, in a flash, the origin of *šm*. If this little word, depending on its context, can have either the spatial or the temporal meaning of "there," then this strongly suggests that in the beginning, when it was formed, it did not yet make a distinction between "here" and "now"; in other words, it is a very primitive, elementary word. It is hard to believe that it was formed out of miscellaneous "here"s and "now"s. Rather, it must have come from their shared use in an emergency. A thing is totally "here-now" when its *sudden presence* captures all attention. Nothing does this so well as a sudden fright. When a volcano suddenly erupts or there is an earthquake, we don't notice anything else; alongside it, everything else fades into obscurity. Events that create this level of convulsive shock are the essence of the "there."

In the early layers of the Old Testament we find the formula *Yahweh zabaoth*, meaning "Lord of the hosts of war," initially in a sense that was completely terrestrial and military—a hint of the extent to which Israel, at the time, imagined its God as a war god. *Yahweh shamah* is Ezekiel's alternative formulation. It gives *shamah* an almost substantive status: "Yahweh, the here-now." On other occasions when "the word came to pass," whether on Mount Sinai or in the visions of the great prophets, Yahweh's "here-now" had been identical with the epiphany of fright. Ezekiel transforms it into the epiphany of salvation. Where Yahweh is the "here-now," all history's misery ends, indeed history itself comes to a halt. The blessed state of eternity has been reached. In the "here-now," the extremes meet.

However, *šmh* also appears in the form of a proper substantive. Here, it is also pronounced *shamah*, but with a short *a* in the first syllable. It means "staring," "horror," or "shuddering." Jeremiah says, "Astonishment hath taken hold on me," as he realizes what his people have done.[24] Psalm 46 speaks of the *shamot* that Yahweh inflicts on earth.[25] Here, the occasional emphasis that the adverb *šm* assumes when *h* is added has become fixed in the noun *šmh*. The sound for the sudden "there," so terrifying that it is felt in the very marrow of listeners' bones, has become an essence. Although it may be next to impossible to feel this empathetically in the era of developed technology, the syllable *šm* must have been a very elementary one, wrung from excited stammering: the hearers must have virtually seen the accompanying gesture, the extended arm and finger pointing that accompanied it: "There it is!" *šmh*, as a noun, already marks a separate substance, a certain degree of inner solidity and distance, as compared to the excited "There!" Even today, we can get a sense of this when a child, suddenly frightened, calls out "There, there!" whereupon the adult immediately wants to know *what* is "there," and the child lacks the routine and distance to name the noun that corresponds to the bird that suddenly flew across the room, or the fire that has broken out next door, even though it is already part of his vocabulary. The noun *šmh* is a solidifying and calming down of *šm*, both phonetically, as a result of the emphasis and breath that the *h* lends it, and factually. "Horror" is related to "There" in the manner of a commentary. It explains what the emergency of the "There" is—something that only succeeds to the extent that it speaks from a certain distance and is no longer so completely overwhelmed as the demonstrative *šm*.

Now comes the point of all this. *Šmh* means "there" when it is pronounced "sham." However, it can also be pronounced "shem," and then it means "name." Both are written the same way; the writers of the Old Testament only marked down the consonants. So whether *šm* meant *sham* or *shem* could only be decided based on the context. The transformation of *a* into *e*, a mere inflection, leads from "there" to the name. This suggests that, in point of fact, the apparently so ordinary "There" is also located in the immediate vicinity of the name.

First of all, *shem* is a very gestural word. It draws on the close relationship between the hand and the mouth. Just as the hand makes a sign of something, inscribing a notch or a mark or adding a label or tag to it, the mouth does the same thing by forming a stable sequence of sounds for it. Speech is mouth-work, and name-giving is an auditory designation, just as pointing is a manual one. To be given a name, in Aramaic, means the equivalent of being decorated, whereby this "decoration" is admittedly essential to life. Without it, a person is exposed and unprotected. To blot out someone's name does not mean just annihilating him and his kin but also destroying everything that perpetuates his memory: buildings, inscriptions, stories. The name, in other words, affords protection, honor, and remembrance. The person who enjoys these three things is "someone," and being "someone" does not just mean being registered and identified but being positively noticed, having a (good) reputation, even fame. The motive for erecting the Tower of Babel, consequently, is: "let us build us a city and a tower, whose top may reach into heaven; and let us make us a name, lest we be scattered abroad upon the face of the whole earth."[26]

The series of the three words *sham, shamah,* and *shem* brings us close to the primary process of language creation. Not in the sense that these were primal words—there is no hope of getting at that original sound. But they do tell us something decisive about the logic of primary word-creation. First of all, they raise doubts as to whether the first sounds that were formed in such a way that we can consider them names were actually names in the grammatical sense: nouns, that is, substantives linked to concrete objects. In nouns, naming has already started to be sedimented, calmed down, consolidated. When it first began, things must have been a good deal more tempestuous. The driving force behind the formation of sounds was traumatic shock, whose excess of stimuli sought exits. One such exit is the constant repetition of cries. It is as if by crying out the organism is trying to eject the shock itself, to push it out. The formed sound that is created in the course of this work of repetition takes on the function of an escape valve. It reduces the pressure and lets some of the horror escape. This, though, means that it is full to the brim with it.

The full word, in the immediate sense, means the word that is full of fright. Here, word and thing are so undivided as to be unbearable. Words are an attempt to create a division between them. When fright grips an organism, the shock is inside and outside; source and sensation are still one. This shock does not yet have the status of an object: it has no thing-like form. Correspondingly, the sound that articulates it does not yet have a name. It has no grammatical identity whatsoever. The closest we could come would be to call it a pre-verb: a kind of preliminary stage of the name. *Sham* has this character. It is the Hebrew overdetermination of the sound of an excitation that does not yet distinguish between "here" and "now," does not yet name any object, and does not want anything except to get rid of the convulsive shock that has penetrated it. As the signature of this elementary stage, where the sound is beginning to be distinguished from shouting or babbling and to take on the repeatable regularity of a word, *sham* means nothing other than "There," and "There" means the same thing as "Go away." It is crying out as a way of making something disappear.

"FORT—DA"

Freud accidentally touched on the origin of the word, without really taking full notice of it, when he recounted an episode concerning his one-and-a-half-year-old grandson Heinerle. He told this story, which has meanwhile become quite well known, in order to explain the nature of repetition compulsion. The child "was on good terms with his parents and their one servant-girl. . . ."

> Above all, he never cried when his mother left him for a few
> hours. At the same time, he was greatly attached to his
> mother. . . . This good little boy, however, had an occasional
> disturbing habit of taking any small objects he could get hold of
> and throwing them away from him into a corner, under the bed,
> and so on, so that hunting for his toys and picking them up was
> often quite a business. As he did this he gave vent to a loud,
> long-drawn-out "o-o-o-o," accompanied by an expression of
> interest and satisfaction. His mother and the writer of the
> present account were agreed in thinking that this was not a
> mere interjection but represented the German word *fort*

["gone"]. I eventually realized that it was a game and that the only use he made of any of his toys was to play "gone" with them. One day I made an observation which confirmed my view. The child had a wooden reel with a piece of string tied round it. It never occurred to him to pull it along the floor behind him, for instance, and play at its being a carriage. What he did was to hold the reel by the string and very skillfully throw it over the edge of his curtained cot, so that it disappeared into it, at the same time uttering his expressive "o-o-o-o." He then pulled the reel out of the cot again by the strong and hailed its reappearance with a joyful *da* ["there"].[27]

Freud, then, interprets the *Fort—da* game as an attempt to come to terms with the mother's going and coming. The child stages the departure himself, repeats it in different variations, takes this "distressing experience" under his own charge, and tells the mother, "'All right, then, go away! I don't need you. I'm sending you away myself.'"[28]

This is the way a child's version of repetition compulsion functions in a comfortable upper-bourgeois household at the beginning of the twentieth century. It is interesting that Freud does not make the connection between this episode and his text, written a decade earlier, "The Antithetical Meaning of Primal Words." The essay is actually only a rather lengthy review of a study of the same title that the scholar Karl Abel had published in 1884. Its thesis was: At the base of archaic languages an "antithesis" is at work. His star witness is ancient Egyptian. There, *strong* also means "weak"; *light* also means "darkness"; *to give orders* also means "to obey." There are composite words like *old-young, far-near, bind-sever,* and *outside-inside.* And once you have become aware of the frequent existence of this kind of antithetical meaning in ancient Egyptian, there are plenty of examples to be found in other ancient languages too. The most prominent is the Latin *sacer,* which means both "sacred" and "accursed"— where, "accordingly, we have the complete antithesis in meaning without any modification of the sound of the word."[29]

Naturally, these examples are far from being primal words. They all belong to highly developed language systems. And Abel has a rather threadbare explanation for the antithetical meanings. "If it were always light we should not be able to distinguish light from dark, and consequently we should not be able to have either the concept of light or the word for it. . . . Since the concept of strength could not be formed except as a contrary to weakness, the word denoting 'strong' also contained a simultaneous recollection of 'weak,' as the thing by means of which it first came into existence."[30] This sounds as if the beginnings of linguistic development were being watched over by dialectical philosophers anxiously striving to make sure every word contained its opposite. To Freud, this seemed much too superficial and rationalistic. He immediately connected the antithetical verbal phenomena to reversal in dreams. There must be something much more elementary at work here than a conceptual comparison between opposites. In Abel's supposed primal words, Freud sensed the eroded remains of a much older linguistic practice, but he didn't really explore it, especially since he didn't realize the relevance of the game with the wooden spool for the theory of language.

"Gone!" and "There!" his grandson had said. Naturally, he wasn't producing primal words but was attempting to repeat things that had often been pronounced for him in the past. And yet "Gone!" and "There!" even if they are more than mere interjections, are still far from representing anything like adverbs in the child's vocabulary. They are words in a state of becoming, words that remain distinctly below the level of names, in the prenominal state that is so characteristic of primal words—except that the prenominal state, in Freud's grandson, is already preformed by the linguistic habits of a highly developed society, for which "Gone!" and "There!" have long since become separated into two disparate, grammatically precisely defined words that no longer have any more recognizable phonetic similarities. This is where the difference between ontogenesis and phylogenesis makes itself felt. The child of a high culture no longer has to traverse the entire pre-verbal horror that the species was unable to avoid, and that set itself, in the Hebrew *šm*, a monument that is as modest as it is unfathomable. Primal words are pre-nouns: interjections. The meaning of their "There!" is no different from "Gone!" The words are unaware of the opposition between them. They want to drive out what they call out. What they name is meant to disappear. The word begins as an exorcist. In its pre-noun form, it is as much a statement as a command, as much an affirmation as a denial. We can take it as a noun, a verb, a demonstrative pronoun, or an adverb. But it is not yet any of these, for the grammatical syntactic distinctions are not yet at work. They are still undifferentiated, encapsulated in each other. Only as the word unfolds and becomes language will the distinctions become separate from each other.

If the primary word is full to the brim with fright, it is also no less full of a wish—the wish to be superfluous. The word wants to end the existence of its cause—fright—and thus end its own existence. This is why it forms the sounds over and over. But precisely by doing this, it attaches itself firmly to the fright. The formation of the sounds recalls the fright again and again; it calls it back and revolves around it. The sounds' agitated, trembling, fluctuating early forms take on their first stability in the encounter with the fright. Thus, it cannot be otherwise than that the fright, as it is formed by words, becomes their subject, their fundus, their purchase on the world. This is the very process that can be observed in the relation between *sham, shamah,* and *shem.* The pre-noun *sham* is hardly anything more than the echo of the fright that convulsed the whole organism. The noun *shamah* is already a word for this process. It is already distant enough from it to be able grasp it as an object: as staring, horror. And *shem?* The small change in the vowel, from *a* to *e,* stands for a change of direction that is without compare—from an exorcising calling, out of fright, to its form of address. To give fright a name is to attempt to transform it from a deadly force into a saving protector, and in this way to make it disappear. The flight forward that was initiated by traumatic repetition compulsion, as it tried to get rid of the fearful event by causing it to happen again and again under its own direction—to make it bearable, graspable, ordinary, even familiar, so that self-made fright actually becomes salvation from suddenly overwhelming terror—this enormous reversal finds its linguistic form in the creation of the name. A name is the stable combination of sounds by means of which traumatic shock creates a breathing space for itself, and the fright is invoked and entreated to be its own opposite, namely the power of salvation. Theologically speaking, the name is the word that hallows fear. Or, the holy is convulsive shock that has been given a name; it is "decorated," salvational fear.

Where "Gone!" means "There!" and "fright" means "salvation"—this is where we find the original antithetical sense of primal words. It is implicit in the pre-noun *sham* and explicit in *shem,* the name. Names are antithetical meaning par excellence. More than this, every meaning is initially an antithetical meaning. Only through the affirmation of fright did meaning come into the world. Originary antithesis lets opposites collapse into each other. Where, by contrast, depending on the context, a word can mean one thing in one situation and its opposite in another—there the collapse of opposites has already given way to a "both-and." Antithesis has yielded to ambiguity. Egyptian *ken*, depending on the situation, can mean both "strong" and "weak"; Latin *altus* can mean "high" and "deep"; *sacer*, "holy" and "damned." All of Abel's examples originate only in the realm of ambiguity and fail to reach as far back as antithesis. To name the fright, in the beginning, precisely does not mean giving it two opposing meanings, namely, holy and terrible, which to modern ears sound like good and evil. Rather, the holy *is* the fright that has been named. Fear, in other words, is not evil; it is precisely what is being affirmed. Even the meaning "damned," which the Latin *sacer* assumed, was initially the same thing as "sanctified." No one is more sanctified than the clan member who draws the lot and is chosen to make the sacrifice that the collective must make to the terrifying, protective power. In the drawing of lots, blessing and curse are still undivided. The person who draws the fatal lot is literally marked; he is *taboo*, as the Polynesians say. Blessing and curse only diverge with the ending of human sacrifice. Where the possibility has opened up of offering animals in place of humans, and where humans are nevertheless killed based on the collective will, "in the name of the people," they are no longer being sacrificed, but executed. Only at this point does "doomed to die" cease to mean the same thing as "chosen," but instead its opposite: condemned. Only now does "accursed" mean the same thing as "evil." Evil is everything that denies the claims of the sacred and that, as a result, is denied its protection. To be exiled, nameless, unprotected, or, in later terms, "damned and accursed"—this is the condition of absolute evil and abjection.[31]

The death drive, which Freud began to believe in later in his life, does not exist. "Life" does not voluntarily seek death. But *need*, in life, does indeed lead to phenomena that in their emergence are inspired by the urge to disappear again. The word is one of these. The laborious forming of sounds came about in order to expel fright. The fright was meant to end—and with it the words themselves. But the opposite occurred. Through constant repetition, words became solidified as names. But they also got stuck there. They did not succeed in getting rid of the disturbing excitation; as an escape valve, they were inadequate. There was always more excitation than could be expelled. But words succeeded in creating a distance from the excitation, by softening it. The regulated (and regular) formation of sounds initiated the regulated (and regular) discharge of stimuli, and the sonic escape valve assumed the opposite characteristic. As names, words offered a place of asylum for stimuli. *Asylon* is the Greek word for the protected place where anyone who takes refuge must not be harmed, even if he is an enemy. This place was the sacred precinct or temple grounds, and it may not even be an overstatement to call the creation of the name the construction of an inner temple. In the attempt to allow excitation to escape, the name gave it asylum: an inner space in which it was moderated and calmed down to the point where it became bearable. We may also say that the name gave it a phonetic setting. It is as if it enclosed it acoustically, the way the sacred site was enclosed spatially. The sacralization of fright, by means of the name, was inseparable from the creation of the sacred precinct: the latter gave fright a double setting. The sacred precinct enclosed anyone who fled to it in fear; and it enclosed terror in the form of the ritual killing of "chosen" individuals, where the fright could recur over and over again until its raging was gradually worn out, without destroying the entire collective. A sacred precinct or temple could not be created without a *genius loci* imagined as floating above it. Sanctuaries were erected "in the name" of the "genius." Names par excellence are the names of such "genii." In them are condensed the excited cries and stammered pre-nouns of collective excitation that accompany the performance of the sacrifice.

The Hebrew *shem* still bears traces of the fact that the names humans confer or have conferred upon them are descended from the holy name. "To invoke the name" is a stock phrase that initially refers to the absolute name, Yahweh. *Kara*, literally, means "to shout," but then also appears as "to appeal to," and finally, "to bestow a name on." Once again, this indicates how the bestowing of names was gradually tempered until "in deepest affliction I cry out to you"[32] became tempered as profane name-giving. If humans receive a name, and through it protection, honor, and memory, they owe it all to the sacred name. The Old Testament, by the way, is not alone in this opinion. All totemism thinks this way. It is not just that the totem, ordinarily an animal—initially a fearful one, but always one that attracts collective attention—has a name; its name is simultaneously the name of the whole tribe or clan. The name of the clan is the name of the totem, and the individuals bear the same name, too. They do not yet have individual names. "One is part of a clan only by virtue of having a certain name. So all who bear this name are members of it in the same right; however scattered cross tribal territory they may be, they all have the same kin relationships with one another."[33]

Every totem not only has its own name, by the way; it also has its own sign. The members of the totem identify themselves by affixing it to their bodies. This is the manual name-giving that is part of the thinking of the Hebrew *shem*, which also gives us a better understanding of the story of the mark of Cain. The sign with which God marks the fratricide Cain, "lest any finding him should kill him"[34] is a naming sign. It only makes sense as the sign of a clan, with which all its members must be indelibly marked because they are all fratricides and in need of protection. The collective, bloody self-marking is a nondiscretionary attribute of the ritual brother or sister murder in which the entire collective must be equally involved. The sign represents both the collective's bloody deed and the protection that it confers on the perpetrators. The "genius" that devours the "chosen" is also the protective power that gives life to the others. To invoke the sacred name and to mark oneself in blood—with the signature of the sacred, so to speak—these are two directly related ways of submitting oneself to a terrible protective power as the only possible salvation.[35]

NOMINALISM—REALISM

"Naming something," says Ludwig Wittgenstein, "is rather like attaching a name tag to a thing."[36] What he failed to notice was the dialectical nature of the little name tag. The place where it is attached to the thing becomes invisible. Little name tags don't just designate; they also cover up the thing they designate. (Mass production, by the way, has turned this into a particularly bad habit.) The name tag of the commodity is its bar code, which can often be removed only with difficulty and then not completely. Large fruit companies even affix their name to every individual piece of fruit—making it unappealing, if not inedible, in the spot where it is attached. The resulting annoyance can serve as the reminder of an everyday phenomenon we easily forget, namely: places that are designated are also places that are covered up. And in the critical situation out of which designation emerged we are not talking about adhesive labels but about enfolding something in a protective cloak that cushions it in order to make it bearable. Indeed, the covering must be large enough for living beings seeking shelter to find a refuge in its enveloping folds. Thus, the sacred name does, radically and inclusively, what the adhesive label does only partially and externally. It covers up—covers up the fright and takes cover from it. The sacred name is an alias.

With this, we have unwittingly laid out the two extreme positions between which all reflection on naming has always oscillated. Plato gave indelible expression to the two positions in his dialogue *Cratylus*. Cratylus represents the view that "a power more than human gave things their first names, and . . . the names which are thus given are necessarily their true names."[37] The second interlocutor, Hermogenes, doubts "that there is any principle of correctness in names other than convention and agreement. Any name which you give, in my opinion, is the right one, and if you change that and give another, the new name is as correct as the old— we frequently change the names of our slaves, and the newly imposed name is as good as the old. For there is no name given to anything by nature; all is convention and habit of the users."[38] Later, in late medieval Europe, Hermogenes' position would come to be called "nominalism." Naming things, in this view, is nothing but a special, customary use of proper names, which we can affix without any rhyme or reason since they have no correspondence in nature. Cratylus's position, on the other hand, led to "realism." Names, to this way of thinking, are not mere combinations of sounds that turn out one way in one language and another way in another. They have a conceptual side: this is where we find the dimension of "natural rightness." This aspect is what different names have in common; it makes them translatable. It also constitutes their generality, which includes all the individual things of a given kind. Names may be particular in their nature as combinations of sounds, but as concepts they are universal. Their role in thinking is the same as the role of species and genus in nature; they give things their real correspondences and are the guarantee of their "rightness."

This was where the fronts were drawn at the beginning of the medieval battle over universals. As Günther Mensching's comprehensive monograph has demonstrated, the battle is by no means over.[39] But why did it continue to smolder, unresolved; why did the attempt by analytic philosophy to reduce objective problems to problems of language fail, and why was metaphysics, which had never been disproven, able to celebrate an "astonishing comeback" among its representatives?[40] The answer is evident as soon as we examine the battle over universals, not from the usual vantage point of the inchoate present, but instead from behind, as it were, from the most distant point of its prehistory in the sacred name. If it really is an alias, what does the sacred name actually accomplish when it names something? Initially, it does the same thing all later names will do: it affixes something external to it. So far, it is nothing but a label, exactly like Wittgenstein's "name tag." But it is a label of a singular kind. It sits atop the thing it names in such a way that it completely surrounds, covers over, and envelops it. It doesn't say what the thing is, but what it isn't; in fact, it says the polar opposite of what it is. Its label is uniquely deceitful. It calls fright good. But this capital swindle is the originator of all morality. With it, the distinction is born between good and evil. It is the primal lie, but it is so elementary that, in a certain sense, it isn't a lie at all. Only thanks to it does the fact of lying even come into existence. Nor can we say that it incorporates lying, given that it lacks all sense of right and wrong. After all, it had no choice in the matter. The primal lie is a lie of necessity that is both completely unaware of its falsity and driven by the best of motives. For it wants to get rid of its need, and thus of itself, as a lie. It doesn't merely want to *say* the opposite of an object; it wants this opposite to *come into existence*. The primal lie wants to become true. It is the source of prophecy.

The sacred name, admittedly, lives above its means. It is meant to be a deed. Calling out to it is meant to transform fright into protection from fright. Naturally, it can't do that. To this extent, those who call out to it have their mouths too full. But the name is not entirely without the power to transform. The odd thing, namely, is this: the terror to which we have given a name is no longer the same as the nameless one. This is difficult for modern humans to accept. After all, an earthquake loses nothing of its shattering force just because it has been given a name. But nevertheless, when it receives a name, it is as if it were breathed on. It is surrounded, covered over, and enveloped in a layer of acoustic protection. The layer is neither here nor there as far as the earthquake is concerned, but it helps the people who are calling out. For them, it forms a protective layer and has the effect of ameliorating the fright, even if the difference is only a breath or a trace. With this, though, the name reveals itself as the trace of wholeness. It offers a tiny bit of relief from the convulsive shock of those who call it out. This is its cathartic effect. The thing that is named may be completely unimpressed, but it is breathed on. In the process, in an utterly elementary sense, it is covered with meaning. The breath of the name tells the terror of nature that it should allow the people who have invoked it to escape unscathed, that it should open itself up and offer them asylum. To this extent, the name is the breath of a pacified nature, the first breath of utopia. When something has been named, its unbearable quality diminishes, if only by the slightest nuance. The name gets a first grip on its unfathomability, however weak and impermanent this hold may be.

All this, if we want to speak in the terminology of the battle over universals, seems to argue for an unrestrained nominalism. If the sacred name is perpetrating an actual swindle with labels, if it breathes on things to impart a meaning that is the opposite of what they are, then it is modeling the world in accordance with its own needs—and this to an extent that a more fully differentiated language, later on, will no longer be able to accomplish. But just at the point where it is acting like a super-nominalist, it does exactly what the conceptual realists demanded. It offers something that corresponds to the thing it names. It may be doing nothing but trying to satisfy its own needs, but it does not do this arbitrarily. It does not affix itself to something or other; on the contrary, there is only one thing to which it can affix itself, because only this one thing has been able to inflame it: traumatic shock. Traumatic shock is the name's absolute point of reference, its "one and only," so to speak. In this sense, a correspondence exists, although it is anything but a foundation promising stability, or a model the name could actually emulate acoustically. The traumatic shock does not correspond to the name; the name corresponds to the traumatic shock, by addressing, calling out to or screaming at it as a way to give its monstrosity a form and to be able to grasp it. Names, in other words, don't sit on their corresponding entities the way the label sits on the apple, but more like the way a boat rides a flood tide after a storm. What the name corresponds to is the overwhelmingly superior power it attempts to grasp hold of. It is, in a twofold sense, the opposite of this power—its polar opposite and at the same time its echo. Thus, the sacred name succeeds maximally in doing what the conceptual realism of the name demands—having a correspondence in the things it designates. No later name is as full of what it names; none adheres so closely and imploringly to its corresponding thing as the sacred name. Except that its correspondence is not the "essence" of the thing, not what holds the world together in its innermost being. Instead, it is what drives it apart and makes it inchoate and frightening. It is what later, in Hebrew, will be called *tohuwabohu*, and in Greek *chaos*. We could also call it the world's un-being, or its un-doing (*Unwesen*).[41]

Unnamed nature does not yet have any essence. It is, however, rich in things that have a characteristic form (*Gestalt*). And there is nothing by which natural things are more recognizable than their form. A strong formal resemblance usually allows us to conclude—usually correctly—that things belong to the same species. The perceptions of color and movement that regulate the flight, hunting, and courtship behaviors of optically endowed animals are themselves already a first step toward the perception of their form. And yet the living form is always only something exterior, never an essence. It would be equally incorrect to think of a species as an essence, even though generations of Platonists confused the two and believed that the species was what remained as individual examples appeared and disappeared—that it was the "eternal and unchanging" reality amid all change, the true being and "idea" in which all terrestrial beings only participate during their life on earth. But, unfortunately for this notion, it is always only individuals that produce offspring. The species itself doesn't do anything. It has absolutely no existence independent of individuals. It is nothing but the name tag for all individual things of comparable consistency. In the case of organisms, consistency has the same genetic basis; we also know it by the name of the genome. But the genome is not the species; it is only a combination of specific acids and proteins that is found in all the organisms of a given species. And the genetic equipment of an organism is certainly not its essence—any more than the interior decoration of a house is already the lifestyle of its occupants. Only as a result of complex developmental processes and with the help of numerous epigenetic factors[42] can a genetic program grow into a complete organism; under different conditions the same organism can take on very different forms.

In short, nature, on its own, never provides us with an essence. It only acquires one by being given a name, and it is given a name so it will cease its un-doing. Only in the fact of nature's terror—its chaotic un-doing par excellence—could its opposite be constructed, as the essence par excellence. The latter is nothing but chaotic un-doing that has been affirmed, terror that has been sanctified—in short, the sacred. And just as all names are descendants of the sacred name, so we can say that whenever Western metaphysics saw an essence in physical things—whether it went by the name of *ousia* in Greek, or *essentia* or *substantia* in Latin—we are dealing with descendants of the sacred. The "essence," or "substance" of natural things was always understood as what gives them their indestructability and stability, their inner and outer coherence. Individual things' essence or substance was conceived as what is exalted in them— the higher something that outshines and outlasts their empirical existence. But this higher something could never be thought without the presumption of a highest something, an absolutely benevolent divine power that allows earthly things a certain participation in those characteristics that only the divine power fully, wholly, and irrevocably possesses. This is especially evident in Genesis. God creates humankind "in his own likeness." Although Hebrew has no word for "essence," Genesis gives us the best possible paraphrase when it mentions similarity to the image of God. This is the acme of goodness, after all the other acts of creation have already been commented on with the notoriously repetitious: "And God saw that it was good."[43] Nor did the Greeks manage to get by without the idea of the good. In Plato's *Republic* it is the overarching idea, which takes precedence over all others. In *Timaeus*, there is even a divine "artificer," who in his wisdom has formed the pattern of the world.[44] In Aristotle, finally, we find the "unmoved mover" on whom "heaven and earth depend," whose "conduct of life is such that the best of it is only given to us for a short time"—namely *theoria*, the clear gaze at true being, in which the god is present eternally and all-encompassingly, "as we [are] only occasionally."[45]

In other words, what is imagined as the "substance" or ultimate "essence" of things is something like their benevolent primal structure, a grounding consistency that remains the same throughout all changes, and that, if only we know how to value it and comport ourselves accordingly, will get us through life's adversities. If, however, we attempt to comprehend this grounding consistency without the theological detour and without recourse to a benevolent deity, we miss the point. Aristotle felt that acutely. The essence or substance (*ousia*) of a thing, in his standard definition, is its *ti ēn einai*, literally, its "what it was to be." Translated a little bit more freely, it is "the thing that has made sure it is what it is," or "the thing that has made it what it is." Even more freely, we could also say "the thing that constitutes it, that gives it its identity."[46] But this does not say very much either, and Aristotle is variously engaged in finding additional names for this thing that founds identity. He often says *eidos* for this, using a word that in Plato first means "form" (*Gestalt*), and later "idea," except that Aristotle does not understand this to be a separate, higher being in which everything physical merely participates, which is what it means in Plato. Instead, Aristotle means an inner force that is at work in every individual thing that exists, and that gives it its concrete unity. This force is meant to have its effect in the material and yet be immaterial itself. Occasionally, Aristotle calls it *energeia*—a word in which potency and reality are blended. To the extent that we translate *eidos* as "form," the way medieval scholars frequently did, we must imagine it as referring to an energetic, a "forming" form. It is no accident that for *eidos* we sometimes find *arché*, the "first cause," or *entelechia*, defined as the "inner tendency toward" or "movement in the direction of a *telos*" (goal, purpose, or end).[47] But in invoking these concepts, are we much the wiser about essences? Each attempt just seems to go from one handle to the next; none of them opens the door. Even the definitions of *essence* that later philosophers came up with—"*an sich*" (per se), "intelligible substrate," "thing in itself," "unique or inner self," and so on—ultimately don't advance matters. There is an ongoing exchange among various concepts, all of which tiptoe around the essence like a cat around a hot dish, but they don't actually tell us *what it is*.

This is not the fault of philosophers' inability to form definitions, but of a misunderstanding of metaphysics itself. So-called being is by no means the ultimate thing as which it is always presented. What it always is, is a cover for something else that is not supposed to exist—impermanence, convulsive shock, or decay. When a natural entity is furnished with a name, it is, by virtue of this very act, endowed with the wish that it should not decay but should remain "whole"—hale and hearty. No profane name is ever completely divested of this hallowing wish. In this, it reveals its descent from the holy name, whether we are aware of it or not. To endow an entity with a name means to grant it this wish, as its "essence."

Being (*Wesen*)[48] is what the thing does not have on its own—the utopian breath of wholeness with which the name envelops whatever it designates. Even the most analytic language philosopher, when he gives his child a name, does not give it nothing but a number. He grants the vulnerable being something that is meant to protect and preserve it on its path through life: an essence. Nowhere is the function of naming expressed more laconically and expressively than in the story of the Tower of Babel, where the name is given "lest we be scattered abroad upon the face of the whole earth."[49] Only in high cultures, in the context of a narrow, well-constructed space of material security, does diversion acquire a positive value, as recreation. Originally, it is a relative of fright. When something is diverted or scattered about, it loses its composure and stability, its very existence. Each time a collective, an individual, or a thing is given a name, it negates diversion, opposes decay, and grants wholeness.

Aristotle sketched out the implications of this act of granting in a few spare words that have yet to find their equal. They compensate for all the eccentricity of his metaphysics. At the moment of its naming, each thing or event, according to his thinking, must be considered to be "individually (*atomon* = atom) and numerically one."[50] Whether the world actually consists of atoms, that is, of very small individual particles, is another question. But for naming they are indispensable. If the name does not refer to a single, indivisible whole, there is nothing for it to affix itself to. "For not to designate One means not to designate anything. But if names designate nothing, the conversation with others is nullified, in truth even conversation with oneself."[51] If we call a certain entity the "brain," we can only take it, at this moment, for *one*, although we know very well that it consists of billions of nerve cells. The person who talks about the "world population" cannot avoid speaking of it as one, even if what he has in mind is a milling multitude.

Thus, the name is not merely a label that is affixed to the thing, but something that seeks to hold it together more powerfully than it naturally is, "lest [it] be scattered." Nietzsche's famous exclamation, "I am afraid we are not rid of God because we still have faith in grammar"[52] did not go far enough. The name is even more theologically infected than grammar is. As long as we still use names, we will never get rid of utopia. The name may become as profane and ordinary as it wishes; it cannot stop conjuring up the wholeness of nature and investing everything that has a name with a hint of this notion. There is no naming without this magic, even if the speaker resists it and affixes a name to the object only as a means of classifying or even annihilating it. In the latter case, he commits an offense against the name like the one a perjurer commits against his oath. The name cannot prevent its misuse, but no misuse can take away the name's magically utopian trace. As long as we continue to give things names, we are preserving this trace—the same way every image preserves the spark of hallucination.

SPEECH ACTS

Archaic name-giving is a speech act; indeed, it is *the* speech act par excellence: catharsis. The modern theory of speech acts knows little of name-giving's intensity and expressive power. Its founder, John L. Austin, approaches language only at that well-tempered, late stage when naming has long since turned into a multifaceted system with an everyday, routine character. Austin then takes this language as he finds it, without further discrimination, to be language in its authentic state, and is astonished by his discovery that words not only have a meaning, but also do something, "performing such an act as: asking or answering a question; giving some information or an assurance or a warning; announcing a verdict or an intention; pronouncing sentence, making an appointment or an appeal or a criticism, making an identification or giving a description, and the numerous like."[53] Insofar as words mean something, according to Austin, they perform a "locutionary act"; insofar as they do something, an "illocutionary" act. And since philosophers are culpable of criminal disregard for the latter, he comes up with a theory of "illocutionary forces."

What sort of forces are these? In Austin, we have a hard time distinguishing them from the speech acts with which they express themselves. If words can form questions, can promise, complain, warn, and so on, they obviously have the "force," or capacity, to do so; just as, to the extent that they mean something, they have semantic capacity. Thus, speech-act theory immediately becomes a means of managing separate capacities. Locutionary and illocutionary forces are no longer supposed to be confounded. The question of whether the two forces might have a common root, even a physiological one, is not explored. And yet, it is quite obvious that a speech act is always a "force" in a quite concrete, physical sense. It doesn't happen without a certain expenditure of strength, skill, and effort. This is also true of its meaning. It would be a mistake to think that the meaning of words was always inscribed in them, like an inlay of spirit. It was formed only gradually, by dint of innumerable repetitions, in the course of the formation of sounds. "Meaning something," in common parlance, is thought of as an automatic function that words perform without any active intervention in their environment. This is the "locutionary" aspect of speech. But historically, "meaning something" required an active combination of sound, gesture, and mimicry, of motor and sensory self-discipline that took thousands of years. Only by dint of protracted processes of condensation, displacement, reversal, and repetition did meaning come into the world—in other words through an action, that, if indeed we want to apply the standard of speech-act theory, is illocutionary in the greatest possible degree. Meaning is a sedimentation of ritual activities, and the so-called "locutionary" is nothing but a patina on the surface of the "illocutionary," like culture on the surface of nature. Asserting the existence of locutionary and illocutionary "forces," and watching to make sure they are not confused with each other, is more of a bookkeeping operation than a deep understanding of the primal dimension of speech acts, in which "locutionary" and "illocutionary" were not yet separate. All later speech carries its original nondifferentiation along with it, as its unmastered past, and for this reason an antiseptically clean bisection of locutionary and illocutionary speech acts is not a very promising undertaking.[54]

Occasionally, Austin became aware of this and risked a look back at the early phase of human word-creation—if only to convince himself, as quickly as possible, of its outdatedness.

> The plausible view . . . would be that in primitive languages it would not yet be clear, it would not yet be possible to distinguish, which of various things that (using later distinctions) we might be doing we were in fact doing. For example "Bull" or "Thunder" in a primitive language of one-word utterances could be a warning, information, a prediction, etc. It is also a plausible view that explicitly distinguishing the different *forces* that this utterance might have is a later achievement of language, and a considerable one; primitive or primary forms of utterance will

preserve the "ambiguity" or "equivocation" or "vagueness" of primitive language in this respect. This may have its uses: but sophistication and development of social forms and procedures will necessitate clarification. [Whereby, however, we should by no means] take it that we somehow *know* that the primary or primitive use of language must be . . . statemental or constative . . . We certainly do not know that this is so, any more, for example, than that all utterances must first have begun as imperatives . . . or as swearwords. . . .[55]

Now, it is possible, without having been present, to know that the first verbal constructs were neither statements nor curses, just as one does not have to have heard primal words in their original tones to gain an appreciation of the logic of archaic word-creation. The scientific ethos that animates analytic speech-act theory resembles that of the geologists who look at a mass of lava and only see the stone in front of them, while they staunchly ignore the volcanic eruption that is petrified in it, since they did not experience it and can no longer reconstruct it in every detail. Out of pure scrupulousness, they set the decisive thing aside. A speech-act theory, though, that does not understand the catharsis that occurred in primal words as its own basis is making the reckoning without the host.[56] There are many details we will never know about the first process of naming, the way from *sham* to *shem*, that is, from the stammered pre-noun, which cries out in terror and seeks protection *from* it, to the solidly constructed name, which calls out to the power of terror and seeks protection *within* it, simultaneously affirming it and enveloping it with a utopian breath. We are still unclear about the length of time it took (probably measurable more in tens of thousands than in thousands of years) or about many details. And yet we can describe the structural course of this epoch-making 180-degree turn quite precisely. We can also say with certainty that even if the name, as an asylum for stimuli, offered a certain pacification and calming, there was still much too much horror remaining for early humanity to have been able to relax in peace. No sooner had the name become stabilized than the urge to escape from it already introduced the era of its profanation.

Over the course of this process, the name unfolded like a bud that becomes a flower, but at the same time it gave up much of its initial character as a "proper name," in the literal sense. To call out the sacred name initially meant to put oneself in the hands of a terrible power, to seek protection from it by giving oneself over to it as its property. In this most literal sense, the name remained a proper name only as long as it was divine or sacred. The "genius" that floated above the sacred site and "accepted" the sacrifice was *one*. Named, it remained the same, and undivided. Every new generation was ritually introduced to the practice of the "genius's" name, which was also theirs. Initially, it was theirs in the sense that each new generation spoke this name exactly as its forbears always had. But gradually, it became theirs in the sense that those who spoke it also related it to themselves. The name of their protector became their own protective sign—an acoustic mark of Cain. The names we give ourselves are always secondary. In cultivated societies, by the time a child begins to name himself, he has long since been named: the child takes the name by which his parents call him. The archaic collective, when it began to name itself, took the name it had previously given another. This is precisely the point of the logic of totemic name-giving: The name of the totem is the name of the clan—and thus of all its members.

With this doubling back on the collective, the name underwent a change. As long as it only referred to the "genius," the sacred, the god, it was exclusive. As the name of the collective, it became inclusive, a collective name that incorporated numerous other things. It turned out that it did not need to affix itself to a terrible power forever but could detach itself from that power and be transformed into a separate, consolidated acoustic entity that could stand for many things. Calling out the name no longer necessarily had to mean subsuming oneself under an overwhelming natural power. It could also mean subsuming many natural powers under oneself! Only through this turnabout, from seeking shelter to seizing power, did the process of subsuming gradually become what the logicians consider to have been its original nature—a process for subordinating individual things under collective names. The name entered the phase of its second great reversal—from the concealing naming of that which is not supposed to be to the ordering naming of what is. Psychologically speaking, it moved from identification with the attacker to identification with its objects. The name, as it became a collective noun, also became the preferred collection point for the forces of profanation of early humankind. And if one name could be transferred from the sacred to the clan, if *one* collective name was possible, then many were possible, not just for terrifying events and things, but also for moderate, regular, ordinary, familiar, pleasant, and joyful ones. In other words, as a collective noun, the name became profane as a tool for ordering natural phenomena, for disposing of them and emancipating oneself from their power and control.

The profanation of the name brought enormous relief from its authentic nightmare. Gradually, it also took away its character as a proper name. It is not that proper names disappeared altogether. They survived as the names of gods and sacred sites. For a long time, people might still speak them with a shuddering sense of awe. But they were no longer the one and only of human language; they were but worn remnants of their prehistoric existence—atavistic special cases in a language system that rests on the pillars of collective nouns. And the personal names of human beings? These already belong to a late period of naming, after clans had become so differentiated that they could no longer make do with collective totem names but had to adopt individual acoustic protective signs for their members. A careful look shows that these were no longer even proper names in the strict sense. Human proper names emerged as specializations of the clan name. Like the latter, they were meant to confer the protection of a divinity on the named person, but they did this in a particular way. If, for example, the Egyptian sun god was called Ra, then an individual who was meant to stand under the special protection of Ra could actually only be called Ramses (Ra-Moses = Child of Ra). Ra is a genuinely individual name; Ramses is only its descendant, not only because the name could only be constructed with reference to Ra, but also because it lacks the unmistakable and exclusive quality that distinguishes Ra. A lot of people can be called Ramses—for example a whole generation of pharaohs. If the pharaoh's individual ancestry is not mentioned or at least implied, the name by itself does not reveal which Ramses is meant.

Only gods have protected individual names—and commodities, which have brand names and "logos." A product's legally protected brand name is a sign of godlike status and openly acknowledges the fetish character of the commodity. It is no accident that children and adolescents, during the uncertain years when they are building their identities, are especially keen on brand-name clothing with its striking logos. In their force field, they believe they find a sense of belonging that they don't have as individuals. No proper name that is given to a person is as exclusively *his* or *her* name as the name of a brand is *its*. This is the difference between "Jesus" and "Coca-Cola." With individuals, we always have to add clarifying information if we want to identify them unmistakably, which is why modern bureaucracy cannot dispense with family names and birth certificates. Human names are only late reminders of the proper name par excellence, which was unequivocal without any additional information and which made your hair stand on end—the holy name. Although most people, nowadays, when they are thinking of names for their children, no longer have any notion of sacred names, the memory persists. It is a shining example of procedural memory.[57] Whether the name that is given to a child belongs to someone whom the parents admire and hope the child will emulate, or they just like the way the name sounds, it always invokes something that is meant to bring the child protection and good luck and to hover over its life like a "genius." The relationship to the sacred name may be nothing but a vague echo, but it will never end as long as names are given.

What hallucinations are for the imagination, names are for language. They began as its one and only, the site of its irritation and its driving force, and gradually became its underground. This occurred by means of a reversal of language's power to turn something into its opposite, a process that was internally contradictory. The consolidation of the prenominal demonstrative pronoun into a proper name was by no means already a unidirectional move in the direction of gradual stasis. A thing that becomes sedimented by means of constant repetition is also constantly changing. Repetition is not just "again and again," but also always "again and again, a little bit differently." As nouns became consolidated, they were reinforced by additions that strengthened and differentiated them and that gave them contours. Linguistically, we call these additions attributes. Attributes not only appeared after the formation of names (or nouns) had been completed; the process itself was already one of unending modification, variation, and addition. In the course of its naming, fright became differentiated—into singular and plural. The times and places of its occurrence, the places that offer protection from it, the reactions it causes—all these began to have an impact in the form of phonetic modulations, and as the fright lost its unfathomability, by dint of constantly repeated and varied naming, the name acquired additions that enveloped and softened it the same way it had enveloped and softened the original traumatic shock. The name experienced something of the very process it imposed on traumatic shock. It too lost the dread that is associated with the divine. And as it became quasi-ordinary and mundane as a result of its constant repetition, it gradually started to become clear that naming itself could be something quite ordinary, and that other things besides the terrifying ones are susceptible to naming. All of nature can be grasped in words. Language is not eternally condemned to be a cover for things that inspire fear. The same way that it itself once emerged from an unarticulated stream of sounds, it can play a role in emphasizing, revealing, and differentiating, and can gradually make the turnabout from covering up fright to discovering nature.

It can only do this by moving beyond names and nouns to form sentences. In the process, it downplays and deemphasizes names—their fearful origin, their role in covering up fright. In other words, it engages in something that philosophy will later call "the negation of the nega-tion." Naturally, this negation does not remove the thing that is negated; it merely denies it. The original cover-up function is still present, as negated. As the prehistory of language, it remains as its underground, which can never be entirely put to rest. It is understandable that so-called ordinary language wants to know nothing of this, its horrific prehistory. Normally, it is completely unconscious of its underground. But wherever there is name-giving it continues to rumble beneath the surface. Just as the mental world of imagination was only able to establish itself by suppressing and denying its hallucinatory prehistory, profane language only exists by virtue of the suppression and denial of its nominalizing prehistory.[58] Humankind could only assemble a regular store of imaginary things, and a mode of speech, by dint of a long struggle and a process of repression that is considerably more deserving of the words *primal repression* than what Freud calls by that term. After all, the primi-tive process described here is much more primal and fundamental; we can think of it as having constructed the mental space containing the repressive processes that psychoanalysis would later consider.[59] This primal repression has two sides: a visual and imaginary side, and an auditory and linguistic one. Only as a result of their interaction could the two become stabilized, interpenetrate, and grow together into the verbally supported power of imagination, or image-supported phonetic power, that we attempt to describe with such makeshift terms as *intellect*, *reason*, or *spirit*.

THE SUBJECTION OF THE NAME

In the first chapter we saw what happened to hallucination when it outgrew itself. Here we will now sketch the analogous career of the proper name. The name was not capable, by itself, of simultaneously concealing its cover-up function and developing its capacity for discovery. To do this, it needed the phonetic additions that grew attached to it, as it were, in the course of its constant repetition and variation. Additions to proper names are the origin of sentences. How names became sentences is something we can no more recapture than the sound of the first, primal words. Everywhere we find human collectives this transition has long since taken place, and we are already dealing with whole language systems. Even the most primitive surviving languages have long since passed beyond the elementary phase of sentence construction that humankind must once have undergone, and that necessarily preceded the evolution of language systems. Nor do modern children, growing up in a fully developed language system, experience this process in the same way. Additions to nouns are sounds that attach themselves to names in a way that softens them—and that have a tempering effect on the nouns not only by virtue of their phonetic value, but also through volume and pitch. We cannot yet assign them to grammatical categories, for example, suffixes or attributes. Grammar, after all, is still in the process of being created. In the beginning, the additions are merely appendages to the names. But as they gradually become familiar they acquire their own solidity, their own habits and quirks—in short, a life of their own. They separate into attributes, verbs, adverbs, conjunctions, and so on. Names acquire a whole team of helpers. Their capacity for discovery becomes broader, deeper, and more refined, and they are able to say things that the names could never have succeeded in saying on their own. On the other hand, in this process the team of helpers also becomes more self-sufficient. The additions turn against the names to which they have affixed themselves. They no longer just modify them; they also express something about them.

When children, later in the course of human history, grow into a language that already exists, this turnabout is hardly recognizable as such. It has long since been integrated into a scheme of gradual and progressive language acquisition and has rubbed off all its sharp edges. It is, nevertheless, remarkable to see the extent to which the linguist Roman Jakobson, when he examined childhood language acquisition, insisted on contours.

> In the beginning, every statement consists solely of a holophrase, a one-word sentence. . . . During the following stage, the holophrastic unity is complemented by a second component. In this way, the first grammatical divisions emerge simultaneously, on one hand words and combinations of words, on the other nouns . . . and adjective-like attributive elements . . ., for example "it ball," "more ball," "little ball." Some observers have tried to identify predication even during this stage, but the detailed interpretation of such complexes as peculiar, situation-determined predicates is a futile broadening of the term "predicate," which already led to long-winded discussions during the nineteenth century and revealed a very special and consequential role that is played by the purely grammatical predicate. Even the word combination "little ball" is still very far from the elementary sentence "the (this, a) ball is little." Neither "little doll" nor the diminutive "dolly" could be seen as equal to the sentence "the doll is little." The primary and non-characterizing function of the adjective is by no means predicative, but markedly attributive, and only the following, third stage of children's linguistic life expresses the elementary sentence—subject/predicate. A provocative example: . . . In English there are three homonymous suffixes that are spoken as "s"—first, that of the nominative plural ("cooks"); second, the possessive ("the cook's hat"), and third, the third person singular of the verb ("mummy cooks"). First, the child develops the ending of the plural, then the ending of the possessive, and finally the ending of the verb. Analogous observations show that aphasics follow the opposite path. An exact mirror image of losses emerges: Of the three homonymous suffixes, the verbal is lost first, followed by the possessive, and finally, in last place, the nominative plural suffix. The cause is evident: When it comes to differentiating singular and plural, only a single word is

involved, while the use of the possessive form already involves the entire verbal complex. But when the person of the verb is at stake, the question extends to the relationship between the predicate and the subject, in other words to the entire elementary sentence.[60]

When Jakobson contrasts childhood language acquisition with the loss of language in adults, his argument points beyond mere ontogeny in the direction of a specific, layered structure in the linguistic capacity of the species as a whole. If it is true that human beings with brain damage who gradually lose their capacity to speak ordinarily deconstruct it the same way they acquired it, but in reverse order—the most recently acquired features first, the first-acquired features last—then they are testifying to the fact that the child's individual language acquisition is a recreation of layers that the species had to lay down and allow to grow together over very long time periods and with great tribulation, with the result that children can recapitulate them with much less effort, and give the impression that they are simply undergoing a continuous process of growth. Jakobson's insistence that predication represents the inception of something qualitatively new in the child's language may never attain the status of an empirical proof; how could it, given that over the course of millennia the new acquisition has been worn down to the point of unrecognizability? But his perspective serves to remind us that in the historical construction of human language, predication was a literally epochal revolution. As the name mutates into a collective name and inclines in the direction of the grammatical noun, as it is modified by additions that enable it to say what it cannot say by itself, as the modifications acquire an independent value and molt from suffixes into attributes, whereby they no longer function as mere attachments to the name but become independent words alongside it, two things happen. On one hand, the name grows in power and reach; on the other, it approaches the point where it will turn into its own weakening.

This point is reached with the creation of verbs. Verbs too are a function of naming. They are part of the team of helpers, naming's royal household, so to speak, but as they perform their role as courtiers they simultaneously carry out a linguistic palace revolution. They make the name into something that the Latin language expresses with enviable clarity: a *subiectum*, literally, something that has been subordinated or subjected.[61] Only literal translation is entirely frank here. Where it is translated as "basis" (*das Zugrundeliegende*)[62] there has already been a significant shift in meaning. Certainly, a thing that has been subordinated may be found at a lower level, that is, at the base. But this means, first of all, that it has been overthrown. If instead we say "base" we have, in the blink of an eye, turned a defeat into a foundation and thus given the impression that the subject of a sentence is the solid foundation on which the predicate rests. This is an ontological falsification, no less than the assumption that the subject of a sentence has a basis, an "essence" in nature outside language.

Only when *subiectum* is taken quite literally as "something subjected"—that is, defeated—does it reveal what predication means. Namely, the very same master-slave dialectic is at work here as in Hegel's *Phenomenology of Spirit*. On one hand, the predicate is nothing but the herald of the subject: it says something about it. To this extent, it is its slave. The subject is in charge. On the other hand, saying is an activity of the predicate. The subject is subjected to its statement. The predicate says what is happening. To this extent, as the slave of the subject it is also the master of the subject; just as, conversely, the subject, as the master of the predicate, is also its slave. In this elementary form, we can see that predication is a specific means of uniting things that are incompatible. It is a performative contradiction. Let us take a sentence like "The lightning flashes." Here the predicate says what the subject is doing, but it is the predicate that is active. By presenting the subject as acting, it itself is acting on the subject. The predicate multiplies the reach of the noun about which it speaks. But at the same time, the noun is reduced in its possible reach: it becomes the subject of the sentence. Every sentence, it is true, is only the expansion and branching out of a subject. Thus grammarians are justified in saying that the subject "rules" the sentence.[63] But to the extent that the name becomes a noun and then the subject that branches out in the sentence, it is also incorporated in the sentence. It ceases to be the absolute word and loses its exclusive position. In a certain sense it becomes anonymous. Only the human custom of giving proper names to certain classes of organisms, and the fact that this name-giving never entirely loses the character of a solemn act still remind us that the name is not just some random word, but was once "the word," in its absolute sense.

It remains the root of the sentence. Except that a root has something very incomplete about it; this is why it outgrows itself. The sentence is a name that has outgrown itself. The name alone was not able to prevail over the superior power of traumatic shock. It was too full of it, had not enough of an escape valve to get rid of it. Hence the enormous pressure to repeat it, through which it acquired a solid form, and the modulations of its constant struggle for relief. These modulations are as much a part of the primary process of language as the emergence of names themselves. If the modeling of names, as they emerged from a tangled mass of excited sounds, is an act of condensation, the modulation of these names is an act of displacement. Only with the help of both was the name able to transform fright into something sacred. The trinity of condensation, displacement, and reversal that was at work in the creation of rituals and dreams is no less constitutive of the creation of language. It works in sound as well as images. And now, after focusing first on phonetic condensation, that is, on the modeling of names, we must turn to displacement: the modulation that, in its variations, both strengthened the phonetic image of the name and pushed it to surpass itself. The modulation of naming is already the driving force of the sentence and of speech; from the perspective of drive theory, it is acoustic stimulus flight. The way to sentences is the flight path of the name, and the name itself is already an implicit sentence, as the sentence is merely an implicit name.

This explication was the work of tens of thousands of years. Very gradually, hardly perceptibly, varying additions become associated with naming. They calmed its shuddering, as they had once calmed the shuddering of traumatic shock. And yet, this was not only a gentle, continuous forward progression. There was a qualitative leap, a reversal, which took place at the precise point where specific additions become so independent, as words, and took on such an independent sense, that they definitively stopped being mere attachments and tapeworm segments. They became additions to the name that worked against the name. These headstrong words were verbs. Only with their emergence did the stammering that surrounded the name become a sentence. Naturally this did not occur from one day to the next, but also very gradually. It is hard to say, and perhaps we will never know with certainty whether the nominal additions had already separated into suffixes and attributes before verbs took on their unique contours, or whether it was the independence of the verbs, their "revolt" against the nouns and ultimately their domination of the latter, that sent a kind of jolt through the phonemic field surrounding names and led to the separation into nouns, suffixes, attributes, and adverbs, thus establishing the elementary measure of phonemic order that deserves to be called grammatical structure.

A remainder of this uncertainty is the borderland where the proper grammatical place of attributes remains a matter of dispute. The adjective may be taken as an excellent object in this struggle. "Little ball" was Jakobson's example. Is "little," here, merely an attribute of "ball," or already a predicate, in other words, the abbreviated form of "is little"? We will hardly be able to decide this based on children's language develop-ment alone. Who is going to decide whether the child, in using the adjec-tive, is adding something to the noun or actually already "means" the predicate? We would have to know how the language of the species devel-oped at moments of transition among suffixes, attributes, and verbs. When additions to the name took the form of separate words, when they became attributes rather than suffixes, was predication already basically at work, just not in an explicit way? Or was it the headstrong verbs, their explicitly predicative force, that, independent of the force of the nouns, had a structural impact on them that made the hitherto indistinct additions to the name begin to separate into suffixes—which remained glued to the nouns—and attributes, which became independent? We may never know.

In any case, predication introduces something qualitatively new into the realm of the word. Words had begun as prenominal, cathartic, exor-cising exclamations. As names, they became calls that sought protection. Both were aural forms of wishing—in grammatical terms, the so-called optative mood.[64] "To call on the name of Yahweh" means to pray to Yahweh—to urge him to provide his protection to the person concerned. The grammatical mode of prayer is the optative—except that prayer began pre-grammatically, as a pleading cry or stammer. We can really speak of the optative only at a point when it has also acquired an antithesis, and for this to be the case the name must have been tempered to the point that another word can appear alongside it. This is the verb, which makes the name into a *subiectum*. Of course verbs, too, can plead and wish. But they don't have to. A new power attaches to them: they can make a statement about the name. Stammering can already express a plea. But only the sentence can make a statement—thanks to the verb. With this, language conquers a new dimension: the indicative. Only now is it capable of saying, of something specific, "This is the way it is." Here, on one hand, a predicate is saying something about a noun, thus making it into the subject of the sentence. This is the inner-linguistic side of the statement. On the other hand, predicate and subject together are saying something about a matter that is named by the noun and that initially is something nonlinguistic. In the beginning, statements do not respond to statements but to concrete physical events and figures. But if "statement" has two meanings, one that is internal and one that is external to language, then it can scarcely be otherwise than that the "subject" too takes on a dual meaning. First, it is the subject of a sentence; second, it is the thing that is designated by the subject of the sentence, a kind of natural subject—here in the literal sense of the term, since, in the statement, language makes a bit of nature into a *subiectum*. It subjects it to the control of its analyzing attention, marks it, and emphasizes its behavior, its actions. Only now does language's emphasizing, identifying, and classifying potential come into play.

THE DREAMTIME OF LANGUAGE

Only with the emergence of the indicative does the optative become a separate mode. Previously, the two were undivided, as they are in dreams. A chief characteristic of dreams, after all, is that we do not immediately know what mode they are in. Is a dream expressing something as it is or as it ought to be? Does it say "This is how things are" or "This is not how things are"; "This is as it should be" or "This is not as it should be"? The interpreter of dreams has to figure this out. The dream itself does not tell him. It has sunk back to the level of representation, where this kind of distinction has not yet been drawn. The distinctions become graspable only when there are sentences. Only then do "yes" and "no," "is" and "ought," "before" and "after" become clearly differentiated. Sentences are characterized not only by a specific mode but by a specific word order, which in turn implies that from now on it is possible to speak correctly and incorrectly—this too in a dual sense. You can create sentences that are correct or incorrect, and you can, in a sentence, say things that are true or false in regard to the things they describe. For example, you can say of an existing thing that it is or that it is not.

Sentences, consequently, manifest nothing less than the reality principle. True, language had to work hard before it arrived at sentences. In its unimaginably long presyntactic phase, it was by no means luxuriating in the delights of the pleasure principle—it was in a kind of dream state. Indeed, the prehistoric era of names is the dreamtime of language. In the attempt to rid itself of fright, it spoke fright's antithesis into language; it smuggled it in via hallucination. The aural side of this hallucination, the sacralization of terror, is the holy name—the absolute name. It is the platform from which language was able to pass through its hallucinatory stage and its dream state, to arrive, gradually, at sentences. With this, inversely, we can say somewhat more precisely what the achievement of the reality principle means for the history of the species. It is, after all, not as if with the invention of the sentence we had suddenly achieved the capacity to say what nature is "really" like. Even statements about which there is no doubt don't tell us that. They merely represent nature and never quite stop presuming something about it. But now the presumption has reached the level of a grounded assertion. Thus the reality principle means the opening up of a becalmed space in which shattering terror and the optative have ebbed and become a moderated, quasi-well-tempered excitement. The space of indicative speech is this kind of space. It is a space within which things are marked, sorted, and organized, and can also be checked for logical coherence. Here, for the first time, the attitude becomes possible that will later be called observant, theoretical, even contemplative.

Theologically speaking, the sentence gave an extraordinary push to profanation—a push that only language could give it. Imagination may also represent nature, but it makes no statements about it. It does not judge. Only with the sentence did the capacity for judgment enter the world of imagination. We can scarcely envision the degradation that was once involved when the sacred name became downgraded to the subject of a sentence. Instead of "calling Yahweh by his name," sentences say something about Yahweh, his commandments and deeds, using verbs and adverbs, adjectives and relative pronouns, whole sentences and speeches to do this—what a tempering of his terrible sacred nature this already was! How inappropriate the distanced focus of judgment, observation, and *theoria*. Strictly speaking, all of theology is already a profanation of the *theos*. The same is true of "holy books," which are skillfully composed on papyrus in a cleverly worked-out alphabet that has long since lost the bloody seriousness of the sacred primal signs that had once been inscribed on one's own body as a means of enduring human sacrifice. Measured against the mark of Cain, the Bible is nothing short of profane writ.

It is easy to underestimate how profane the primitive sentence already was. Nor, as we know, did things stop there. Subject and predicate were joined by objects, adjectives, adverbs, pronouns, and conjunctions. The sentence developed into complex speech, and to the extent that speech always traversed the same aural tracks, it gradually became sedimented into a whole system of language. To put this another way, the cathartic stimulus flight that began by calling out a name branched out, in the course of innumerable and varying repetitions, into a whole network of flight paths, which also appears as a complex of grammatical-syntactical structures. These are no less leftovers from specifically human stimulus discharge than are the types of imaginative activity that had crystallized earlier in the creation of rituals. The modeling and modulation of names was, at first, also nothing but the acoustic side of ritual creation. And just as ritual structures change over the course of time, grammatical structures are also subject to change. The structures themselves are never graspable, anyway; what we grasp is always only their use in a specific case. Human collectives do have at their disposal a grammatically regulated vocabulary, in what Ferdinand de Saussure called *langue*, as opposed to *parole*, which is the actualization of this repertoire in concrete speech.[65] But what does this tell us about the extent of *langue*? At least this much: that there is a grammatical arsenal that extends beyond individual national languages, such as French, English, or German; otherwise they would not be mutually translatable. Yet this arsenal is not so comprehensive that every individual language is completely translatable into every other one. Each language, apart from its phonemic particularities, also possesses a semantic and grammatical remainder that immediately raises the question: Should we neglect this remainder, as a kind of byproduct of a generalized grammatical structure, or is it already proof of the fact that no such structure exists?

UNIVERSAL GRAMMAR AND CATEGORIES

Structuralism naturally supported the first claim: "that all languages are cut to the same pattern," namely according to a "system of rules . . . that can iterate to generate an indefinitely large number of structures," as Noam Chomsky says. He assumes, in asserting this, that this system consists of "formal universals" that work as so-called "formatives" in all languages, but not in such a way "that there is any point by point correspondence between particular languages," or that there "must be some reasonable procedure for translating between languages." Rather, Chomsky's grammatical universals are conceived as a "deep structure"[66] that has to be filtered out of individual grammars before it becomes possible, in turn, to derive individual grammars from it. This brings the old battle over universals back to life in a new linguistic guise. It is striking how obliviously structuralism sails along in the wake of the old metaphysics, viewing linguistic structures as immemorial, always preexisting sources of order, like the genera and types of the Platonists. Grammatical "deep structure" is the spitting image of Aristotelian "substance," the *ti ēn einai* of individual grammars, that is, the thing that made them what they are. Just as in Aristotle, the *eidos*, as forming form, constituted individual things, so grammatical deep structure "generates" the individual grammatical practices—except that the entire linguistic toolkit is not able to catch the "generation" process *in flagrante*, even once. It has always already happened. The linguist always only finds its results, its impact on individual grammars and practices. He is unable to say how it takes place, any more than the metaphysical philosopher could say how a substance manages to "appear." And deep structure itself? Here again, the crux is the same as with Aristotle's "substance," which he was only able to surround with a nimbus of alternate concepts, without being able to say what it is. We learn as little from Chomsky as regards grammatical deep structure. Certain elements of which it is supposed to consist, like empty strings and sentence generators, are introduced as if they were self-explanatory, without being clear about the extent to which they are fundamental. We search in vain for clear boundaries between universal and particular grammars, or at least for precise descriptions of their minimal extent. That all human languages have subjects, predicates, and objects is correct, but didn't we already know that? With all its transformation rules, universal grammar can't even answer the question whether a particular sequence of subject, predicate, and object is the authentic one, and thus represents the fundamental pattern and universal "deep structure" of which other sequences represent specific deviations.

This is a consequence of Chomsky's theory's unmastered linguistic Platonism, the fact that it treats those linguistic structures that Saussure calls *langue* no differently, in principle, than ancient metaphysics treated being—as something immemorial, primal, and existing *an sich*—in itself. But just as this so-called being is nothing but a nonbeing that has been covered up by being given a name, *langue* is nothing but the covered-up language of names. Naturally, in language there are universal forces that create structure. Everywhere on earth where prenominal demonstratives emerged, these forces were already at work. This was true when names first emerged, and again when the additions to the names turned against them, when the names were degraded and became subjects, when they were profaned and incorporated into an architecture of grammar, and, finally, when the optative was tempered and became the indicative. Nevertheless, the forces at work here are none other than the pre-grammatical, energetic forces of stimulus flight: they are called condensation, displacement, and reversal. By modeling and modulating sounds, they brought sense into the world, as antisense. In short, they constitute the primary linguistic process. Grammatical structures, on the other hand, are always already precipitates of and are already woven through with the many chance events that the collectives creating the language experienced under diverse natural-historical, geographic, and climatic conditions. To put this another way, grammatical structures are always already tinged with particularity, are only ciphers of the universal linguistic primary process that they always also involuntarily recall, even as they deny it. Grammar is always something secondary: *ens per aliud*, not *ens per se*.[67]

Somehow, Aristotle must have had an intuition about this. In his *Organon*, it is no accident that before he starts to discuss the construction of sentences he lays out an index of structures that he claims are innate in all human speech and precede all grammar—categories. *Katēgoria* literally means "accusation"—the claim that is solemnly brought against someone in the agora (meeting place, ritual site, execution site, and only then marketplace). Later, it means the content of the accusation, a crime. More generally, then, it is what people say about someone—gossip, slander, and the (good or bad) repute or reputation the person acquires as a result. Gossip and slander are viewed by Aristotle so generally that they turn into a kind of anticipated repute. After all, what remains after speaking is, at the same time, the preparer and path-maker of all the speech that follows. It precedes and prepares it not only temporally, but structurally as well. The currently accepted philosophical interpretation of category, then, sees it as a function of expression. This is not wrong, but it is also not very characteristic. Linguists may easily conflate categories with *langue*, the grammatically structured repertory of words. But what Aristotle means by it is something expressly pre-grammatical. And the way he gets there is as awkward as it is brilliant. First, he takes language as he finds it, namely his Greek mother tongue, which as *logos* (word, speech, and also argument) is at the zenith of ancient word and sentence creation. Then he breaks the sentence down into its components, the individual words. Finally, he formulates, for each of these words, a partic- ular aspect, we could also say a unique condition, which he identifies either with interrogative pronouns or with verbs.

And the result of this is the famous catalog, given in a virtually telegraphic style, of the ten categories that for Aristotle, like most of his writings that have come down to us, were probably no more than a brief outline prepared for an extensive oral presentation. "Of things said without any combination, each signifies either substance or quantity or qualification or where or when or being-in-a-position or having or doing or being-affected. To give a rough idea, examples of substance are man, horse; of quantity: four-foot, five-foot; of qualification: white, grammat- ical; of a relative: double, half, larger; of where: in the Lyceum, in the market-place; of when: yesterday, last-year; of being-in-a-position: is-lying, is-sitting; of having: has-shoes-on, has-armour-on; of doing: cutting, burning; of being-affected: being-cut, being-burned."[68]

The first item in Aristotle's catalog is the naming of a "substance" (*ousia*); his examples are also as simple as can be: a human being or a horse. But watch out. Here, he expressly does not mean a human being or a horse as a species, an idea, an *eidos* or *ti ēn einai*, but instead refers to this individual human being, this very horse with which I am concerned at this moment. He calls this here-and-now being *protē ousia*, "primary substance," and his thought, in doing so, is that if there is not even a word in existence to name this person and to preserve it as a being, then all our ruminations about what constitutes a truly existing thing or what founds the identity of a particular person have nothing to which to attach them- selves. They hang in the air. So, from the perspective of concrete language, the *eidos*, the forming form or thing in itself, is only the "secondary substance" (*deutera ousia*).[69] For the "primary substance," Aristotle now offers a formula that is as simple as it is unfathomable: *tode ti*, "this," or "this there."[70] Every concrete form, every isolated thing is a "this there." This immediately recalls the gestural context in which human word formation originated. In the period of their emergence, words were extended index fingers—pointing toward something that is simply *there*: a here-now that wholly absorbed the attention and for which, initially, there were no words except stammering demonstratives. But the language-creating "there" par excellence is traumatic shock. Thus, the *tode ti* immediately and straightforwardly opens up the energetic, pre-grammatical dimension in which languages are actually greater than any culture, not to say universal. To the best of our knowledge, Aristotle did not have any acquaintance with Hebrew, was unfamiliar with the Old Testament, and had no clue about the complex of issues surrounding *sham*, *shamah*, and *shem*. Nevertheless, with the sure-footedness of a sleepwalker, he and his *tode ti* both grasped this complex and distorted it to the point of unrecognizability. The first, archaic level of the *tode ti* is the prenominal, demonstrative, and highly excited "there" (*sham*); at a second level, it has been stabilized as a name (*shem*); at a third, it has been tempered to become a noun that no longer has to provide a moderating cover for being that is here and now, but can emphasize, identify, and mark it: human being, horse, and so on. At this point, it already tends toward the collective noun that subsumes individual things, as well as toward the subject of which predicates speak.

The terms "this there," and "primary substance"—in Aristotle these designate a thing that is not only numerically first but also primary in rank. All other statements are about *it*. Only with reference to a "this there" can we speak about conditions like number, composition, place, time, situation, activity or passivity, and so on. The status of this manner of speaking is admittedly unclear. Kant, in particular, took issue with it. His *Critique of Pure Reason*, in its first part, is concerned, for long stretches, with deepening the Aristotelian categories so they can serve as an incontestable foundation for all knowledge. "It was an enterprise worthy of an acute thinker like Aristotle to make search for these fundamental concepts. But as he did so on no principle, he merely picked them up as they came his way. . . ."[71] Aristotle's procedure, to Kant's way of thinking, was much too confined by empirical reality, his categories were merely distilled from chance linguistic processes, rather than grasped as "pure concepts of the understanding which apply *a priori* to objects of intuition in general,"[72] in other words, as prelinguistic forms of thought that are already there the moment someone starts to speak. Kant famously accorded these forms of thought a special status, that of the "transcendental." *Transcendental*, for him, means "something other than 'metaphysical.'" Categories should not be things in and of themselves that provide the foundation for the restless work of the senses; they should be a set of rules that have no function other than to create concepts. And yet, at the same time, this set of rules is supposed to have a crucial commonality with metaphysical substances: it is meant to be equally free of becoming and provenance and hence "pure," in other words untroubled by any empirical inconstancy or imponderability.

Viewed from this "pure" perspective, Aristotle seems quite impure. He ignores the merely concept-creating function of categories and mixes them up with the foundational forms of perception, or "intuition" (*Anschauung*), of which Kant allows only two: "space" and "time." For Kant there are three modes of pure sensation"—"when," "where," and "lying." He subordinates them to the pure forms of intuition (space and time), but denies them the status of independent categories. He takes the same approach with "doing" and "suffering," which he counts only as belonging to the "derived concepts," although he does not consider them to be "modes of sensation." Instead, he places them—without any discussion, as if this were self-evident—under the category of "relation." According to Kant, other things that he himself subsumes under the rubric of "concepts" (for example "being" and "nothingness," or "affirmation" and "denial") have gotten lost, in Aristotle, in the as yet not fully matured "post-predicaments," which, in fact, do bear an unclear relationship to the "predicaments" (= categories).

But this whole furor over the order of categories alters nothing about the fact that the whole concept of the transcendental misses the point. While it might seem, from the vantage point of a highly developed human culture, as if the capacity to create concepts formed a part of humankind's basic natural endowment, in reality it had to earn its place there laboriously, over long periods of emergence in the Stone Age. Kant is not simply the historic victor over Aristotle. Undoubtedly, the latter's categories are underdetermined; but what they lack is certainly not the fact that they are not "pure." Nor did he simply confuse them with forms of perception.

Rather, he was feeling his way forward, without yet being certain, toward something very remarkable: the neuralgic point of indifference between modes of perception and expression. Let us take another look at his telegraphed list of categories. The ten aspects that it lists remain utterly disparate from a linguistic point of view; they are single, staccato words. It is all the more remarkable that they nevertheless evoke an image of perception: the scene of a white-robed, literate human being several feet tall, who is sitting in the Lyceum wearing shoes and who is cutting or burning something. A bizarre scene, it seems more like a dream than the content of waking consciousness. But in both cases, its existence is not dependent on something being said about it. It could also be a completely wordless visual impression. In any case, the ten aspects, each of which is marked by a word, resolve themselves first into an image, not a sentence. With this the question arises: Are they really primary means of expression—or, rather modes of perception?

Modes of perception are much older than the means of speaking. Primitive organisms, when they always react in the same way to changes in light, temperature, or humidity, already demonstrate that they have a well-rehearsed repertoire of modes of perception. Modes of speech, on the contrary, are only a thin layer, or veneer, on top of modes of perception. They emerged only in a single, highly developed species, and then only when the nervous system of this species developed the capacity to translate isolated points of perception into subsequent, lasting perceptual states: representations. Word and representation could only develop in tandem, which does not mean that, from the very beginning, they represented each other, nicely organized, in a reciprocal one-to-one fashion. The first stammering creation of words and diffuse images, over the course of many millennia, was in absolutely no condition to do this. Phonemes could only be regularly connected with images at a point when the representations had become sufficiently solidified for words to attach themselves to them repeatedly in an always identical fashion. Modes of speech can only become sedimented along the traces of modes of perception, and this only after the perception itself is no longer flickering but has been transformed into an inner mental state. And now we also see why it is "states" with which Aristotle associates the individual words (always in the singular) on his list of categories. Words can only dock onto states—and in the process also help to preserve them.

It looks as if Aristotle's category concept focuses on the precise historical moment when regular modes of speech were stepping into the footsteps of well-rehearsed modes of perception. In actual history, of course, this "moment" lasted thousands of years. We will not go wrong if we identify it with the Early Stone Age. A more precise dating is simply not possible.[73] The first attempts at regular modes of speech will have occurred at a point when the modeling and modulation of names and additions to names had begun to recur regularly, always taking the same pathways—in other words, long before there was grammar. These modes of speech, over a long period, had prepared the road to grammar, not the other way around. Aristotle didn't know this, but he intuited it. Hence we can certainly define his categories as pre-grammatical modes of speech that form their unique pathways in the traces of well-rehearsed modes of perception. Aristotle innervates the moment when they became pathways within pathways, where the two overlapped to the point of indifference, and where, at the same time, their difference also came into existence. The latter supervened, at first, mainly by breaking down into words what in mental representation had previously been condensed as an image. Where words dock onto an image of this sort, the image is like the host, and the words are its parasites. They burrow in and break down the host. They work analytically, as harbingers of the reality principle, so to speak, but not yet up to its standards, for they do not reintegrate what they have broken down to form sentences or judgments. This very moment of breaking down is what the bizarre scene of the person sitting in the Lyceum represents. It is visually homogeneous but linguistically disparate; thus it not only simulates a dreamlike image, but the presyntactic stage of language, too—its dreamtime, as it were—where optative and indicative, what should be and what is, yes and no, are not yet sundered from each other. And thus it makes sense that Aristotle does not place affirmation and negation, as Kant would have liked, among the primary categories but only provides for them to be located, as "post-predicaments," at the stage when sentences and judgments have been fully developed—as a kind of final seal on the reality principle. His sparse concepts are marvelously shadowed by a deep memory of whose implications he himself can scarcely have been fully conscious. The same way his lapidary *tode ti* has proven to be a formula in which the entire history of name-giving is condensed, his catalog of categories condenses thousands of years of linguistic development into a couple of laconic sentences. The scene is no less filled with history than the episode in the Sinai, only more coded.

PSYCHOANALYTIC STRUCTURALISM

Of all this, structural linguistics knows . . . nothing. What's more, it doesn't want to know. To its founder, Ferdinand de Saussure, "The question of the origins of language is not as important as is generally assumed. This question should not even be asked. The only true object of linguistics is the normal and regular life of an already existent idiom." This is the approximate equivalent of saying that the only true object of the interpretation of dreams is the manifest dream content. How it comes to be is not so important—we can confidently ignore the primary process of dream construction. This is exactly how structuralism deals with the primary linguistic process. Words are only worth considering in the cultivated context of a fully differentiated *langue*, with a ramified grammar and syntax within which they play the role of profane, well-tempered signs. "Since I mean by sign the whole that results from the associating of the signifier with the signified, I can simply say: *The linguistic sign is arbitrary.* . . . I mean that it is unmotivated, i.e., arbitrary in that it actually has no natural connection with the signified."[74]

In 1916, sentences like those were viewed as a pioneering act of demythologization. Words in themselves were nothing but sequences of sounds; they were not linked with natural things by any inner or outer sense, any *adaequatio rei et intellectus*.[75] To this way of thinking, linguistic communities are sound-formation communities. One calls a certain thing a "tree"; others say *arbre* or *Baum*. None of these sound sequences is more true, meaningful, or appropriate for the designated thing than any other. All three, by their nature, have nothing to do with any tree. They are arbitrary in relation to their object and have been assigned to it without any evident motive. Only after the assignment has taken place does it cease to be arbitrary. Then the community that happened to adopt the sound sequence "tree," and is thus committed to it, must keep it cleanly separated from similar sound sequences like "sea," "key," "bee," "knee," and "we." Only in the mutual interrelationship of these sound sequences and with respect to the rules that differentiate and connect them can there be something like sense and appropriateness. In other words, these qualities emerge only between signs and not between signs and the things for which they stand.

This superficial diagnosis initiated an entire analytical and semiotic discourse about language—at the expense of a major failure of memory. That originally signs were by no means merely arbitrary means of identifying arbitrarily chosen events; that word creation was by no means "unmotivated," but was strongly motivated by traumatic shocks that were not intended to be held on to, but instead were to be gradually gotten rid of by means of ritualized cathartic expression—the structuralist discourse simply ignores all this. In so doing, it does not exactly recommend itself as the main source of guidance for psychoanalysis. But Jacques Lacan famously selected it precisely for this purpose—and inserted it into the philosophical gap that Freud had left behind when he failed to show how the "foremen" of dreams—condensation, displacement, and reversal— actually accomplished what he claimed for them, namely "primitive thought activity." Where, in the interplay of unconscious, preconscious, and conscious notions, or (as they would later come to be called) of id, ego, and superego, are the imaginative and logical structures of thinking to be found? Lacan knows the answer: They are "always already there," he says: *"The unconscious is structured like a language."*[76] If it is true that language is the ceaseless play of signs that, for their part, play with something they designate, then the unconscious must also be understood as a similar kind of play. It should be read structuralistically. "Linguistics, whose model is the combinatory operation, functioning spontaneously, of itself, pre-subjectively—it is this linguistic structure that gives its status to the unconscious."[77]

Lacan's linguistic pleadings are thus not at all aimed at reconstructing the primary linguistic process that we have described in this chapter. Instead, they inject a preconceived structuralist notion of language into psychoanalysis, in order to apply it to the primary process of dream creation as analyzed by Freud, and to show that it too follows the same basic pattern. What language *is*, what it *means* for language to have been formed from the congealed movements of stimulus flight—this sort of question is never posed. After all, the play of signs and the things they designate is "always already there." All this is quite self-evident—and hence the key for understanding everything that follows. Thus, for Lacan, we only grasp displacement and condensation correctly if we see them as linguistic processes, which he renames metonymy and metaphor. Because structuralism is convinced that designations (= signifiers) and the things they designate (= signifieds) belong to different orders, or "registers," in the "interplay of combinations," the signifiers at first are all alone, so to speak. They change places, intersect, and occasionally form whole chains of metonymies (= renamings). This is constantly occurring even in ordinary speech, but it is especially pronounced in poetry. Lacan cites Quintilian, who, when he wants to refer to a fleet, says "thirty sails," thus creating a chain by omitting its middle link, namely the ships. But since signifiers not only tend to form chains but also have a tendency toward willfulness, everyday speech leads not only to metonymies, but also constantly to metaphors, which according to Lacan come to occupy the place of other words in such a way as to cover them up. "Love is a pebble laughing in the sun" is his poetic example. Condensation and displacement, for him, are essentially games with signs, which in prose and poetry may take on more elaborate forms than in dreams and the unconscious but are structurally no different. There too, displacement is essentially just metonymy ("word for word"), and condensation is metaphor ("a word for another word").[78]

Linguistics is meant to give psychoanalysis increased precision, but it results in a physiological loss. The energetic achievement of the primary process, the neural effort that is required to replace one visual or aural shape with another, is transmuted into language. In other words, it is dissipated until it becomes nothing but a relationship among signs. And the critical case of condensation and displacement, in which the word or image is by no means a mere translation or cipher for another word or image, but instead a nameless and image-less excitation that must be compressed and transformed in order for primary names and images to even *come into existence*—this case is not contemplated at all. Lacan actually sensed this lack, and compensated for it by a twist that we may regard as the beginning of post-structuralism. It introduces into structuralism an irritation that reduces its stasis (Derrida will later say of this move that it "de-sediments" Lacan's thought), and that undermines it with thoughts that are not affected by its blinkers but do not fundamentally break with Lacan's ahistorical point of departure. Post-structuralism is irritated—and irritating—structuralism. It can be conveniently studied starting from the prohibition of questioning that Saussure imposed at the inception of the linguistic order of signs (also often termed the "symbolic order"). But looked at in the light of day, the interdiction is not nearly as soberly scientific as it pretends to be. Signs, which are considered "unmotivated," and for which there is, in the things that are designated, neither a stimulus, a cause, nor a reason, are rendered mysterious, whether intentionally or not. They become a symbolic order that is simply *there*, for no reason. But where are we presented with such a thing? In the theater, when, suddenly and without any preparation, a deus ex machina appears, straightens the furniture, and restores the order that from now on everyone must follow.

This is Lacan's point of departure. His own unique post-structuralist theater begins with the psychoanalytic elaboration of the deus ex machina. On this stage, the unmotivated symbolic order appears as spontaneous, sovereign, and self-erected. What then could be expected to occur to a psychoanalyst but the male organ that, in erecting itself, makes its owner capable of procreation? And—lo and behold—the erection of the symbolic order is declared, without further ado, to be the work of the phallus. The latter is not one signifier among others, but the instigator of all the others, the force by means of which they are all related to signifieds. But the phallus itself is not a signifier. Naturally, it is not the penis of some empirical person either. In male sex organs it only finds its imperfect embodiments. And what is the phallus as such? How does it erect the symbolic order? For Lacan, these are the wrong questions; after all, we always already find ourselves existing within a symbolic order. The phallus that erected it, by contrast, does not belong to it at all. In erecting it, it falls out of it. It is the signifier that all our signifiers never reach, the signifier that not only has no signifier, but that can never become a signifier—the blind spot in the symbolic order. Or, even more drastically, it is the absolutely impossible. But now comes the staggering result. The impossible is—the real. How so? Apparently, quite easily. A symbolic order may always be striving to catch reality in its net, but it only succeeds in catching images of it. It always only reaches as far as the imaginary. None of its signifiers is ever able to catch up with the real. Hence, the real is the impossible, and the impossible is the real.

We can hardly claim that Lacan learned nothing from the Jesuits. The way he builds a false bottom under the impossible is really impressive. The "impossible" is represented first by what is inaccessible to us; Kant would call it the "thing in itself," which all our human powers of intuition and conceptuality are never able to actually reach. Lacan stands there like a worthy Kantian. However, the "impossible" does not only designate the things we can't reach but also the nonexistent, the non-thing, the wooden iron—whatever cannot possibly exist. And Lacan slips this second kind of impossibility in under the first in a way that is truly virtuosic. The phallus as such, which erects itself into the symbolic order, is a non-thing of this kind. Precisely for this reason, in Lacanian reading, the phallus is the thing in itself; it is what's absolutely real. Its impossibility is its badge of identity as *ens realissimum*. With this, Kantianism comes to a full stop. Lacan, here, is proceeding like theologians when they talk about the *Deus absconditus* (the hidden God). Human beings can't know anything about Him, for He is intangible; He is the absolutely inaccessible—and in this context they assiduously propose that it is *He* who withholds Himself— He, of whom the credo claims to know all sorts of things, for example that He founded the order of the universe, is embodied in the world, and has oriented it toward a good end.

Deus ex machina, *Deus absconditus, Deus phallus*—in our context, this is much more than a rhetorical phrase; it is the Lacanian credo. And whoever joins the congregation of the faithful is richly rewarded by the fact that *Deus phallus* lends an even more elevated meaning to even the most dubious teachings of Freud, while forcing them into a closed psycho-analytic worldview. An example is the theory of penis envy, which little girls supposedly feel automatically if they catch sight of naked boys or their own father in a state of undress.[79] It is hard to deny that there is such a thing as penis envy. Under conditions of patriarchy, where the idea that males are more valuable than females colors even the education of small children, female children cannot fail to interpret the penis as a sign of the greater value that they lack. Except that Freud understood penis envy as something given by nature. The female body, in his view, was actually incomplete, and female feelings of inferiority were the natural conse-quence of this natural inequality. The deficits of the male body, on the other hand, its incapacity to bear or breast-feed children and the feelings of envy that result from this, which were very much a socially constitutive factor in the matriarchal high cultures of antiquity, went entirely unno-ticed by Freud. His penis envy theory is patriarchal. In Lacan, an over-arching transpatriarchal metaphysics generalizes the phallus to become the epitome of perfection. Girls lack this perfection in any case: they have no penis. But boys also lack it. Their penis is the threatened organ per se. The Damocles sword of castration is constantly hanging over them. The childlike penis, after all, is only the impoverished empirical embodiment of the phallus, the visible sign of what he lacks—and of what, for this very reason, threatens him. Thus, the Damocles sword of the phallus—and, as such, the "law of the father"—hangs over the male child.

With this, another Freudian theory finds its higher justification—the theory of the murder of the primal father. Lacan leaves open the question of whether it can be taken as literal historical fact. But he takes its consequences very seriously. In the "brothers'" renunciation of their capacity to treat the women of the horde the same way the father does, he sees nothing but the primal form of phallus-erection: the constitution of the symbolic order. By founding and then falling out of it, the phallus is the primal father, now transmuted into the "impossible," and the symbolic order is nothing other than his "law"—the permanent threat of castration. Even quite ordinary symbols or signifiers further extend this threat by virtue of the fact that they do not reveal the real but precisely make it disappear, cover it up, and put themselves in its place. By naming things, they cry "Gone!" just like Freud's grandson Heinerle. What should be "There" symbolically must, itself, be "Gone." The "law of the father" is only "fully there" when the father is "gone," that is, has been murdered. "Thus the symbol first manifests itself as the killing of the thing, and this death results in the endless perpetuation of the subject's desire."[80]

Desire too is a result of the erection of the phallus. Desire makes it unreachable. As a result, the natural tension of drives, which press toward release, becomes symbolically stretched—it becomes a tension that reaches for the unattainable, the very phallus itself. This is the point of Lacan's "desire." Not only does it not achieve release; it doesn't want it. It wants to remain what it is, or, in Nietzsche's words, it "wants eternity." Except that Nietzsche was talking about pleasure. Pleasure, however, is a drive that has been satisfied, while desire is an unsatisfied one—an endless state of tension directed at the phallus. In other words, it is *ananke*, the fate within which human existence has been suspended, Sisyphus-like, ever since the mysterious erection of the phallus broke it apart, symbolically, into signifier and signified. To recognize desire in language, or to recognize that desire is the authentic language—this is the ultimate goal of Lacan's analysis and therapy. As long as it is only *I* who speak, I am at odds with language. It does not do what I want. It disguises *itself* in relation to me, and it disguises *me* in regard to myself. Only when I speak in such a way that *it*, namely desire itself, speaks from within me, am I no longer subjected to it, no longer its *subiectum*. Then I become one with it, I arrive in it, so to speak. This is what is meant by Lacan's idiosyncratic translation of Freud's "Where id was, there ego shall be" (*Wo Es war, soll Ich werden*), as "*Là où fut ça, il me faut advenir*"—literally, "Where it was, I should arrive."[81] "I" should arrive in desire. "In order to free the subject's speech, we introduce him to the language of his desire, that is, to the *primary language* (*language première*), in which—beyond what he tells us of himself—he is already speaking to us unbeknown to himself, first and foremost, in the symbols of his symptom."[82] And when it has learned to speak this language consciously, it is liberated—is at one with language, because at one with desire. Lacan calls this state of oneness "full speech."[83] The "full" word, for him, is not, for example, a word that could possibly be freed of torturous fullness by means of catharsis; instead it *is* free. It is not the *fulfillment* of desire that makes it free, but our becoming reconciled with it. To accept desire as fate and, like Camus' Sisyphus, to learn to understand it as happiness—this is where I should "arrive."

With this, the phallus is alpha and omega in the precise theological sense of these words. When we desire, we ultimately desire *it*—for it is the ultimately desirable thing. It is omega. But at the same time, it is the thing within us that desires, for it is the originator of all desiring. It is alpha. When desire speaks in us, it is ultimately the phallus. It is present in our desiring as the perfect thing that we lack—and that desires our lack. It excites us to enjoy, and simultaneously turns all our enjoyment into a lack, so that we can only enjoy what we do not have—what is absent, unreachable, nonexistent, dead. The embodiment of the dead, however, is the murdered father. There is nothing more real than he, and nothing is more desirable. Desire, in orienting itself toward him, shows itself to be "a desperate affirmation of life that is the purest form we can find of the death drive."[84] Thus ultimately even the Freudian death drive is "salvaged"—admittedly with the help of a construction that is in complete opposition to Freud. Desire is the death drive; life and death drives collapse into one.

That the phallus as such, very much in the manner of a genuine Platonic archetype, constantly generates copies of itself, so the newborn self-evidently can see nothing but a phallus in the mother's nipple and has a castration experience when it is taken away; that the mother initially greets the baby that emerges from her womb as a phallus and suffers for the rest of her life from the disappointment that it isn't one; and that, finally, in coitus the woman becomes a phallus for the man and he desires, in her, the unattainable "other," while she misunderstands herself to be this other, and as a result the two constantly copulate past each other—these are all consequences of a phallo-theology whose paranoid characteristics, after all, may attract notice. This is scarcely an option for the adepts of this theory. Their worldview is a closed one; even psychoanalysts are not immune to the need for a closed worldview. Lacan was much more skilled, when it came to satisfying it, than Freud. That the erection of the phallus is no less mysterious than the virgin birth turned out to be only an advantage, especially considering the fact that Lacan did not just lecture dryly about his theory, but understood how to transform its mysteries into theater. The constant scholarly or polemical digressions from his own thoughts, before they have even been developed, their constant complication by means of insertions and accretions, the sparing use of explanations, the breathlessness and mercurial leaps that make it difficult to cite a single passage in a coherent way—all this is as different from Freud's style of speaking and writing as night and day, but is on a par with professional theater. Lacan was able to provide a rhetorical form that was congenial to the central content of his theory—the inaccessibility of the phallus. Particularly in the oral context of his year-long "seminars," this had an unbeatable impact and ensured the constant curiosity of participants about something that, in each session, rose up before them anew and never ceased to deny itself to them.

A closed worldview can nevertheless contain a wealth of insights, and if Lacan's work were without charm and intelligence it would not be worth talking about. But we may comfortably let go of the hope that his linguistic turn could lead us to the primary process of language. The opposite is closer to the truth. That even language went through a primary process is something that does not even enter his field of vision. Instead, the primary process of dream creation is transposed into the terminology of an ahistorical, structuralist model of language, in which it tends toward dissolution. Energetic processes dissolve into semiotic ones, neural results into signifieds, drive-related tensions into a symbolically extended and eternalized desire. The occasional claim that language is "not immaterial," but a "subtle body,"[85] is only the other side of this coin, the permission to say "language" for "body" and to ignore the fact that language, while it may always *have* a body, *is* spirit or intellect. Even if this spirit consists in nothing other than the reflexive turning of energetic forces against themselves, it remains the self-overcoming, even the self-transcendence of the merely corporeal—something that the Lacanian concept of language precisely covers up. Freud, in contrast, helped to discover it. The two key concepts of his *Interpretation of Dreams*, condensation and displacement, which go much deeper than metaphor and metonymy, opened the sluice gates of prehistory and enabled us to read what in Freud is called dreamwork as the cipher for something much more fundamental: the origin of culture, the emergence of humanity.

THE TALKING CURE

The emergence of humanity has two sides, an imaginative (primarily visual) one and a sonic one. Freud's *Interpretation of Dreams* emphasized the first, for good reason. "Primitive thought activity" is first of all hallucinatory activity. Nevertheless, it depends on the word. It is not just that dreams, if they are to be retained, interpreted, and managed, require verbal communication. Freud's own path to the interpretation of dreams also began with verbal interpretation. A word is "a complex image that proves to be composed of acoustic, visual, and kinesthetic elements," he writes in 1891, in his early study of aphasia.[86] In its time, this was pathbreaking, insofar as it did not make physical brain damage alone responsible for the pathological inability to speak, or speak correctly. Instead, it showed that extreme fatigue or excitement can also lead to malfunctions, abridgments, and verbal mistakes and confusion. The language center of the brain must not only be organically unharmed if it is to be capable of forming words; it must also associate its neurons in such a way that the complex structures "of acoustic, visual, and kinesthetic elements" that we call words actually come into existence. This associative accomplishment is not the function of individual organs. It is a synthetic achievement of the whole, in which the various regions of the brain come together to form the "concrete field of association that is language."[87] It is this achievement that the young neurologist Freud claims as being genuinely "psychical." If it fails or is weakened, paralyzed, or blocked, "psychically" conditioned aphasias can occur. These are states in which a tormenting excess of stimuli finds no means of discharge, not even the way to the word, and the entire organism experiences a diffuse, urgent suffering for which no organic defects are responsible.

If we wanted to reduce Freud's life's work to a formula, we could say, "to overcome aphasia." Latin *infans* literally means "without language," and usually stands for "young child." That Freud found early childhood so interesting has to do with the fact that he himself experienced it with enormous intensity as *infantia*—the time of life when impressions are so exceptionally urgent and formative because there are no words that could temper them.[88] And thus, via the detour of an experimental phase during which he frequently hypnotized his patients, Freud gradually arrived at the talking cure. The decisive breakthrough in this direction was his insight that the diffuse pressure of suffering that, in particular, plagued the genteel ladies who suffered from hysteria at the close of the nineteenth century, was experienced as so unbearable because it was elusive and unbounded, so that it was possible to understand the hysterical neuralgias, spasms, paralyses, and so on, as attempts, through concrete pain, to give a graspable, limited form to the diffuse source of the torment. To discover in localized bodily pain an emergency exit and an image of ungraspable suffering was the first step on the way to the talking cure— and at the same time a *mémoire involontaire* of human imagination's anarchic, primary achievement—making the ungraspable graspable. The second step was to give the bodily image of pain, or, as Freud has it, "memory symbol"—itself already an initial but completely inadequate emergency exit—a second emergency exit: the word, with which it could express itself in the most literal sense and thus make itself disappear, the way one of Freud's hysterical patients did. As she was reporting a deeply hurtful remark of her husband's, "she then suddenly grasped her cheek, crying aloud with pain, and said, 'That was like a slap in the face.' With this, both the attack and the pain came to an end."[89]

This too is an exemplary *mémoire involontaire*. To cry out in pain, to cry it out as a way of getting rid of it—this is the archaic, elementary achievement of the word. The psychoanalytic talking cure starts there. It is procedural memory in a dual sense. For one thing, it is a revival of that stage in the patient's life history when she was a traumatized *infans*, the stage she now, under therapeutic guidance, is meant to experience again so as find words that do not merely sit externally atop her suffering but are internally so replete with it that they are able to express it in the full sense of the word, in other words, to drive it out. But at the same time the talking cure is also a species memory. It always also touches the point when humanity as a whole was still entirely *infans* and was slowly beginning to stammer. Its particular way of churning up a patient's interior stirs up the primal history of the word more than any other manner of speaking. In it, the most primitive forms of this history come back to life as an underground that has never quite been put to rest, and it turns out that the talking cure owes its identity to the fact that humanity's primal words were, themselves, already a talking cure. It walks in their footsteps.

One thing is missing from this picture. Only because the first, archaic talking cure did not have the desired effect does human language exist. When words emerged, they were filled with painful excitation and were accompanied by a wish to be cried out and thus to disappear again. But there was always more pain left over than could be cried out. Instead of disappearing, words became solidified. Without ceasing to serve as an escape valve for stimuli, words became their refuge—names. The name was intended to sanctify fright, in other words, to turn it into a protective power, but there was much more fright left over than it was able to transform. It was intended to lend integrity to the thing it named, but there was always much less integrity created than was conjured up. So the name was provided with attachments, which became independent, turned against it, reduced it to the profane constituent of a sentence, and pushed its sanctifying, conjuring impulse down into the underground of language, where it continues to lead a repressed existence as language's subcutaneous site of excitement and unease. In this way, the word attempted to cure itself of itself, just like hallucination, which had begun as a mental means of healing traumatic stimuli but was itself unbearable, required additional healing mechanisms, and drove the world of mental images out of itself. At this, hallucination was reduced to a mental underground that since then, as a source of impulses and a general troublemaker, has not ceased to lash out persistently at the world of the imagination. This attempt at self-healing is what, above, was dubbed "primal repression."[90] Its imaginative and its linguistic sides are inseparable. Only together do they constitute our mental space.

It is fantastic how Hesiod sensed this. His *Theogony*, which celebrates the victorious struggle of the young gods against the older ones, is not only the mythological echo of clan feuds and generational conflicts in the Mediterranean region; it also simultaneously describes the course of primal repression. From the turning of words against themselves, sentences emerged; by the turning of hallucination against itself, representation was created. Representation and the sentence are children who turn against their parents, making them into subjects and only then into the orderly world of thought and speech—the same way Zeus turned against his father, Cronos, castrated him, and in the struggle against him and his allies generated the world order as we know it. Zeus himself is a Titan, as well as the force that rebels against the Titans and forces them down into the underworld, indeed turns them into the underground of his new, Olympic order. One of the characteristics of the new order is that it can never come to rest, because the forces that were overthrown never stop rumbling and, as it were, fomenting a counterrevolution against the "palace revolution" that representation and the sentence once carried out against hallucination and the word.[91]

The orderly world of the imagination and of speech are the result of the attempts at self-healing carried out by hallucination and the word. On one hand, these attempts were a major failure, for neither was able to save or to cure anywhere nearly as much as it desired. On the other hand, they are a grandiose success—for they went far beyond the horror of the hallucinated "genius" and the fright-laden demonstrative. Admittedly, they were able to do this only with the help of a repressive process that we should by no means imagine as mute or psychologically inward. It was a hair-raising social drama, of which Hesiod's description of the battle of the Titans provides a notable echo. "Horrific, the endless ocean resounded. The wide earth roared. The broad heavens groaned, quaking, high Olympus was shattered from the ground up."[92]

Whether primal repression was much less horrific that what it suppressed, we don't know. Nevertheless, it is one of the signal achievements of the Early Stone Age, if not its greatest accomplishment. We owe it one of the most precious things we possess—ordered imagination and speech. When Aristotle defines human beings as *zoon logon echon*,[93] that is, as the "animal that has words," indeed words in the sense of ordered, reasonable speech, we must add: He has these words because he has repression, and repression is the primal form of human self-referentiality—reflection. Repression, first of all, was an epochal achievement of emancipation. Without it, no one could construct consistent mental representations or reasonable sentences. The repression that psychoanalysis sets its sights on is a comparatively late special case. There, the barrier between unconscious mental underground and conscious surface sphere, between the underground of the name and spoken language—a barrier that itself, after all, is a product of repression—has long since been erected. A relatively high cultural level has been attained, where intensely felt, traumatically unfulfilled wishes are suppressed by the above-mentioned barrier because they contradict customs that have been sedimented in collective rituals, images, and ways of speaking. In the attempt to rid the organism of these feelings, instead of working through them, the other side of repression makes itself felt—its paralyzing side, which torturously returns cultivated human beings to the *infans* stage and prevents their stored-up excitation from breaking out in liberating words.

This is the launching point of the psychoanalytic talking cure. It is a revival of the archaic talking cure, the catharsis of primal words. Because the archaic talking cure did not succeed as its practitioners may have wished, it became not only the prime mover of human speech but also its unfulfilled promise. Nowhere is this promise more thoroughly recalled than in psychoanalysis. In actualizing the archaic talking cure at a high cultural level, it is practical language philosophy—a much better one than the adoption of a structuralist concept of language can ever produce. The talking cure is an active recollection of its own archaic origin, an act of reflection lacking which all philosophy of language only taps blindly at the surface of its object. But this origin also incurs a big debt. The psychoanalytic talking cure cannot take the original promise of the word seriously without attempting to fulfill it. To do this, it has no other means at its disposal than the very same one that led to the failure of the archaic talking cure—understandably ordered speech. The latter may be able to breathe new life into the cathartic primal function of the word, but it cannot fulfill the primal promise it contained—that the tormenting excitation could be gotten rid of by means of words. In this regard, the second, psychoanalytic talking cure shares the fate of the first one. It always lags far behind its intention of healing with words. That is why its success in healing is so controversial—and rightly so. It is true that the right word at the right moment can be a virtual balm. Yet words are never sufficiently healing. Only a supernatural, divine word could close all wounds.

Every responsible talking cure must therefore be accompanied by the awareness that it is *not* the thing itself, but actually only a symbol; and that even where it can show very respectable success, it only stands for something that in any case can never be created by words alone, and that could at best be simulated by collective action—namely the pain- and deprivation-free overall state for which the Old Testament found an unsurpassed metaphor: the "land flowing with milk and honey."[94] When psychoanalysis, in this promised land that Israel puts in the mouth of its god Yahweh, recognizes the primal promise of the word, which psycho-analysis carries forward as its own most intimate act, then it is recalling its Jewish roots much more thoroughly than when it recalls that its founder was a Jew. Besides this, a talking cure that sees itself as a symbol is relieved of the pressure to be the only true cure for the soul. The working alliance it fosters between therapist and patient can be broadened into a working alliance among various methods—not indiscriminately, but in such a way that the original meaning of *methodos* shines through, namely "access." The best access, the most appropriate method, always emerges from the perspective of the thing that is to be investigated. Differing individual and social pathologies demand different methods. It is quite possible to imagine well-organized settings in which the talking cure would no longer be seen as being in strict contradiction with art, music, or Gestalt therapy, or even the occasional use of hypnosis—but above all not with the incorporation of social-critical discourses and movements—settings that, at the same time, are likely to avoid the misunderstanding that it would be enough to do away with repressive barriers for society to become free.

As surely as there is false repression—repression is not, in itself, necessarily false. Anyone who sets out to tear down the barriers that primal repression has erected between hallucination and representation, naming magic and the sentence, is proceeding to tear down mental space and language itself, for they live from this repression. Without them, there is neither reflection on the cathartic primal function of the word, nor the escape valve of ordered speech, which no cultivated catharsis will never be able to do without. Certainly, in the "land [of] milk and honey" we would no longer need repression. But until then, primal repression is our warranty that we will not forget the prophecy of that promised land. This warranty is absolutely worth keeping—but the fact that it is necessary to emphasize this shows that it is no longer held to be obviously so. Primal repression is no longer the peaceful foundation of human thought. It has come within reach of mental archaeology, social technology, and bio-power. The barrier that separated mental space into an "Olympic" upper realm and a "Titanic" underground is once again at risk. It falls when the "Titans" storm Olympus with the help of advanced technological weapons. But it also falls when "Olympus" sucks the underworld up into itself, the way Freud, toward the end of his life, imagined it when he demanded, "Where id was, there ego shall be" (*Wo Es war, soll Ich werden*).[95] Both outcomes are equally opposed to the logic of reasonable catharsis. The latter demands neither the unleashing of the id nor the final victory of the ego, but rather, as the young Freud so beautifully put it, that "the pain [should be] spoken away."[96] But in order to be able to speak it away, what is needed is to make the barrier of primal repression as soft and sustainable as possible; to provide it with plenty of pores that allow a return to the unfulfilled cathartic primal function of the word, and to transform it into a kind of semipermeable membrane that is suffused with reflection, can breathe freely, and, between excitation and the word, permits that reconciliatory exchange to occur that in theology is called *communicatio idiomatium*—the "reciprocal exchange of characteristics."

AFTERWORD: HIGH-TECH DREAMTIME

THIS BOOK ASKS THE QUESTION of origins. But it would be a profound mistake to read it as only a new version of the old philosophy of origins, like Aristotle's unmoved mover, Rousseau's nature, or Bloch's hope—as a philosophy that takes traumatic repetition compulsion as the *principium* that defines the world's meaning and determines its course. To understand traumatic repetition compulsion as a *principle* is to fail to grasp what it *is*, namely a form of reaction—initially a mere reflex, a particular kind of stimulus flight untainted by any higher, much less cultural intent. Only after the fact, when the stimulus flight had gone over into the flesh and blood of a number of hominid species, including at least Neanderthals and *Homo sapiens*, did it prove, with all its shortcomings, to be the high road to culture. But culture was never its goal. "Everywhere we seek the absolute, and always we find only things," wrote Novalis.[1] This is more or less the way things went with human evolution. What early humans sought was salvation, what they found was culture. It was not Auschwitz that "demonstrated irrevocably that culture has failed."[2] Culture's emergence in the Early Stone Age was already the failure of something other than culture itself.[3]

Traumatic repetition compulsion is the phylogenetic needle's eye of culture. It has no alternatives, but at the same time it is not a principle, if only because it is profoundly at odds with itself. Its flight from traumatic shock is always also a flight from itself. It wants to cease; so it constantly repeats the thing it fears. In this sense, it is the human drive par excellence and demonstrates in an exemplary way what drives want, namely to be satisfied so they will go away. In their headlong movement, however, they do something very clever: they negate their fright by affirming it, so that the negation is affirmation and the affirmation negation. Thus, it fulfills in an exemplary way Hegel's definition of dialectics as the "unity of unity and difference, or the identity of identity and non-identity." If there is an original dialectician, it is neither Hegel's absolute spirit nor Engels's dialectical nature—it is traumatic repetition compulsion. Much more reliably than Hegel, traumatic repetition compulsion shows us where dialectics comes from, namely not from a pure "being . . . without any further distinctions,"[4] but from nameless need. Dialectics does not obey eternal laws of nature; it is driven by the urge to come to rest, to be dissolved— not into pure spirit but into a pleasure that is free of all wishing.

To claim that all the rituals, customs, laws, grammars, and institutions formed by human culture are the result of traumatic repetition compulsion is not to fall into the trap of a monocausal explanation. For the effects of traumatic repetition compulsion derive in equal measure from its impact and its tendency to cease. It comes to rest somewhere in between, but where it will end can only be ascertained after the fact. In the individual instance, it is never possible to predict whether negation through affirmation will wind up stubbornly circling around itself, with no means of escape, or will enact its own gradual deconstruction. And the fact that culture has actually endured successfully only following a considerable breaking down of compulsive repetition must not let us forget the enormous sacrifices that this process has cost—not only the sacrifice of the actual ritual victims but also the innumerable individual nervous collapses that traumatic repetition compulsion had to work its way through, so to speak, over long periods of time, during which it gradually became tempered to form the rites, customs, and conventions that undergird human communities. Its tempering is nothing other than its profanation. Just as the name was absorbed into the sentence and became profane, so traumatic repetition compulsion was absorbed into culture. There, it lives on as a restless remainder, a pathological leftover from prehistory, in a context that may consist of its precipitates but that has managed to overcome itself by transforming its outcomes into valued achievements—an ensemble of uplifting rituals, familiar habits, and routine processes. Every culture needs them. They are the foundation of every form of individual development.

Until the beginning of the modern era, repetition was a synonym for a tendency toward de-escalation and calming down. Then a ground-breaking discovery was made—automatic machinery. Since there have been humans, there have been tools. But "auto-mobiles," tools that as if of their own volition make the same movements over and over again, have existed only since the dawn of the modern era. Their prototypes, machines driven by steam, gasoline, and ultimately electricity, took over movements that had previously been performed by humans. This can be a marvelous relief. We no longer walk but travel by train or car; we no longer saw, plane, and grind but have a machine do it for us. But even during the first industrial revolution, which began in England in the nineteenth century, the demoralizing impact of machines outweighed their positive impact. Their human accessory, the proletariat, was literally used up in a workday that lasted twelve to fourteen hours and that consisted of nothing but stupefying service to and waiting on the machines. This continued until the proletariat battled for and won conditions that made this existence endurable. Steam engines made life easier mainly for the capitalists who owned them and forced others to work at them. The unequal division of the impact of machinery—making life easier or more burdensome—is the capitalist birthmark of the industrial age. It changes, but it never goes away.

As machines took over processes of human motion, repetition encountered something qualitatively new: it became removed from the human organism and hence objectified. Mechanical movements can be made repeatable significantly more successfully than human ones, notably by means of programming. The quality of a mechanical program consists in its capacity to repeat itself over and over again with utter reliability. Thus, machines bring with them a new, quasi-superhuman capacity for repetition. What machines do they generally do far faster and with much greater precision and persistence than human beings, even though there must always still be human beings there who do something to them. This means that all the repetitions humans transfer to machines have a reciprocal impact on humans. Medieval crafts were already well acquainted with routinized, constantly repeated sequences of movements.

They even provided a sort of model for the construction of machines, since the schemas for mechanical functioning were based on these movements. But then came the backlash. Factory workers were forced to accommodate the motions of their organism to the automatic movements of the machines. No machine, even the most sophisticated one, can be operated unless the people who deal with it adapt themselves to its program and the sequence of its movements. But "assimilation of one ego to another one"[5] is Freud's standard formula for identification. Indeed, human beings are not capable of steering or operating machines (and only if you operate one can you also steer it) without identifying with them to a certain extent. Identification, however, is always oriented toward a higher authority, which has or can do something we ourselves lack. And machines can always do something that the person who operates them cannot do. The feeling of superiority that their efficient use gives us is the feeling of participating in their superiority. It is only the reverse side of the feeling that *they* are the superior ones, in other words of a feeling of inferiority toward them. Günther Anders called it "Promethean shame." He says that we humans—as Prometheus, as makers of the world of machinery—have gotten ourselves into the embarrassing situation of feeling permanently inferior to what we have made, of feeling ashamed in front of it.[6] Shame is a feeling we would rather not have and that we therefore like to suppress or distract attention from. This requires effort, however, and this effort is the subcutaneous, sublime, hard-to-put-your-finger-on stress that underlies our human relationship to the mechanical world—the price of the greater ease that the machines offer.

The steam engine adopted processes of movement. The image-making machines adopted processes of perception. The camera makes images appear on chemically prepared surfaces or electronic screens, in a way that is similar to the way the eye makes them appear on the retina. The camera preserves the images exactly as they impress themselves on it, in a process that we can literally think of as imagination (*Einbildung*).[7] Then the camera also makes these images available to untold numbers of people. What progress! While we humans have to work our way laboriously from diffuse impressions to distinct perception, from perception to imagination, and, what is more, are only able to convey what we imagine to others indirectly, by means of gestures and words, the technical imagination of the camera does all this simultaneously and immediately. It is understandable that identification with this marvel made the "assimila-tion of one ego to another one" more intensive than when people were dealing with the steam engine. Soon, the technologically produced images also began to move, and the audience sat as if spellbound watching the first short films, although they showed only such mundane events as workers leaving their factory at the end of the day, or a train arriving at a station. The fascinating thing was that an apparatus managed to imagine these events, to store them, and to make them publicly visible as often as was desired.

At first, this capacity gave the fantasy of the cinematic pioneers and their public one jolt after another. New means of expression and percep-tion opened up; images seemed to acquire hitherto unsuspected force. "Soviet cinema must hit people over the head," said Sergei Eisenstein. It must feel "like a tractor that plows over the psyche of the viewer in the sense of the desirable class perspective."[8] Walter Benjamin saw in cinema the promise of the "heightened presence of mind"[9] that the proletariat urgently required for the overthrow of capitalist society. The nearly messi-anic expectations that the new medium awakened echoed even in Claude Lévy-Strauss, when he wrote "of the excitement into which I was plunged by the newest painting by Picasso, the latest work by Stravinsky, or the films that I went to see, when I was still in secondary school, with posi-tively religious fervor, every Saturday afternoon, in a little dark hall in the Latin Quarter or Montmartre."[10]

There was one thing that the hopeful proponents of the new medium overlooked. It was the extent to which their own imaginations still belonged to the "world of yesterday," and were still formed by traditional, relatively contemplative media and spectacles. Depending on their social position and predilections, these included letters, newspapers, books, popular festivals, concerts, plays, and the like. The movie-goers brought this imagination with them into the cinema as if it were a secure mental property that could only grow broader in the force field of the films, without suffering any losses. And they did not notice, at the time, that the early blossoming of cinema was due not only to the charm of its novel images, the intoxicating fantasies of its directors, or the gold-rush atmo-sphere surrounding the new medium, but to the simple fact that at first film showings were rarities—festive evening or weekend events. Between the individual films, there was plenty of time to allow the experience to settle down again. The next filmstrip, talk show, or news program didn't follow right on its heels. It was only when, thanks to their speedy victory, films became inflationary—no longer high points but quite ordinary— that they gradually reached the point at which their mechanical operation could have its full impact on the individuals it touched.

The ideal members of the cinematic audience are anachronistic, old-fashioned viewers, people who are still able to recount the plot of a film they have just seen, to reflect on it, discuss it, possibly critique it—in short, people who follow it with a certain amount of stamina and who embrace it with behaviors that they have learned from childhood crafts and games of skill, from looking at and making art, and from reading and writing texts— not from the cinema. Film's principle, as Benjamin clearly saw, is "constant, sudden change" of places and focus, "which periodically assail the spectator . . . The spectator's process of association in view of these images is indeed interrupted by their constant, sudden change. This constitutes the shock effect of the film, which, like all shocks, should be cushioned by heightened presence of mind."[11] Benjamin, admittedly, thought that the intensification of the present on which he placed such great hopes for revolutionizing capitalist society was a gift of film itself, a kind of automatic dowry it brought with it. The opposite is the case. Only a presence of mind that has been practiced outside film is capable of being heightened during the watching of a film, and that only to some extent. When films have become so ordinary that they fill up most of our free time, then it is all over with the "cushioning" of its shocks by heightened mental awareness. Looking back, we can see that this cushioning, basically, was already imagined as a movement of resistance, a sort of sensory judo move that accepts the opponent's attack in such a way as to transform it into a force of one's own, and that overwhelms him. To want to absorb the daily television program by means of heightened mental awareness is more like wanting to throw a company of sharpshooters on its back using judo.

It is true that the shock effect is lessened when screen images have become an everyday background, but the shocklike "changes of place and focus which periodically assail the spectator" by no means stop as a result. They become ever present. Every cut continues to have the effect of an optical jolt, which says, "Look!" "Watch out!" to the observer while dispensing a new little injection of attention, a tiny bit of adrenaline—and in doing so breaks down his attention precisely by constantly stimulating it. The shock of the image exercises psychological power. The eye is magnetically attracted by the abrupt change in light and can only be pulled away from it by a big effort of the will. The shock of the image exudes an aesthetic fascination; it is always promising new, still-unseen images. It habituates us to the ubiquity of the market, its "Look over here!" praises the next scene like a fishmonger hawking her wares. And since the screen has become a part of the computer, as well as television, and no longer fills only our leisure time but often our entire working life as well, the shock of the image and the tasks of the workday collapse into each other. The facts that I can call up so abruptly call on me to work on them equally abruptly—or to worry about being fired.

With all of this, the shock of the image has become the focus of a global regime of attention that dulls human attention by constantly overwhelming it. It has been a long time since the people who make television programs could count on viewers watching a longer program from beginning to end. They assume from the outset that at the least reduction of tension the viewer will change the channel, and are happy when they can at least get him to stick around for the highlights of a program that they have announced in spectacular previews. For *this* viewer, the regime of attention imposed by the shock of images is congenial. The same cannot be said of the film critic, whose profession it is to rework the impressions made by the cinema, television, or computer screen; who writes articles and books about them and literally limps after them. It is true that the resulting written work increasingly participates in the new regime of attention. A print product that wants to attract attention has to impose itself with jolts that resemble those in a film. We only need to compare the front pages of today's leading daily newspapers with those of twenty years ago; in comparison, our current newspapers look like illustrated magazines. They can scarcely do without big color photographs. Newspapers are becoming more and more "appealing," that is, they have less text and more pictures, and book design is moving in the same direction. Even academics' eyes are more and more in need of a clever layout to guide them. Increasingly, they want to have a graphic image here, a little photo there, if they are even to manage to decode the signs. Among the unspoken assumptions of all print design is that there is hardly anyone who still possesses the concentration and stick-to-itiveness to study a text from the first line through to the last.

These are all manifest symptoms of attention deficit. So-called "attention deficit disorder" (ADD) or "attention deficit hyperactivity disorder" (ADHD) is only a crass special case. Here we are dealing with children who do not succeed in concentrating on anything, dwelling on anything, developing a friendship, finishing a game that involves others—children who start all kinds of things but can't finish anything. They are driven by constant motor agitation that finds no escape valve or place of rest and that makes them a disruptive presence at school, in the family, and in youth groups. To calm them down, there is, however, one very effective method. "When you take children who cannot sit still for a second, who swivel their eyes from right to left, searching and avoiding, and you put them in front of a computer, their gaze becomes clear and fixes on things, their activities are goal-directed and patient," writes child analyst Wolfgang Bergmann. "In any case, it is more than striking how well hyperactive children and adolescents, who seem lost in the real world, are able to orient themselves on computers, and how, in computer games and online contacts, they move with a sureness they do not possess in the so-called 'first reality,' of their everyday lives." And why does the machine feel instantly familiar to them? "Only a few hand motions are enough to bring a desired object close enough to use, or to call up a communication partner for the exchange of some fantasy, some contacts or other—everything is ready, seemingly at our beck and call." And yet: "Everything is aimed at a person's own *immediate satisfaction*. As soon as it has been achieved, the representation of the longed-for thing disappears, whether it be an object, an action, or contact with others. With a tap of the finger, a click on the keyboard, they are removed . . . as if they had never existed."[12]

Here, again, "Gone!" and "There!" is being played, very much the way Freud's grandson played it, but in reverse: "There!" and "Gone!" Whereas little Heinerle threw out the spool in order to be able to say hello to it again, thus practicing bringing back something that was absent, for the hyper child everything that is gone is simply no longer there—it is over and done with. He hasn't yet reached the Heinerle phase. He has never profoundly experienced something absent that he can still name and hold mentally present, even though it is physically "gone." Thus, the playmate he has just been looking for is forgotten as soon as he has had to go home; the promises they have just made, in tears, to follow a particular set of rules in the future, vanish the minute he leaves the room, like the big fight they had earlier, or the soccer game they won yesterday. Nothing settles down, nothing endures; wishes don't combine into a stable will; successes don't produce self-confidence.

Naturally, the attention deficit of these children is initially the one that they themselves have *experienced*. The attention that they are incapable of paying has previously been withheld from them. So is a lack of parental care likely responsible for ADHD, after all—not "television"? Empirical studies that start with questions like this never produce intelligent results, even with the utmost expenditure of methodological effort, because they have no concept of what a *regime* of attention is—namely not an apparatus, but a force field that affects the whole of society, children first of all. What small children have are superfine antennae for relations of attention. And once they have already spent their entire life as newborns in front of a televised backdrop, they have good chances of making the early, traumatic experience of how the attention of the people they are closest to is divided between them and this backdrop. They can feel how, against the backdrop's permanent claims on attention, interpersonal warmth and affection become flat and unreal. Empirical research has a hard time grappling with traumatic denial of attention when it occurs in early childhood in such an unspectacular way. There are no obvious shocks, no significant periods of parental absence—and yet there must have been a vital denial. Otherwise there would not be this continuous motor agitation, the constant search for something that has not yet even taken the form of a lost object. Only afterward, when the affected individuals fly to the visual media like a collective swarm of moths to the flame, can we recognize where their agitation comes from. Long before they could perceive visual media as objects, or the television screen or computer monitor as a thing, they experienced the attention-absorbing power of their flickering: as withdrawal. This withdrawal demands repetition in order to be mastered. It tries to satisfy its desire in the place where it originated. And, thus, the hyper children seek calm and purchase from the very machines that they have experienced in diffuse ways, still preobjectively, in a quasi-ghostly but nevertheless formative way as the origins of their agitation and preventers of their inner stability. This is the logic of trauma: "I feel drawn to the very thing that terrifies me." This is the logic that led humanity to the first, diffuse, still spectral imagination of the "genius," the first sacralization of fright. In the behavior of the hyper children it celebrates its high-tech resurrection.

That such children should have relationship problems only with computerized devices, but not with their mother and father, is by no means true as a result. On the contrary, they suffer from the fact that, in the force field of new relations of attention, the primary human relationships no longer acquire contours firm enough to offer an elementary measure of stability and orientation. New " 'maladies of the soul,' " writes Julia Kristeva, have "a common denominator—the inability to represent. Whether it takes the form of psychic mutism or adopts various signs experienced as 'empty' or 'artificial,' such a deficiency of psychic representation hinders sensory, sexual, and intellectual life. Moreover, it may strike a blow to biological functioning itself."[13] These unrepresentative, fluctuating forms of suffering, which scarcely, anymore, assume the concrete form of palpable pathologies, have represented a significant trend only since the new regime of attention developed significant contours. To deny that there is a meaningful link between the two is like denying that infection and fever have something to do with each other.

This is not to say that narrow causal explanations are warranted, for example those claiming that "children who spend a certain number of hours in front of the TV every day get ADHD"—something that depending on social status, gender, and individual mental resilience can either be confirmed nor denied. Explanations of the medical variety, which immediately think they have found the actual cause of the problem in the neuronal abnormalities that occasionally appear in ADHD children, are equally unjustified. It is quite obvious that the diffuse phenomenon that goes by the name of ADHD—the term is more of a stopgap than a clear pathological diagnosis—cannot possibly be appropriately conceptualized other than from the perspective of a comprehensive theory of culture. ADHD is not simply an illness that crops up in a healthy environment. The opposite is true: Only where there is already an attention deficit is there ADHD. And it is truly no exaggeration to describe the "concentrated distraction"[14] that with its billions of tiny shocks focuses human attention precisely on something that breaks it down, as attention deficit. It is possible to defend ourselves against the effect of this situation; in the immediate future it will not be possible to prevent it. But if you can count to three you can also figure out that what currently goes by the name of ADHD—in Germany approximately every sixth child is affected, according to a conservative estimate—is just an overture, a beginning, a tuning up, announcement, and anticipation of the main themes, just as in music.

At the same time, it is also important to see the high-tech regime of attention from an overall cultural perspective if we want to comprehend what an epochal caesura it represents in the history of human repetition. With machines' takeover of identical human series of repetitive motions and the reverse impact of this takeover on humans, a process was initiated that we could call the turn of mechanical repetitiveness against its creator, organic repetition. With the invention of imaging technology, this recursion entered a new phase. Now the process affected not only external muscular processes of motion but also the inner sensory process that had been laid down in a network of stimulus flight paths. Laying down these paths took *Homo sapiens* the greater part of its early life, during which hominids had to mobilize unprecedented powers of condensation, displacement, and reversal in an infinite number of repeated efforts, in order to transform traumatic fright into an inner presence; to moderate its diffuse image by means of many additional images; to limit, contour, and synthesize it; and thus ultimately to unfold it into an inner world of imagination. And then came the miracle of technical imagination, which not only took care of all this in an astonishingly simple way, with a tap of the finger, but was also able to turn the images that were produced in the interior outward in such a way that they also attracted external attention and were no longer, like human beings' inner images, forced to live a blurred, pale existence imprisoned in interior mental space.

The identification of human beings' faint imagination with the powerful technical one, and the reverse impact of the technical imagination on the human one, proclaimed the triumphant victory of technical imagination. But with this, at the same time, a new kind of repetition compulsion has befallen humankind. Imaging technology, always accompanied by sound and occasionally by haptic or olfactory trimmings, the better to suggest comprehensive experience, runs twenty-four hours a day, constantly beaming out its attention-demanding impulses, but it no longer reiterates the repetitive processes that become sedimented in the form of rituals and habits. That complicated designs have to be invented in order to lift regularly broadcast shows, such as news and TV series, above the amorphous mass of programming, shows precisely that the dynamics of machine repetition is moving in the opposite direction. It is de-ritualizing, de-sedimenting. This is because it has no need of ritualization and sedimentation—in complete contrast to Paleolithic humans, who were still in the process of becoming and needed nothing more than this. The traumatic excitation that once drove them to create culture and repetitious rituals, the wish to rid themselves of these stimuli and find rest—all of this is alien to technical repetition compulsion, which simply runs on automatically. There is no pain, no fatigue, no wish, no goal. And the enormous force of its needlessness and self-satisfaction instantiates nothing less than the reversal of the human logic of repetition. Until the modern era, that logic was aimed at de-escalation, sedimentation, calming down. With the turn of the technical imagination against the human one, a repetition has begun that is traveling backward down the history of repetition. Its de-ritualizing, de-sedimenting effect begins to stir up the mental ground of culture, which had been forming gradually ever since the Early Stone Age. "Mental archaeology" is more than just a metaphor.

To borrow the language of Hesiod's *Theogony*, Zeus, the Titan who opposed the Titans in a world-changing struggle and erected the world order by forcing them down into the underworld, brought forth a power that emerged from his head wholly complete and fully armed. Now this child of his mind is turning against his world order the same way he turned against the Titans. Except that the new power is not in a position to bring forth a higher order; it merely decomposes the existing order, erodes the barrier between the underworld and the terrestrial one, and damages the achievement of primal repression by means of which hallucination once mastered itself, broke apart into a fermenting underground and a light, pale world of ideation, and thus, for the very first time, made mental space what it has been until today.

For hard-boiled empiricists, there is, of course, no mental space, because they can't touch, see, hear, or quantify it, but always only its expression. Talk about mental space is therefore, in a certain sense, speculative. We can only deduce it. But a science that doesn't do this never gets past registering things, without any concepts. It will never get to the primary processes that make it possible for human beings to represent, imagine, think, and speak. Primary processes are certainly not perceptible and palpable—including what is being said about them here, namely that their existence is threatened by the regime of mechanical repetition. No plan of empirical research can prove this. But the conclusion is nevertheless hard to avoid if we look again, more closely, at the triumph of the technical imagination.

It can do something human beings can't—namely turn what it has imagined toward the outside. With this, however, it not only uses its superior mechanical means to take over the work that human nerves do when we imagine things, it also takes over the focal point that was also the point of origin of this labor. In the Bible it is called "here-now" (*shamah*), in Aristotle "this there" (*tode ti*). Its archaic form is the sudden fright encountered in nature, and it has been sufficiently demonstrated, in the course of this book, that it is only as a result of the traumatic power of this shock, and the necessity of working it off through innumerable repetitions, that the merger of condensation, displacement, and reversal was able to take place at all. This merger created first rituals and then the mental space of human imagination. And now, after nature's terrors have faded away and have been tempered and sedimented in the form of multiple cultural institutions, the technical imagination is singing their chorus. Its unceasing image shocks turn it, itself, into a "here-now" or "this-there" machine. Each individual shock is, of course, a completely harmless, scarcely noticeable touch—but it does not stop being a shock. It is a shock that is far from traumatic, but repeated millions and billions of times it has the effect of wearing down. Thus, with its mechanically produced mini-shocks, the mechanical repetition that is performed by the technical imagination has the effect of breaking down *human* imagination, as it was constructed, once upon a time, in response to mega-shocks. Shock versus shock, repetition versus repetition, imagination versus. imagination—this reversal has started a global process of de-sedimentation. After all, the technical imagination is so compelling precisely because its images are genuine, sensual, and presentable. They are direct replicas of the external reality that can be turned outward in an equally direct manner. With this, the technical imagination not only puts to shame its human competitor with its nonpresentable images; it also takes back one of the greatest achievements of human imagination—the distinction between hallucination and representation. Mental images only turned properly pale and abstract after they had thinned out into the sphere of the imagination and forced the site of their hallucinations underground. Only with the use of abstract representation did it become possible to invent a technical imagination that then held the mirror of their own pallor up to these imagined things and finally, with a flood of saturated, full-bodied, aggressive images, posed the question: Who are you, pale beings? Don't you want to capitulate?

Cinematic images, whether documentary or fictional, impress themselves upon the viewer with hallucinatory intensity. Whether we like it or not, we see them through the mechanical eye of the camera, which does not know the difference between hallucination and imagination. When we let our gaze become one with that of the camera, we enter into a technically precise, externally focused dream scenario—a scenario that others have already dreamed for us, so to speak. We don't need to create it ourselves, by condensing, displacing, and reversing latent motifs, and we are able to dream it so effortlessly because we have retained only the outside of the dream—its manifest dream content. There is no question that cinema, thanks to its special similarity to dreams, opened up a new dimension of world experience. Paul Klee's famous definition applies, without reservation, to its great works: "Art does not reproduce the visible; rather, it makes visible."[15] But it exacts a high price. Even in its great works, technical imagination makes no distinction between hallucination and representation—and inevitably contributes to making human imagination, as well, less habituated to making it.

If only it were possible to limit this relapse into indifference to a few restorative hours at the movies. Everyone needs some regressive phases, needs a chance to sink into a relaxed, distracted state in which representation and hallucination playfully intermingle. We need this precisely in order to retain our capacity to deal with reality. The problem is *concentrated* distraction—the regime. In great films, it celebrates its finest hours. In the lowlands of the everyday, imagination's backward journey toward hallucination takes the shape of desolation and misery. The ADHD children bear witness to this. The things they imagine are nothing but outgrowths of whatever they happen to be experiencing or wanting. As they abandon themselves to this here-now, as they sink ever deeper into its increasingly fitful flickers and jerks, they come close to entering into a new kind of daydreaming—but not the contemplative daydreaming where they gradually become lost in thought. Instead, the things they imagine are reduced to images and take on, for a few moments, a hallucinatory vividness. But it is a hectic daydreaming, where states of dream and wakefulness collapse into each other, in such a way that the affected children neither dream intensively anymore nor are able to achieve the structured quality of waking behavior. Where the space of mental representation no longer has any volume worth mentioning, even the space for dreams shrinks. It no longer deepens to create a mental "back office," where the remains of the day, unprocessed by waking consciousness, can be reworked and something can take place that the human nervous system needs as much as sleep: mental homework.

"In every century, humanity has to be kept in after school," Benjamin said.[16] Yet, in the twenty-first century, its capacity for doing homework has decreased significantly, so that—like the hyper children—it is no longer so easy to get humanity to sit at the desk. More rapidly than anticipated, what Benjamin saw so accurately when it came to the miniature format of cinema has come about in a big way: "The spectator's process of associa- tion in view of these images is indeed interrupted by their constant, sudden change."[17] In other words, the images themselves prevent the audience from lingering over them, daydreaming about them, reworking them, staying after school to do its homework on them. But when this prevention is not merely a sporadic, isolated incidence, but becomes systematic and is transformed into a regime of attention, then being contemporary can only mean being *up to date*, being in tune with the latest developments, giving the day's "this there" the attention it demands. Presence of mind, under these circumstances, comes to mean only devoting one's mind to the present—the here and now. And, indeed, the essence of contemporaneity is *updating*[18]—the activity to which all Web site owners are condemned. Today, this is the identity card that counts. By constantly threatening to make us outdated and relentlessly requiring us to be informed about the latest state of affairs, *updating* proves to be the activity that actually creates identity—the high-tech version of the Aristotelian *te ēn einai*.[19]

Updating comes to be perceived as the essence of dealing with reality. Its success consists in reducing reality to newsworthiness, that is, momentary relevance. But precisely in this respect, updating involun- tarily comes close to the type of perception that we find in dreams, which know no measure of time except the present, and which know nothing other than what is occurring in them *right now*. Whenever the current regime of attention is fully in charge, the perceptual world of a film, of manifest dream content without any latent mental "back office," is applied to the perception of all presently relevant facts. Among stock-market professionals, for example, who tensely watch the rise and fall of stock prices on their monitors, this leads to states of waking dream similar to those of children staring at their computer games. Motor agitation, states of constant tension and distraction are the reliable accompaniments of such activities. And it is thus inevitable, among the avant-garde of updating, on the stock exchange and in upper management, that attention deficit disorder and hyperactivity syndromes are no less prevalent than among hyper children–only in a much more comfortable way and at a much higher level. But extremes meet, and what they have in common is the rapid decrease in the capacity to sit and do homework. This is true both literally and metaphorically. Updating, we might say, is de-sedimentation of the mental capacity for stick-to-itiveness.

The de-sedimentation process that is underway presents itself to social critics primarily as the deregulation process of neoliberal capitalism. Its corrosive effect on social and cultural institutions, on authority, family, enterprise, and forms of production could not be dealt with in this book. *The Philosophy of Dreams* had to dig down a layer to find its starting point, namely the effect of this process on mental archaeology. It needed to find the link between the Stone Age and high technology, in order to free up the view of the world-historical turn that de-sedimentation has begun to take. Hegel spoke of the "return to the ground."[20] We are gradually finding out how prophetic this remark was. The return may still be in its early stages, but we can already see that mechanical repetition compulsion, the power of concentrated distraction, not only does not stop at social and cultural institutions of whatever kind, it also does not stop at the mental substratum that this book has shown to be the hallucinatory dregs of all imaginative and linguistic achievements. In Freud, it is called primitive thought activity. We could also call it dream power. Its entire drama needed to be sketched out. After it had been dethroned in the Early Stone Age and was relegated from the essence of mental power to its underground, it is now at risk of dissolution—ironically by its most advanced descendants. The dreamlike, hallucinatory sequences of images that are constantly broadcast by the globally installed image machinery make living dream power look old. *Its* images are comparatively pallid. Their actions seem to lag behind. They are never up to date, but always reworking events after they have already taken place—eternally too late, incomplete, and confused. Dream power against dream power—the technologically outfitted and simulated one against the one that is alive and antiquated—this is the paradoxical constellation in which human beings' capacity to do their homework is beginning to diminish. But a culture that can no longer do its homework puts in doubt mental space itself—the only latitude for "deferred action"[21] that ever opened up in natural history. Without the space for deferred action, there would be no patience, no commitment, no looking forward or preparation for the future. We only begin to gain an appreciation of what an enormous achievement the space for deferred action is at the moment when we can no longer take it for granted because it has fallen under the influence of a global regime of concentrated distraction, and a fusillade of attention-getting sensations is permanently digging into it like innumerable little spades. Only when this process is seen from the perspective of an entire culture do we gain a more acute sense of its tempo. How many millennia were required before the traumatically excited rituals of early humanity became sedimented in the form of well-tempered processes of repetition, and how much of that has started into motion again in just a few decades! Even if the mental-archaeological digging were still to require three or four centuries to get to what is buried there, it would be breathtakingly fast.

Global de-sedimentation, however, is no more a mono-causal, one-dimensional process than was the sedimentation of traumatic repetition compulsion into the rituals and institutions of culture. And it is not fated to be. From the beginning, it has evoked opposing forces. One of the darkest is fundamentalism—the mindless fixation on rituals and articles of faith that are as shaken as they are dubious.[22] But there are also other opposing forces. There are signs of them—as weak as they are hopeful—in the sustainability projects launched by NGOs critical of globalization, the stubborn resistance of teachers to the presence of concentrated distraction in education, or civil society initiatives involving shared homework after visits to exhibitions and experiences of reading. They prove that de-sedimentation can also generate re-sedimentation. Homework can become a practice. In the era of its existential endangerment, it can even become a virtue in ways that were not previously known. A culture, on the other hand, that cannot bear to do any homework is an unbearable culture. It begins to become feverish, like the person who can no longer find his way from the waking state to sleep and who, as a result, is also abandoned by the protectors of sleep—dreams. But where there are no dreams, there is no rest, no contemplation, and no hope.

NOTES

TRANSLATOR'S NOTE

1. The "complete and definitive" variorum edition (New York: Basic Books, 1955) comes in at 674 pages.

2. *The Interpretation of Dreams*, trans. A. A. Brill (London: G. Allen & Co., 1913). Brill was the first person to practice psychoanalysis in the United States.

3. Arnold D. Richards, review of *Dreaming by the Book: Freud's Interpretation of Dreams and the History of Psychoanalytic Movement*, by Lydia Marinelli and Andreas Meyer. From: http://internationalpsychoanalysis.net/wp-content/uploads/2008/01/interpretation-of-dreamsreview.pdf, downloaded March 13, 2013.

4. For an in-depth consideration of the question of terminological consistency and its relation to Freud's views on science, as well as a discussion of the issues involved in Freud translation, see Darius Gray Ornston, Jr., ed., *Translating Freud* (New Haven: Yale University Press, 1992), especially the essays by Ornston and Patrick J. Mahoney; and Mark Solms, "Controversies in Freud Translation," in *Psychoanalysis and History*, 1:28–43 (1999).

5. Ornston, *Translating Freud*, xi.

6. Cited in an interview with Mark Solms by Jason B. Jones, Bookslut (http://www.bookslut.com/features/2007_05_011064.php, downloaded March 29. 2013).

7. According to Bettelheim, "the translation . . . makes Freud's direct and always deeply personal appeals to our common humanity appear to readers of English as abstract, depersonalized, highly theoretical, erudite, and mechanized—in short 'scientific'—statements about the strange and very complex workings of our mind." Bruno Bettelheim, *Freud and Man's Soul* (New York: Vintage Books, 1984), 5. Strachey's use of Latin terms has recently been defended by

Mark Solms and others on grounds that the practice was already common in English and in other translations from the German. See "Controversies in Freud Translation," in *Psychoanalysis and History*, 1:28–43 (2009), 32–34.

8. Solms is also preparing an edition of *The Complete Neuroscientific Works*, to be published by Karnac and The Institute of Psychoanalysis (English) and Springer Verlag (German) and is due out in 2015. Personal communication.

9. In Strachey's words, "today I should probably suppress the tiresome hyphen in the word psycho-analysis." Cited in Darius Gray Ornston, Jr., "Alternatives to a Standard Edition," in Ornston, ed., *Translating Freud*, 97–113, 108.

10. Sigmund Freud, *The Unconscious*, trans. Graham Frankland (London: Penguin Books, 2005).

FOREWORD

1. For additional information, see Friedemann Schrenk, *Die Frühzeit des Menschen: Der Weg zum Homo sapiens* [Human prehistory: The road to *Homo Sapiens*], 4th ed. (Munich, C. H. Beck, 2003), 71, 77ff, 98, 100, 113, 115, 117.

2. This developmental aspect was lost when the Jewish Platonist Philo introduced the word *archetype*, which he used to refer to the "image of God," according to which the Bible says man was created. With this, along with its connection to origins, the *archetypos* also assumed aspects of eternity, of something not characterized by becoming. Carl Gustav Jung gratefully followed this lead. Today when we speak of archetypes we understand primarily what he understood by them: unconscious images that form the deepest collective level of human psychological life. "These images are 'primordial images' in so far as they are peculiar to the whole species, and if they ever 'originated' their origin must have coincided at least with the beginning of the species." (Carl Gustav Jung, "Psychological Aspects of the Mother Archetype," trans. R. F. C. Hull, in C. G. Jung, *The Collected Works of C. G. Jung*, vol. 9.1, 75–110 [Princeton, NJ: Princeton University Press, 1968], 78.) It makes quite good sense to speak of archetypes when the cost of their historical development is taken into account and they are not immersed in the fog of the always-already-existing, the immemorial.

3. Ulrich Bahnsen, "Heiliger Würger" [Sacred strangler], *Die Zeit*, December 14, 2006, 44.

4. "Technik war der Zündfunke unserer Evolution" [Technology was the spark for our evolution], interview by Frankfurt paleontologist Friedemann Schrenk on the great moments in the history of humanity, *Süddeutsche Zeitung*, February 11–12, 2006, 24.

5. Jeremy Rifkin, *The Biotech Century: Harnessing the Gene and Remaking the World* (New York: Putnam, 1998), 14.

6. Walter Benjamin, "The Work of Art in the Age of Mechanical Reproduction," trans. Harry Zohn, in *Illuminations*, 217–51 (New York: Schocken Books, 2007), 237. Cited as "Work of Art."

7. Siegfried Kracauer, *Theory of Film* (New York: Oxford University Press, 1960), 164–65.

8. Christoph Türcke, *Erregte Gesellschaft: Philosophie der Sensation* [Excited society: Philosophy of sensation] (Munich: C. H. Beck, 2002), 271.

9. Jacques Derrida, *Of Grammatology*, trans. Gayatri Chakravorty Spivak (Baltimore, MD, and London: Johns Hopkins University Press, 1976), 10.

10. Sigmund Freud, *The Interpretation of Dreams*, trans. James Strachey (New York: Basic Books, 2010), 566. As with other works of Freud translated by Strachey, this is a reprint from the so-called *Standard Edition* of Freud's *Collected Works*, which were originally published in cooperation with the Institute of Psychoanalysis by the Hogarth Press (London) and Clarke, Irwin (Toronto).—Trans.

11. Ibid., 324. The standard translation of Freud's term *Werkmeister* is "governing factors," which indeed sounds schoolmasterly. A more literal version of Freud's code word for condensation and displacement would be "foremen," or "head mechanics." Hereafter, *Werkmeister* is translated throughout as "foremen."—Trans.

12. Sigmund Freud, "The Unconscious," trans. Graham Frankland, in *The Unconscious* (London: Penguin Books, 2005, 47–85), 71. Cited as "The Unconscious."

13. Sigmund Freud, *Totem and Taboo. Some Points of Agreement between the Mental Lives of Savages and Neurotics*, trans. James Strachey, 174–81 (New York and London: W. W. Norton, n.d.), 3.

CHAPTER 1: DREAMS

1. This and the next two paragraphs are drawn from Mark Solms, "The Interpretation of Dreams and the Neurosciences," available online at http://www.psychoanalysis.org.uk/solms4 (accessed March 2, 2013).

2. Mark Solms even goes so far as to turn the tables and regard Freud's work as a "guide for the next phase of our neuroscientific investigations." Ibid.

3. Freud, *Interpretation of Dreams*, 240ff.

4. Ibid., 245.

5. Ibid., 245–46. Freud quotes Johannes Volkelt's *Die Traum-Phantasie* [Dream Phantasy] (Stuttgart: Meyer & Zeller, 1875), 34.

6. Sigmund Freud, *Introductory Lectures on Psycho-Analysis*, trans. James Strachey (New York and London: W. W. Norton, n.d.), 122. Translations from the Standard Edition have been modified here and elsewhere to modernize spelling.

7. Along with Mark Solms's project of a "neuro-psychoanalysis," see, for example, François Ansermet and Pierre Magistretti, *Die Individualität des Gehirns* [The individuality of the brain] (Frankfurt: Suhrkamp, 2005). Cited as *Individuality of the Brain*.

8. Freud, *Interpretation of Dreams*, 148.

9. Freud, *Introductory Lectures*, 107–9.

10. Ibid., 107.

11. Freud, *Interpretation of Dreams*, 253.

12. Ibid., 149.

13. Ibid., 253.

14. For a detailed theory of repetition and memory, see chap. 2.

15. Gerhard Roth, *Das Gehirn und seine Wirklichkeit* [The brain and its reality] (Frankfurt: Suhrkamp, 1994), 186.

16. The word *fake* is English in original.—Trans.

17. Eugen Bleuler, *Textbook of Psychiatry* (New York: Arno Press, 1976), 59.

18. Ibid., 60. Translation modified.

19. Immanuel Kant, *Critique of Pure Reason*, trans. Werner S. Pluhar (New York: St. Martin's Press, 1965), A 115ff.

20. See Carl Gustav Jochmann, *Die Rückschritte der Poesie* [The regressions of poetry] (Hamburg: Felix Meiner, 1982), 5ff.

21. Freud, *Interpretation of Dreams*, 566.

22. Freud, *Introductory Lectures*, 211.

23. Freud, *Interpretation of Dreams*, 316.

24. Freud, *Introductory Lectures*, 51–58, 76–77.

25. Ibid., 150.

26. Freud, *Interpretation of Dreams*, 295; *Introductory Lectures*, 147.

27. Freud, *Introductory Lectures*, 171–81.

28. Exodus 20:2, etc. All Bible quotations are taken from the King James Version.

29. Plato, "Socrates' Defense (Apology)," in *The Collected Dialogues of Plato, including the Letters*, ed. Edith Hamilton and Huntington Cairns, trans. Hugh Tredennick, 12th ed., Bollingen Series LXXI. (Princeton, NJ: Princeton University Press, 1985), 31d.

30. The term "cathexis" was chosen by James Strachey, the translator of the *Standard Edition* of Freud's works, to translate the German word *Besetzung*. It refers to the investment of emotional or mental energy in a person, idea, or thing.—Trans.

31. Freud, *Interpretation of Dreams*, 295.

32. Sigmund Freud, "Remarks on the Theory and Practice of Dream-Interpretation" (1923), available at http://www.freud.org.uk/education/topic/10576/subtopic/40035/ (accessed December 4, 2012). Also see Franz Morgenthaler, *Der Traum: Fragmente zur Theorie und Technik der Traumdeutung* [Dreams: Fragments of a theory and technique of their interpretation] (Frankfurt: Campus, 1986).

33. See Immanuel Kant, *Groundwork of the Metaphysics of Morals*, trans. and ed. Mary Gregor (Cambridge: Cambridge University Press, 1997), 21ff.

34. August Kekulé, "Rede im Rathus zu Berlin am 1. März 1890" [Speech in the Berlin City Hall on March 1, 1980], in Richard Anschütz, *Werke von August Kekulé in zwei Bänden*, vol. 2. (Berlin: Verlag Chemie, 1929), 942. Cited as "Speech."

35. C. H. Jung, "The Psychology of the Transference," in *The Practice of Psychotherapy: Essays on the Psychology of the Transference and Other Subjects*, trans. R. F. C. Hull (Princeton, N.J.: Princeton University Press, second edition, 1966), 168.

36. August Kekulé, "Speech," 944.

37. Alexander Mitscherlich, "Kekulé's Traum: Psychologische Betrachtung einer chemischen Legende" [Kekulé's dream: Psychological consideration of a chemistry legend], *Psyche* 9 (1972), 653ff.

38. In German, *Schwanz* (tail) is a slang expression for penis.—Trans.
39. Freud, *Introductory Lectures*, 215.
40. Ibid., 148–49.
41. For this reason, André Breton's idea that the productive image-making power of dreams could be elicited by means of "automatic writing," which disconnects mental control and allows the unconscious source of imagination to flow directly into the writing hand, was doomed to failure. Instead of the hoped-for flow of images, what emerged was the half-digested mass of the bourgeois cultural matter that the surrealists, previously, had gulped down no less eagerly than other contemporary intellectuals. See also André Breton, "Manifesto of Surrealism," in André Breton, *Manifestos of Surrealism* (Ann Arbor, MI: Michigan University Press, 1972), 1–47.
42. Josef Breuer and Sigmund Freud, *Studies in Hysteria* (New York: Nervous and Mental Disease Publishing, 1936), 129.
43. Freud, *Introductory Lectures*, 184–85.
44. Ibid., 186–88.
45. Ibid., 190ff.
46. Ibid., 186.
47. Ibid.
48. Stefan Zweig, *The World of Yesterday: An Autobiography*, trans. Harry Zohn (New York: Viking Press, 1964).
49. In general, it was not until the globalizing movements of the 1960s that it became obvious how Western psychoanalysis actually is—namely, when there were not only European psychoanalysts traveling to Africa or Southeast Asia but Africans and Southeast Asians training to become psychoanalysts. The latter were forced to discover that certain basic notions about reason and faith, customs and the law, individuals, the family, and society, as they had evolved exclusively in modern European bourgeois society, had been embedded in the fabric of psychoanalysis from its earliest beginning. Marie-Cécile and Edmond Ortigues, from the Psychoanalytic School of Dakar, opposed this programmatically with their book *Oedipe africain*, in which Senegalese children expressed themselves with the help of a therapeutic setting that had been developed especially for them.
50. Hesiod, *Theogony*, trans. M. L. West (Oxford and New York: Oxford University Press, 1988), 8–9.
51. Ibid., 29–31.
52. Aeschylus, *Agamemnon*, 205ff.
53. See Walter Burkert, *Homo Necans: the Anthropology of Ancient Greek Sacrificial Ritual and Myth*, trans. Peter Bing (Berkeley, CA: University of California Press, 1983).
54. All quotations in this paragraph are from Carl Gustav Jung, *Psychological Types: or The Psychology of Individuation*, trans. H. Godwin Baynes (New York: Harcourt, Brace, 1933), 601–2.

55. Johann Wolfgang Goethe, *Maximen und Reflexionen* [Maxims and reflections], in Johann Wolfgang Goethe, *Sämtliche Werke*, vol. 9, (Zurich: Artemis, 1950), 639.

56. Walter Benjamin, "Work of Art," 222.

57. Walter Benjamin, *The Origin of German Tragic Drama*, trans. John Osborne (London and New York: Verso, 1998).

58. Freud, *Introductory Lectures*, 216.

59. Ibid.

60. See Michael Foucault, *This is Not a Pipe*, trans. James Harkness (Berkeley, CA: University of California Press, 2008).

61. In the beginning, language too had its problems with this; see chap. 3 ("Fort–Da" section).

62. Freud, *Introductory Lectures*, 222.

63. Ibid., 223.

64. Freud, *Interpretation of Dreams*, 572ff.

65. Hans-Martin Lohmann, *Sigmund Freud* (Reinbek, Germany: Rowohlt, 1998), 36.

66. Wilfred R. Bion calls these elementary excitations "beta elements." For him, these are impressions and sensations in a "prototypical" stage of development— so diffuse that they are literally not yet able to be identified. Only "alpha elements" are "mental." They are elementary patterns of smelling, hearing, seeing, etc., and are already stable enough to set off dream images. For Bion, it should be noted, we may think of "alpha" only ontogenetically, primarily in the mother-child relationship, and as a function. He has developed a special grid on which elementary mental tasks such as functions and factors can be positioned with mathematical precision. It is a masterwork of instrumental reason. See Wilfred R. Bion, *Learning from Experience* (Lanham, MD: Jason Aronson, 1994).

67. Freud, *Interpretation of Dreams*, 296ff.

68. Ibid., 322ff.

69. Ibid., 326.

70. Ibid., 493.

71. Ibid., 353.

72. Ibid., 354.

73. Ibid., 342. (The note added in 1909 is included in this edition.—Trans.)

74. Freud, *Introductory Lectures*, 215.

75. Ibid., 224. Translation modified.

76. Freud, *Interpretation of Dreams*, 159.

77. Ibid., 493ff.

78. Freud, *Introductory Lectures*, 168–71.

79. Freud, *Beyond the Pleasure Principle*, trans. James Strachey (New York and London: W. W. Norton, n.d.). Cited as *Beyond Pleasure*.

80. Freud, *Beyond Pleasure*, 11.

81. Ibid., 36–37.

82. For additional detail, see chap. 2 ("Death Drive" section).

83. Freud, New *Introductory Lectures*, 36.

84. Freud, *Beyond Pleasure*, 25.

85. Freud, *Beyond Pleasure*, 38.

86. On one hand, fright is internal—a feeling that penetrates the organism to its core; on the other hand, it is external—the power of nature that brings it about. If, in the following, we speak of "fright" in general, both sides are always intended. The point of the experience of fright is the discrepancy between inner and outer, subject and object. It is the terrible counterpoint to the *unio mystica*. Both are inexpressible. *Fright* is a word that is used for something words cannot express, but in connection with which words were initially created. For further details, see chap. 3 (Primal words section).

87. Friedrich Nietzsche, *Thus Spake Zarathustra*, in *The Portable Nietzsche*, ed. and trans. Walter Kaufmann (New York: Viking Press, 1954), 434.

88. When reference is made in the following reflections to "early humanity," what is meant is primarily early Paleolithic *Homo sapiens*, but not excluding Neanderthals.

89. This is equally true of later scientific experiments, where the researcher attempts to isolate a bit of nature and free it from all disturbances, so that it reacts only to his interventions and he can filter out the reaction without any impurities. The production of experimental conditions always has a ritual character. The person who wants to enter must first cleanse herself, put on special clothing, and strictly follow the rules that are meant to keep the location free of dust—as if she were entering an archaic sanctuary.

90. "Continuous" repetition, in this volume, always means the intermittent return of an action at certain intervals, not just doing the same thing for twenty-four hours a day without a pause.

91. Max Horkheimer and Theodor W. Adorno, *Dialectic of Enlightenment*, trans. John Cumming (New York: Herder and Herder, 1972), 72.

92. Many things speak for the protective space having originally had the form of a circle. For one thing, the motif of the "charmed circle," into which evil spirits are banned, always points to very archaic mythological material. There is also a physiological indication that penetrates even deeper: the fact that organisms in intense pain curl themselves around the painful spot as if they wanted to afford it the protection they were unable to give it beforehand. The gesture of protection after the fact is one of circling in on the traumatic blow (whereby we must naturally not think of the circle in a strict, geometric sense; it is merely a closed curved shape, which can also be oval). Against this background, the mandala, a rounded image that is surrounded in turn by a rectangle, represents a highly stylized aesthetic memory of archaic events. The elementary process of securing the protected space is mirrored in the shape of the mandala. The original form of the protected space is round, curved, but as soon as this space is meant to be not only marked, but also secured, by either a fence or a wall, or later by an entire building, the physiological problem of dealing with pain is joined by the physical problem of construction. Buildings are only secure, initially, if they are four- sided. This where the famous quadrature of the circle has its origin. It is by no means, as Carl Jung suggested, an archetype that was always present in the collective unconscious (Carl Gustav Jung, *Psychology and*

Alchemy, trans R. F. C. Hull, in *The Collected Works of C. J. Jung*, 2nd ed., vol. 12, [Princeton, NJ: Princeton University Press, 1968], 95–223), but is quite definitely an archaic rationalization, common to many cultures, which is deeply embedded in the human imagination. To secure the basic protected space by transforming it into a long-lasting ritual and sacred space—this can only be effectively accomplished by turning a round shape into a square one. Building something round is not impossible, in principle, but it is a high art that could only be learned relatively late—after the laws of statics had been acquired through long experience with rectangular structures. Curves are always less accessible than corners. It is no accident that the squaring of the circle lives on in calculus, which breaks curves into tiny angles and then takes the angles for the curve, as more or less round.

93. Jonah 1:7 and 15.

94. The Hebrew word for lot, *goral*, is associated with gravel and small stones (early forms of dice). The Greek word *kleros* is associated with branches and small trees.

95. Euripides, *The Bacchae*, 1101ff. Much speaks for the assumption that this horrible fantasy is an echo of real historical practices. The cult of Dionysos is vitally connected with the tearing apart of individuals by a collective. The remark that "the Titans tore Dionysos limb from limb" (Callimachus, *Fragment 643*) should be read as an authentic memory, precisely because it tends to cover up its horror rather than reveal it, by condensing the cultic practice into a single event and moving it to a misty prehistory where the Titans, who have long since been consigned to the underworld, were still committing their terrible acts.

96. In Homer, the heifer that has been selected for sacrifice is pelted with sacred barley, before the "whetted ax" falls on it (Homer, *The Odyssey*, trans. Robert Fagels (New York: Penguin, 1996), 498, 495.

97. Genesis 4:15. In other passages of the Hebrew Bible (Old Testament), this mark appears only as something forbidden or meaningless. "Ye shalt not make any cuttings in your flesh for the dead, nor print any marks upon you," it says in Leviticus 19:28. In I Kings 18:28, there is quite a scornful reference to the priests of Baal, who "cried aloud, and cut themselves after their manner with knives and lancets, till the blood gushed out upon them" whereupon the people "slew them."

98. See Christoph Türcke, *Vom Kainszeichen zum genetischen Code: Kritische Theorie der Schrift* [From the mark of Cain to the genetic code: Critical theory of writing] (Munich: C. H. Beck, 2005), esp. chap. 1, for evidence that writing begins with the mark of Cain.

99. Genesis 4:10.

100. Friedrich Schiller, *On the Aesthetic Education of Man*, trans. Reginald Snell (Mineola, NY: Dover Publications, 2004), 80 (15th letter). Translation modified.

101. The German word here is *Vorstellung*, literally "placing before." In the history of translation of German philosophy into English, it is possible to mark

the point at which the translation of *Vorstellung* into English changed from "presentation" (Kant, Hegel) to "representation" (Schopenhauer). –Trans.

102. Isaiah 65:17ff. The past that has sunk into blessed oblivion and the things that have simply passed us by without notice are strict opposites. One has been worked through and brought to rest; the other is a lost past. And yet, what distinguishes blessed forgetting from never having been noticed? In the end, the opposites meet, if they are not transformed into each other.

103. Resistance to this notion is embodied by Gilles Deleuze. According to Deleuze, representation not only takes on false forms; it is the basic thought error. "The primacy of identity . . . defines the world of representation. But modern thought is born of the failure of representation, of the loss of identities, and of the discovery of all the forces that act under the representation of the identical." (Gilles Deleuze, *Difference and Repetition*, trans. Paul Patton (New York: Columbia University Press, 1994), xix. Thus, we should shake off representation—and nevertheless keep right on remembering, interpreting, and combining. This is as if we wanted to get rid of the brain so that we could finally think in an unlimited way—a wish that, by the way, was one of the decisive motivations for the feverish research that inspired the pioneers of artificial intelligence in the 1940s.

104. Aristotle, *Metaphysics*, trans. Richard Hope (New York: Columbia University Press, 1952), 1072b.

105. Georg Friedrich Wilhelm Hegel, *Hegel's Science of Logic*, trans. A. V. Miller (Atlantic Highlands, NJ: Humanities Press International, 1969), 401.

106. Nietzsche came close to this realization. In the famous passage where he talks about his "hypothesis on the origin of bad conscience," he says: "All instincts that do not discharge themselves outwardly *turn inward*—this is what I call the *internalization* of man: thus it was that man first developed what was later called his 'soul.' The entire inner world, originally as thin as if it were stretched between two membranes, expanded and extended itself, acquired depth, breadth, and height, in the same measure as outward discharge was *inhibited*." (Friedrich Nietzsche, *On the Genealogy of Morals and Ecce Homo*, trans. Walter Kaufmann and R. J. Hollingdale [New York: Random House, 1989], 84.) Here the source of our bad conscience amounts to nothing less than the birth of humanity itself. Nietzsche surrounds it with lovely, anticipatory metaphors that nevertheless lack a foundation, namely, the insight into the role and culture-creating power of traumatic repetition compulsion. More exact knowledge about this would have given a much more solid physiological foundation to the often rather empty trumpeting of the "revaluation of all values." A theoretician of the image and ethnographic dilettante, Aby Warburg, saw more clearly. The snake ritual that he had an opportunity to observe among Indians in New Mexico seemed to him to be a moving image that sought to gather within itself nothing less than the forces of the cosmos, by circling around the snake that had been condensed into the symbol of the world. Warburg experienced the snake dance as "danced causality," carried out with "devotional zeal," in which

he saw a model of research into nature. The ritual "space for devotion" was, in his mind, a prefigured "space . . . for reflection." (Aby Warburg, *Images from the Region of the Pueblo Indians of North America*, trans. Michael P. Steinberg [Ithaca and London: Cornell University Press, 1995], 48, 54.) It is true that there is always "thought" in "devotion." It is already a sublime cultural state that, for its part, has much cruder ecstatic precursor forms. Nevertheless, Warburg renders a decisive genealogical structure thematic. His suspicion that a "space . . . for reflection" could only open up within the "devotional space" is very much in line with the thesis that is proposed here, but in a more principled form: Only within a ritual space was it possible for an imagined space to open up.

107. Not even in its highly developed cultural forms does mental life lose its spatial associations. Neither philosophical logic nor psychoanalysis can do without topology. As soon as we are dealing with concepts that *cover* a subject, or the *reach* or *scope* of judgments and conclusions, there are spatial connotations at work. Models of our psychic apparatus cannot help thinking of unconscious, preconscious, and conscious, or id, ego, and superego, as being layered on top of one another.

108. This is the ground as an abyss (in German: *Grund als Abgrund*—Trans.). The figure of thought is familiar from the neo-Platonic theory of the creation. There is nothing more abysmal than the original unity (*hen*) that for Plotinus (*Enneades* 9.1ff.) stands at the beginning of the world, empty, undetermined, and bottomless, and that nevertheless must be thought of as the primal power if duality, multiplicity, and the fullness of the world are to emerge from it. The idea of the creative abyss is still present even in Schelling, where God plays the role of both absolute ground (*Grund*) and abyss (*Ungrund*) and is meant, in this way, to be made plausible as an unfathomable, metaphysical world potency. (*Philosophical Investigations into the Essence of Human Freedom*, trans. Jeff Love and Johannes Schmidt [Albany: State University of New York Press, 2006]). But now we can see where this thought comes from. It is a screen memory for the "genius." It covers up the horror, attempts to soften it retroactively by turning the abyss into its opposite—from a yawning chasm into a bottomless cornucopia of creative power. This reversal is the subtext of the gradual spiritualization of the divine, from the "genius" that stands at the beginning of ritual to the world-founding creative spirit. Mythology has traced this process in its own way. It begins with stories of the founding of ritual and only gradually moves on to stories of the creation of the world. Only in its late phase, for example in stories about the Garden of Eden, golden age, or dreamtime, has the screen memory of the "genius" advanced to the point where the founding state is imagined without sacrificial victims or violence, as blessed. Only in retrospect is there talk of a tribute to reality, in the form of tales of original sin.

109. There is no reason not to characterize the "genius" as an archetype—for example, of the final cause (*Zweckursache*), primal ground, or godhead—as

long as we do not forget even for a moment that it has emerged by means of an elementary achievement of imagination, a remarkable meshing of reversal, condensation, and displacement, and does not rest somewhere in the murky depths of a "collective unconscious," as Jung claimed. In this way, Jung himself disqualified the concept of the archetype, while the Freudian concepts for primary psychological processes, if we only take them somewhat more fundamentally than Freud himself did, can accomplish something that Jung was never able to do, namely, explain how archetypes are created. Freudians are able to make the concept of the archetype more fruitful than it was in Jung—and in the process also show how misleading the contradiction between individual and collective consciousness is. Each person may dream for herself, but all over the world this happens in a way that displaces and condenses excitation. The dream is individual in the concrete; the mechanisms of individual dream creation, on the other hand, are a capacity common to all humans—they are collective. The reverse is also true: no one could know anything about the profound archaic strata that Jung sees as belonging to the depths of the "collective" unconscious if it weren't for the individuals in whom they rise up, and through whom they take on an always personal coloration. Like the individual and society, the individual and the collective unconscious are mutually mediated in each other. They are not two stories of a building. The dual structure of the unconscious is personally determined; there is no evidence for an archetypically undetermined one.

110. Eugen Bleuler, *Textbook*, 59.
111. Rudolf Otto, *The Idea of the Holy: An Inquiry into the Non-Rational Factor in the Idea of the Divine and Its Relation to the Rational*, trans. John W. Harvey (London, New York, and Toronto: Oxford University Press, 1923), 126.
112. If we concede that animals also dream, that they too rework unmastered stimuli in their sleep, it is necessary to add that they do this in a precultural, precultic stage of development. It follows that their dreams are prehallucinatory.
113. Drawing on the container terminology that was introduced by Bion (*Learning from Experience*, 146), we could speak of mental "self-containment," whereby, however, individual and collective selves are not at all sharply delineated.
114. See chap. 3 ("The Oath" section) for a detailed discussion of how the modeling of mental representations is linked to the creation and development of specifically human language.
115. Sigmund Freud, "Repression," trans. Graham Frankland, in *The Unconscious*, 33–45 (England: Penguin Books, 2005), 37.
116. Robert Craan, *Geheimnisvolle Kultur der Traumzeit: Die Welt der Aborigines* [The mysterious culture of dreamtime: The world of the Aborigines] (Munich: Knaur, 2000), 88.
117. Ibid., 126ff.

118. In chap. 3 we will discuss what a word is. Everything that is said about language in chap. 2 aims merely at setting the stage for later comprehension, or—in Hegelian terms—at establishing a precondition that must still be fulfilled.

119. This struggle also conceals archaic rituals, whether we are thinking of the divine judgment that decides who is "chosen," i.e., designated as the sacrificial victim; or the sacrificial process itself, in which two "chosen" individuals, the victim and the priest, meet in such a way that the priest subsequently has cause to give first voice to the dirge.

120. *The Epic of Gilgamesh*, trans. Andrew George (London: Penguin Books, 2003), II, Y100ff. Square brackets enclose text that has been restored where tablets are broken. Italics are used to indicate insecure decipherments and uncertain renderings in the text. Passages in square brackets and italics are conjectural and have been added by translator Andrew George.

121. This conjectural passage is imagined very differently in the German translation, which has Enkidu tell Gilgamesh, "The mountain that you saw [*is Humbaba*]."—Trans.

122. *Gilgamesh*, IV, 7ff.

123. From the commentary to the German translation, *Das Gilgamesh-Epos: Neu übersetzt und kommentiert von Stefan M. Maul* [The Gilgamesh Epic. Newly translated and with commentary by Stefan M. Mail] (Munich: C. F. Beck, 2005), 163.

124. Literally: "House of the *Zaqiqu*." "The Babylonian word *zaqiqu* means "wind, breath, spirit, dream god" (ibid., 164).

125. *Gilgamesh*, IV, 101–3.

126. *Gilgamesh*, IV: OB Ni 20' and IB NI 14.

127. Homer, at any rate, still names the individual who is carrying out the sacrifice, the seer, and the interpreter of dreams in a single breath, as if they were a troika (*Iliad* 1.63).

128. *Mutatis mutandis*, this is even true of modern historical consciousness. Its visions of the future, the so-called political utopias, are now, as ever, memory in reverse. "[They] are nourished by the image of enslaved ancestors rather than that of liberated grandchildren." Walter Benjamin, "Theses on the Philosophy of History," trans. Harry Zohn, in *Illuminations*, 253–64 (New York: Schocken Books, 1969), 260.

129. The famous Old Testament story in which Joseph, confronted with the dreams of Pharaoh, interprets the seven "fatfleshed" cows that are eaten by seven thin cows as seven fat and seven lean years (Genesis 41), belongs to a much more highly developed dream culture and is probably more than a thousand years younger than the Gilgamesh epic. Nevertheless, it is an archetypical example of the way dream interpretation and awareness of the future belong together. Knowledge of the future, namely, is a very practical matter: it shows people how to prepare. The storerooms that are filled at Joseph's suggestion are places where foodstuffs are displaced and condensed for later use. The two "foremen" of dreams, turned toward the future, become foreman in a practical, economic sense.

130. In this respect, dream censorship resembles repression itself. In his Vienna biotope, Freund almost always experienced repression as a source of fear, although it originally emerged as the exact opposite, as an emergency barrier for warding off fear. Only the latter is "primary repression" in the full sense.

131. *Gilgamesh*, I, 180ff, 288ff.

132. Ibid., I, 243ff.

133. Anu is the father of the gods, including Ishtar.

134. See Sigmund Freud, "Fetishism," in Freud, *The Unconscious*, trans. Graham Frankland (England: Penguin Books, 2005), 95–100.

135. The *ius primae noctis*, or right of the first night, which Gilgamesh practices in the second tablet of the epic, also began as a ritual duty, not an escape valve for princely lasciviousness. The priest must consecrate the virgins to the divinity before the virgins can consecrate themselves to their husband, no matter how the pair may feel about it.

136. For the comprehensive study that ought to follow here, it is not only the possibility of acquiring material evidence that I lack. It is also questionable whether capitalist society is already at a point where its effects on dream life could be captured by standardized empirical surveys in ways that are beyond doubt. Studies of hyperactive children (Bernd Ahrbeck, ed., *Hyperaktivität: Kulturtheorie, Pädagogik, Therapie* [Hyperactivity: Cultural theory, pedagogy, therapy] [Stuttgart; Kohlhammer, 2007]) can be read as indications that this stage has already begun (see the afterword). But here it is a little like the situation with nuclear energy plants. That they produce radiation we can count on three fingers. But a legally prosecutable case is difficult to establish and as a rule only succeeds after the pollution has had serious consequences.

137. Friedrich Engels, *Socialism: Utopian and Scientific* (New York: International Publishers, 1972, among other editions).

138. Freud, "Observations on 'Wild' Psychoanalysis," trans. Joan Riviere, in Freud, *Collected Papers*, vol. 2 (New York: Basic Books, 1959), 297–304.

139. Jacques Lacan, "The Unconscious and Repetition," trans. Alan Sheridan, in *The Seminar of Jacques Lacan, Book XI: The Four Fundamental Concepts of Psychoanalysis* (New York and London: W. W. Norton, 1981), 17–66.

140. Jacques Lacan, "The Instance of the Letter in the Unconscious, or Reason Since Freud," in *Écrits*, trans. Bruce Fink, 412–41 (New York and London: W. W. Norton, 2006), 425ff. For a more detailed discussion of Lacan, see chap. 3.

141. Thus the sentence "The unconscious is structured like a language" reverses itself, for us, to become "Language is structured like the unconscious." See Alfred Lorenzer, *Die Sprache, der Sinn, das Unbewußte* [Language, sense, the unconscious] (Stuttgart: Klett-Cotta, 2002), 84f.

CHAPTER 2: DRIVES

1. *Trieb* is often translated as "instinctual drive," or "instinct." James Strachey, in his influential translations for the *Standard Edition*, follows this pattern. Nonetheless, the translation of *Trieb* as "instinct" is nowadays generally considered inaccurate. In the following, *Trieb* is generally translated as "drive," and citations from the *Standard Edition* have been silently corrected. In a few

cases, such as the newborn's urge to suck (*Saugtrieb*), and in a quotation from *Beyond the Pleasure Principle* that is repeatedly cited as the point at which Freud comes closest to the author's views, "instinct" or "instinctual" as been retained as the more natural expression, i.e. "sucking instinct" And "more primal, more concentrated, more instinctual."—Trans.

2. "Ontic need" is actually only another word for "drive"—and not to be confused with the "ontological need" that Theodor W. Adorno found so unpleasantly striking in his contemporaries. Numbers of them took "Being," which Heidegger believed he had discovered as the ground of all beings, for whole cloth (*bare Münze*), while Adorno proved it was a big empty word-bubble. But even if we pop it, we have not seen the last of ontological need. In living beings that think, ontic need can do nothing except become ontological: it becomes a need for thoughts that provide purchase and orientation. Adorno was self-evidently also concerned with this; no question but that his *Negative Dialectics* was intended to serve as a central point of purchase and orientation for his epoch—a time when we are no longer able to believe sensibly in the supportive power of a "Being." Ontological need cannot be done away with. But we can reflect on it from the perspective of drive theory and bring it to reason.

3. Sigmund Freud, "Drives and their Fates," trans. Graham Frankland, in *The Unconscious*, 11–31 (England: Penguin Books, 2005), 15.

4. Sleepers do not sin, but neither do they enjoy, as was noted in chap. 1. The need for sleep longs for something that sleep cannot provide: the enjoyment of complete stimulus discharge. It longs for something other than sleep. The same is true of the purported drive for dissolution of the self. In actuality, it seeks something else.

5. Freud, *Beyond Pleasure*, 67.

6. Sigmund Freud, "Project for a Scientific Psychology," in Freud, *Standard Edition*, vol. 1, 295–397, (London: Hogarth Press, 1957), 296–97. Cited as "Project."

7. Freud, *New Introductory Lectures*, 118. Where I have translated this well-known passage using "drives" for *Triebe*, James Strachey's translation, in the *Standard Edition*, has "instincts."—Trans.

8. The essay was originally translated into English as "Instincts and their Vicissitudes."—Trans.

9. Freud, "Drives and their Fates," trans. Graham Frankland, in *The Unconscious* (London: Penguin Books, 2005, 11–31), 14–15.

10. Ibid., 16.

11. Freud, "The Unconscious," 59.

12. Only one version is possible: A thing can be either a representative or it can be represented; it cannot be not both at the same time in the same constellation. To what extent Freud was aware of this contradiction does not concern us here. The editors of the *Studienausgabe*, at any rate, attempt to paper it over. In his second attempt, they note, drives "are no longer regarded as psychic representation of physical actions, but as, in themselves, something non-psychic. These obviously divergent views of the essence of drives are both also found elsewhere in Freud's later writings, with the latter predominating. It is possible, however, that the

contradiction is more apparent than real, and the key could lie in the double meaning of the concept itself—precisely as a borderline concept between the physical and the mental" (editor's introduction to the *Standard Edition*). Here, the very inconsistency that is inherent in being both a "borderline concept" and a "psychic representative" is presented as the key to resolving the contradiction.

13. Freud, "Repression," trans. Graham Frankland, in *The Unconscious* (London: Penguin Books, 2005, 33–45), 40.

14. Hegel, *Science of Logic*, 479. The sentence precedes the section on appearance.

15. All quotations in this paragraph are taken from Gerhard Roth. Cited as *The Brain*, 69ff.

16. The word *highlights* is in English in the original.—Trans.

17. Roth, *The Brain*, 228.

18. Freud, "Project," 314ff.

19. Ansermet and Magistretti, *Individuality of the Brain*, 36ff.

20. Roth, *The Brain*, 235ff.

21. It is as if Plato had already gotten a whiff of this when he invented allegorical parents for Eros. His mother is Penia, personified neediness; his father, Poros, the inexhaustible resource and way out. (Plato, *Symposium* 203b).

22. See Jacques Monod, *Chance and Necessity, An Essay on the Natural Philosophy of Modern Biology*, trans. Austryn Wainhouse (New York: Alfred A. Knopf, 1971).

23. In English, although the third meaning of *moment* is less common, it has found its way into the language of philosophy. Webster's *New World Dictionary* has, for example, "in philosophy, any of the constituent elements of a complex entity; momentum."—Trans.

24. James Strachey's influential translation of Freud's works introduced the terms *id, ego,* and *superego* in English. Drawn from the Latin, they tended to give the things they describe a scientific, medicalized aura, thus helping to make psychoanalysis acceptable in the United States. Bruno Bettelheim, among others, has criticized the use of the Latin terminology. Freud himself used the ordinary words *ich* (I) and *es* (it). He invented the term *über-ich* by combining the preposition *über* (over) with the word for "I." See the Translator's Note.—Trans.

25. English in original.—Trans.

26. Plato, *Menon* 81c ff.

27. *"Vor dem mir graut, du dem michs drängt."* The line, by an unknown poet, is cited by Rudolph Otto as the essence of the holy in his book *The Idea of the Holy.*—Trans.

28. Walter Benjamin, *The Arcades Project*, trans. Howard Eiland and Kevin McLaughlin (Cambridge, MA, and London: Harvard University Press, 1999), 118. Translation modified.

29. From the Nicene Creed, in the Episcopal Book of Common Prayer, http://en.wikipedia.org/wiki/Nicene_Creed#English_translations, accessed May 4, 2013.—Trans.

30. "The message is a discrete or continuous sequence of measurable events distributed in time." Norbert Wiener, *Cybernetics: or Control and Communication in the Animal and the Machine*, 2nd ed. (Boston: MIT Press, 1965), 8.

31. This little difference was simply ignored by the great theoretician of difference, Jacques Derrida. See my critique of his "Crypto-ontology of Writing," in Türcke, *Vom Kainszeichen zum genetischen Code* [From the mark of Cain to the genetic code] (Munich, C. H. Beck, 2005), 170ff.

32. Freud, "The Unconscious," 73ff.

33. Sigmund Freud, *The Ego and the Id*, trans. Joan Riviere (New York and London: W. W. Norton, n.d.). Cited as *Ego and Id*.

34. Ibid., 19.

35. Ibid.

36. Ibid.

37. Ibid.

38. Ibid., 8.

39. See Sigmund Freud, "On Narcissism: An Introduction," trans. James Strachey, in *Standard Edition*, vol. 14 (London: Hogarth Press, 1957), 67–81.

40. See also Janine Chasseguet-Smirgel, *Das Ichideal* [The ego ideal] (Frankfurt: Suhrkamp, 1987), 12ff.

41. Sigmund Freud, *An Outline of Psycho-Analysis*, trans. James Strachey (New York and London: W. W. Norton, n.d.), 16. Cited as *Outline*.

42. Theodor W. Adorno, "Der Begriff des Unbewussten in der transzendentalen Seelenlehre," in *Gesammelte Schriften*, vol. 1 (Frankfurt: Suhrkamp, 1973), 79–322. Cited as "Concept of the Unconscious."

43. Freud, *New Introductory Lectures*, 100.

44. Adorno, "Concept of the Unconscious," 203.

45. Adorno's conclusion is similar, in its problematic nature, to Freud's appropriation by structuralism, of which Lacan is a prominent exponent. See chap. 3 ("Psychoanalytic Structuralism" section).

46. Cf. Freud, *Outline*, 14, where the word *Rindenschicht* is actually translated as "cortical layer."—Trans.

47. The German word *Geist* is notoriously difficult to translate. Since *Geist* suggests both intellectual and spiritual capacities, I translate it throughout by combining the two realms, for example as "mind and spirit," "mind, or spirit," and the like.—Trans.

48. Friedrich Nietzsche, *Thus Spake Zarathustra*, trans. Thomas Common (New York: Random House, Modern Library, n.d.), 32.

49. Freud, *Ego and Id*, 44–45.

50. Nietzsche, *Thus Spake Zarathustra*, 256.

51. St. Augustine, *Confessions*, trans. Henry Chadwick (Oxford: Oxford University Press, 2008), 176.

52. English in original.—Trans.

53. Carl Gustav Jung *Wandlungen und Symbole der Libido* [Transformations and symbolisms of the libido] (Munich: DTV, 2001), 161–64.

54. Freud, *Totem and Taboo. Some Points of Agreement between the Mental Lives of Savages and Neurotics*. Trans. James Strachey (New York and London: W. W. Norton, 1950), 175–76.

55. Ulrich Raulff, "Afterword," in Aby Warburg, *Schlangenritual: Ein Reisebericht* [Snake ritual: A trip report] (Berlin: Wagenbach, 1996), 78.

56. Max Raphael certainly projected many notions into this system that are untenable, for example the claim that it "sought to prevent the rule of humans over other humans," expressed "a kind of holy reverence for being as such," or that "every animal of the Paleolithic and, to an even greater extent, every animal species" conceals the face of a human being or group whose own ultimate needs and ideals it recognized in the animal." (Max Raphael, *Prähistorische Höhlenmalerei* [Prehistoric cave painting], new ed. [Cologne, Germany: Bruckner and Thünker, 1993], 24, 28, 29.) It is astonishing how much bombast a Marxist with a bourgeois education was prepared to inject into human prehistory. Nevertheless, it remains Raphael's achievement to have recognized the cave paintings as a totemic representation system. Recently, this system has come under attack: "In particular, the homogeneity and consistency of the animal motives, the complete lack of object and plant totems . . . as well as the diversity of signs and their topographical distribution . . . do not jibe at all with totemism as we know it today in primitive societies." (Michael Lorblanchet, *Höhlenmalerei: Ein Handbuch* [Cave painting: a handbook], 2nd ed. [Stuttgart: Thorbecke, 2000], 87.) This, actually, only shows the relatively nonprimitive nature of "totemism as we know it today" and the extent of its change and development since the Aurignacian era. It does not prove that it was not totemism in the earlier period. Otherwise, we would have to conclude that fish, because in many respects they "do not jibe at all" with mammals, do not deserve to be classed as animals.

57. Translator's definition.

58. Plato, "Symposium," trans. Michael Joyce, in *The Collected Dialogues*, ed. Edith Hamilton and Huntington Cairns, 526–74 (Princeton: Princeton University Press, 1985), 189e–190a, 190d, e.

59. Plato, "Symposium," 191a.

60. Plato, "Symposium," 193a.

61. Freud, *Beyond Pleasure*, 70.

62. See chap. 1.

63. Freud, *Beyond Pleasure*, 46.

64. Ibid.

65. Ibid., 48–49.

66. Ibid., 43.

67. Ibid., 45.

68. Ibid., 46.

69. Freud, *Totem and Taboo*, 164.

70. To suggest, with the gesture of a connoisseur, that Odysseus's horror at his actions was nothing but Freudian denial, and secretly there was nothing he longed for more than to carry them out, is to ignore the particular logic of Sophocles' tragedies and impose on them a psychoanalytic schema that they specifically do not conform to. See, in refutation, the fruitful

philosophy-of-religions approach of Klaus Heinrich, *Arbeiten mit Ödipus: Begriff der Verdrängung in der Religionswissenschaft* [Working with Oedipus: The concept of repression in the science of religion] (Basel, Switzerland: Stroemfeld / Roter Stern, 1993), especially 120ff.

71. Lewis Henry Morgan, *Ancient Society, or, Researches in the Lines of Human Progress from Savagery through Barbarism to Civilization* (London: Macmillan, 1877).

72. *Gilgamesh*, I, 194ff.

73. *Ius primae noctis*, or "right of the first night," is the right feudal lords are said to have had to have sexual relations with the daughters of their serfs before the latter married.—Trans.

74. Freud, "On Narcissism," 84.

75. Meister Eckhart (c. 1260–c. 1327) was a German mystic and Dominican theologian. He was judged heretical by the Inquisition, but his sermons survived and influenced Luther, among others.—Trans.

76. This does not mean that Eros is part of the child's genetic equipment. Rather, the idea is that an epigenetic process occurred in the course of which the capacity for eroticism became a general human disposition. The term *sedimentation* is a perhaps unusual but accurate way to express this, just as the word *pathways* can be used to characterize highly complex neurochemical processes.

77. Melanie Klein calls this process the way from a "paranoid" to a "depressive" position. If her discoveries are not repeated word-for-word here, it is because she has decked them out in an extremely demanding specialized vocabulary that runs like clockwork. There, the newborn already possesses an "ego" and "object relations." He experiences a "fear of destruction" that is evoked by the "Death Instinct" and expresses itself as "fear of persecution." He is at once busily absorbed in introjection and projection and the denial of internal and external reality, and already splits and idealizes the mother's breast, which is always already given as an object, into "good and bad aspects," without our having any knowledge of what makes him capable of all this. It is as if inborn trigger mechanisms are activated. Melanie Klein, "Notes on Some Schizoid Mechanisms," *International Journal of Psycho-Analysis* 27 (1946), 99–110.

78. Freud, "On Narcissism," 87.

79. Freud, *Interpretation of Dreams*, 565.

80. Sigmund Freud, "Formulations on the Two Principles of Psychic Functioning," in *The Unconscious*, trans. Graham Frankland, 3–10 (London: Penguin, 2005), 6. Cited as "Two Principles."

81. Ibid., 9–10, note 4.

82. Freud, *Interpretation of Dreams*, 597.

83. Freud, "Two Principles," 3.

84. Freud, "On Narcissism,"73.

85. Ibid., 77.

86. Ibid., 82.

87. Freud, *Interpretation of Dreams*, 566.

88. Freud, *Beyond Pleasure*, 25, 38. Thus, anyone who believes in the pleasure principle is almost required, by necessity, to believe in the death drive, just as theologians have a hard time believing in God but denying the existence of the devil. So the attempts at justifying the death drive, the new rationales and genuflections it receives, continue as unabated among psychoanalysts as the arguments about God's adversary do among theologians.

CHAPTER 3: WORDS

1. The phrase appears above all in the gospel according to Matthew; see Matthew 1:22; 2:15; 4:14, and elsewhere.

2. Matthew 5:33, 34, and 37. The radical nature of this statement speaks for the assumption that Jesus actually said this or something similar. The parts of the sermon that have been omitted here are certainly not by him. They attempt to soften it with labored reasoning that breathes with the spirit of the early Christian community.

3. This, by the way, is exactly the point of Thomas Mann's "Felix Krull," a story about a con man who works very earnestly at his simulations. In doing so, he is not disguising, but revealing himself. It is his essence to simulate things, and his confidence tricks and impostures are the offshoot of truthfulness and authenticity. They are art, and by no means in an ironic sense, unless we assume that art as such is something ironic because it can never be cleanly distinguished from imposture. But then Krull is not making ironic art, but rather revealing art itself as incurably ironic—a galvanic point of intersection between art and the oath.

4. Bertholt Brecht, *The Threepenny Opera*, trans. Ralph Mannheim and John Willett (London: Penguin Books, 2008), 33.

5. Genesis 15:1.

6. Jonah 1:4:

7. Genesis 9:13.

8. Genesis 1:3.

9. Exodus 19:16–19; 20: 1–3.

10. Exodus 20:18–19.

11. In Homer, "earth-shaker" is a regular attribute of Poseidon's. It is no less fitting for Yahweh in the Sinai tradition.

12. Joshua 6:4–5, 16, 20.

13. Conductors have to remind their orchestras repeatedly that *diminuendo* does not mean "softly," but "becomes softer." Usually, it starts out loud.

14. Walter Burkert, *Homo Necans*, 11ff.

15. For a more detailed discussion, see Christoph Türcke, "Zurück zum Geräusch: Die sakrale Hypothek der Musik" [Back to noise: The sacred debt of music], *Merkur* 6 (2001), 509ff.

16. "It is a long time since I heard the sounds of the shofar," writes Theodor Reik, "and when recently, in the interest of this work, I heard the shofar blown on New Year's Day, I could not completely avoid the emotion which these

four crude, fearsome, moaning, loud-sounding, and long-drawn-out tones produced—I do not attempt to decide whether the reason for my emotion was the fact that I was accustomed to this sound from youth, or whether it was an effect which everyone might feel." (Theodor Reik, "Das Schofar," in Reik, *The Psychological Problems of Religion, I: Ritual: Psychoanalytic Studies*, trans. Douglas Bryan. [New York: Farrar, Straus, 1946], 236.) Reik's study is still worth reading. It is convincing in its evidence that the "original cultural significance of music has developed out of the religious cults" (304) and acute in its analysis of the origins of horn blowing as deriving from the cult of sacrifice of bulls and rams. It is exaggerated only starting from the point when the horn sound of Sinai, together with the (ram?)-horned Moses that Michelangelo sculpted in stone, and Israel's dancing around the golden (bull) calf are seriously invoked as historical verification of Freud's fairy tale of the murder of the father by the primal horde. Here, Reik writes as if Yahweh had actually been the "father" whom the "son" Moses killed as the leader of a band of brothers, and as if the secret behind the replacement of bull sacrifice by the sacrifice of a calf or ram were the "revolt" of "sons" against a primal father. It is remarkable, by the way, how hesitant Freud was in accepting Reik as an ally. He did write a foreword praising Reik's religious writings, but never adopted his Moses interpretation.

17. Exodus 19:19. Translation modified; the King James Version has "answered him by a voice."—Trans.

18. Exodus 20:19.

19. The inspired thing about Exodus 19:16ff. is that here, with the shofar's similarity to the word, the word's similarity to the shofar, and their association with the storm and the volcanic eruption, it marks the common point of origin of music and language, which is also the point at which they diverge. Both emerged from a fright inspired by nature; both are natural sound that is formed, but formed in different ways. Music explores the whole realm of possible generation of sound. Words, on the other hand, are limited to a section of the human vocal register, and producing them requires particularly fine adjustment in order to be able to accomplish what distinguishes the transfer of something soundless, namely, meaning. At their origin, however, music and language are hardly distinguishable from each other, and both begin at the edge of the unbearable. They are emergency exits, attempts to form unbearably shattering experiences in such a way that they become bearable.

20. Roman Jakobson, *Kindersprache, Aphasie und allgemeine Lautgesetze* [Child language, aphasia, and phonological universals] (Frankfurt: Suhrkamp, 1969), 26, 31.

21. Genesis 2:8.

22. Psalm 14:5.

23. Ezekiel 48:35.

24. Jeremiah 8:21. The King James Bible, which is cited here, sometimes varies considerably, in its translation of the Hebrew, from the Luther Bible, which is the basis of the arguments made here.—Trans.

25. Neither the Luther Bible nor the King James Bible does a very good job of rendering this word; Martin Buber, in his translation of the Psalms, has "*Geht aus, schaut seine* [i.e., God's] *Werke, der Erstarren einsetzt auf Erden,*" which might be translated (in biblical language) as "Go forth, look upon the works of Him who strikes terror on earth." Martin Buber, *Das Buch der Preisungen* [The Book of Psalms], vol. xiv of *Die Schriftwerke: Verdeutscht von Martin Buber* [The holy scripture: Translated into German by Martin Buber] (Cologne, Germany, and Olten, Switzerland: Jakob Hegner, 1932), 74.—Trans.

26. Genesis 11:4.

27. Freud, *Beyond Pleasure,* 13–14.

28. Ibid., 14–15.

29. Freud, "Antithetical Meaning of Primal Words," in *Standard Edition,* vol. 11, 153–61 (London: Hogarth Press, 1957), 157–58.

30. Ibid.

31. Giorgio Agamben starts here, i.e., at a relatively late stage of *sacer,* when he adopts a definition by Sextius Propertius: "The sacred man is the one whom the people have judged on account of a crime. It is not permitted to sacrifice this man, yet he who kills him will not be condemned for homicide." (Giorgio Agamben, *Homo Sacer: Sovereign Power and Bare Life,* trans. Daniel Heller-Roazen [Stanford, CA: Stanford University Press, 1995], 71.) Obviously, this definition is intended to put paid not only to the antithetical but also to the ambiguous meaning of *sacer*—to cut it loose from human sacrifice and henceforth to use it only in the sense of "cursed." What this profanation is intended to achieve is unclear. In Festus, it comes up in the context of one of the great challenges to the unity of the *res publica,* namely, the secession of the Roman plebeians and their move to a sacred mountain (*mons sacer*). Although we do not know exactly how this happened, it must have been a concession to the growing power of the plebeians. Agamben, admittedly, stretches the Festus quotation way beyond its limits—after all, it is only a late, context-dependent redefinition of *sacer.* Agamben, however, turns it into *the* definition par excellence: "sacred life—that is, life that may be killed but not sacrificed" (83). Not satisfied with this, he wants this little Festus find to prove that *sacer* is not a genuinely religious term at all, but a political-juridical one: the keyword for political sovereignty. The latter, namely, is not meant to have any stability without *homines sacri,* people who are both in- and excluded in their society and who find themselves in a legally constituted space that is free from law—in a kind of "state of exception," for according to a famous definition by Carl Schmitt, the political sovereign is the person who decides on the state of exception. To translate *sacer* as "existing in a state of exception" may be original. But the sacrificial victim was already in this state when he was "chosen," removed from his normal life context, and prepared for ritual killing, which could only occur without punishment to the extent that the victim was both completely excluded from the clan and completely included in it. Except that this act of in- and exclusion, the decision on the state of exception, was originally

not an act of political sovereignty, but the un-sovereign, fright-induced reaction of hominid collectives to the terrors of nature. It is awkward when someone has no concept of how deeply early humankind was sunk in ritual and cult, knows the state of exception only from political philosophy, and therefore believes that where it is concerned he is dealing with something guaranteed to be free of cults—the foundational act of a purely political sphere. This sphere was naturally never free of the cult. Only by shutting out millennia of cultic history can someone come up with the idea of looking for the "actual place" of *homo sacer*, "outside both human and divine law," and of claiming that it this "figure may allow us to uncover an originary *political* structure that is located in a zone prior to the distinction between sacred and profane, religious and juridical" (73–74).

32. Johann Sebastian Bach made this line famous in his setting of Luther's version of Psalm 130. It was Bach who actually added the word *affliction*, where Luther had "depths."—Trans.

33. Emile Durkheim, *The Elementary Forms of Religious Life*, trans. Karen E. Fields (New York: Simon and Schuster, 1995), 100.

34. Genesis 4:15.

35. For more on this subject, see Christoph Türcke, *Vom Kainszeichen zum genetischen Code* [From the mark of Cain to the genetic code] chap. 1 and 2.

36. Ludwig Wittgenstein, *Philosophical Investigations*, trans. G. E. M. Anscombe, P. M. S. Hacker, and Joachim Schulte, rev. 4th (bilingual) ed. (West Sussex, UK: Blackwell, 2009), 15.

37. Plato, *Cratylus* 439c.

38. Ibid., 383d.

39. See Günther Mensching, *Das Allgemeine und das Besondere: Der Ursprung des modernen Denkens im Mittelalter* [The general and the particular: The origin of modern thought in the Middle Ages] (Stuttgart: Metzler, 1992).

40. See Peter Bieri, "Was bleibt von der analytischen Philosophie?" [What remains of analytic philosophy?], *Deutsche Zeitschrift für Philosophie* 3 (2007), 339.

41. *Unwesen*, in contemporary German, exists only in the formula *sein Unwesen treiben*, which means "to make trouble, to be a nuisance." The root is *Wesen* (being, essence). Heidegger, in his inquiry into being, created a neologism, the verb *wesen*, which has been translated as "to unfold essentially" or "to come to presence" (from the "Heidegger Glossary," by David Fidel Ferrer). Putting this together with the negative particle *Un*, meaning "non," results in another neologism, *Unwesen*, a noun that may, literally, be read as "nonessential unfolding," or "failure to come to presence."—Trans.

42. On epigenesis, see chap. 2. ("Pathways" section).

43. *Genesis* 1:4, 1:10, et al.

44. Plato, *The Republic* 505a ff.; *Timaeus* 29a ff.

45. Aristotle, *Metaphysics*, trans. Benjamin Jowett, in *The Complete Works: Revised Oxford Translation*, ed. Jonathan Barnes, Bollingen Series LXXI.23–24 (Princeton: Princeton University Press, 1984), 1072b.

46. A special case is omitted here for the moment: what Aristotle, in his essay on categories, calls "first substance" (*protē ousia*).

47. See Aristotle, *Metaphysics* 983a, b, 988a, 1038b, 1042b.

48. *Wesen* can be translated as "being" or "entity." Volumes could be written about the implications of these synonyms for translation from Greek to Latin, German, English, and other languages.—Trans.

49. Genesis 11:4.

50. Aristotle, *Categories*, trans. J. L. Ackrill, in *The Complete Works: Revised Oxford Translation*, ed. Jonathan Barnes, Bollingen Series LXXI.23–24 (Princeton: Princeton University Press, 1984), category 3b.

51. Aristotle, *Metaphysics* 1006b.

52. Friedrich Nietzsche, *Twilight of the Idols*, ed. and trans. Walter Kaufmann, in *The Portable Nietzsche* (New York: Viking Press, 1954), 483.

53. John L. Austin, *How to Do Things with Words* (Cambridge, MA: Harvard University Press, 1962), 98–99.

54. Austin himself came across borderline cases such as "I know that . . .," where the statement that follows is considered locutionary but the sentence as a whole can be regarded as illocutionary. This led to debates within analytic philosophy as to where different things should be assigned. (See Eike von Savigny, "J. L. Austin Theorie der Sprechakte" [J. L. Austin's Theory of Speech Acts] in John L. Austin, *Zur Theorie der Sprechakte* [Stuttgart: Reclam, 1975], 18.) It is a fortunate individual who has this kind of worries. In the meanwhile, speech-act theory has developed a whole set of instruments for the regulation of borderline cases. See John Searle, *Speech Acts: An Essay in the Philosophy of Language* (Cambridge: Cambridge University Press, 1969).

55. Austin, *How to Do Things with Words*, 72–73.

56. Is this gradually becoming clear to its adherents? At least Brandom, who rediscovered expression as the elixir of language, could be read this way. Expression instead of representation is his motto. (Robert B. Brandom. *Making It Explicit: Reasoning, Representing, and Discursive Commitment* [Cambridge, MA: Harvard University Press, 1998]). Admittedly, he takes up expression not in its cathartic elementary stage, where it sought to get rid of itself along with the fright, but only in the well-tempered state of differentiated standard languages. For them, he shows, with all the rules of linguistic art, that single words are already exponents of a judgmental and expressive behavior that claims language as a whole and is not satisfied with representing and sorting things out. One thing, though, is omitted: the fact that the continuous survival of expression is also a result of physiological failure. Highly developed languages are ersatz constructions. They only exist because evolving language did not succeed in letting the entire compressed excitation escape. As a result, language was condemned to continue acting as an escape valve (for expression) and becoming a place of asylum (for its representative). This primary process of expression is not to be found in Brandom.

57. On procedural memory, repetition, and remembrance, see chap. 1 ("The Mental and the Physical" section).

58. This prehistory was anything but a paradise. The "naming language" that Walter Benjamin claims Adam spoke when he gave names to the animals in the Garden of Eden ("On Language as Such and on the Language of Man," trans. Edmund Jephcott, in Walter Benjamin, *Reflections: Essays, Aphorisms, Autobiographical Writings* [New York and London: Harcourt Brace Jovanovich, n.d.], 314–32; also available in a trans. by Rodney Livingstone, in *Walter Benjamin: Selected Writings*, ed. Marcus Bullock and Michael W. Jennings, vol. 1, 1913–1926 [Cambridge, MA, and London: Harvard University Press, 1996]) is nothing but the fictional theological antithesis of the real historical language of naming, from whose terrified stammering the articulated system of phonetics developed. The two must not be confounded, but represent mirror images of each other. The real language of naming aims at the absolutely alien being that reveals itself in traumatic shock; its mirror image, in paradise, aims at the absolutely familiar being that reveals itself absolutely and without reservation. The terror that has no equal and the incomparably individual state that is blissfully ignorant of terror are extremes that meet. (See Christoph Türcke, *Erregte Gesellschaft* [Agitated Society], 164ff.) It should, however, be noted that the naming language of paradise can be made fruitful for linguistics only if it is not taken at face value but instead is understood as standing for the utopian breath that emanates from the true name.

59. See chap. 1 (Dreamtime section).

60. Roman Jakobson, "Der grammatische Aufbau der Kindersprache" [The grammatical structure of children's language], in Elmar Holenstein, *Von der Hintergehbarkeit der Sprache* [On deceiving language] (Frankfurt: Suhrkamp, 1980), 176f.

61. The Greek *hypokeimenon*, by the way, means almost the same thing and can hardly be adduced as a counterargument.

62. Various dictionaries translate *subiectum* as "substratum," as "material substratum," or as "substance."—Trans.

63. The subject rules the sentence even if the predicate is in the passive voice ("The lightning bolt is hurled"); so even in this case, the contradiction between active and passive, ruling and being ruled, does not simply disappear.

64. The optative does not exist in English or German but is a feature of many ancient and some modern languages, including Sanskrit, ancient Greek, and Sumerian.—Trans.

65. Ferdinand de Saussure, *Course in General Linguistics*, trans. Wade Baskin (New York: McGraw-Hill / The Philosophical Library, 1966).

66. Noam Chomsky, *Aspects of the Theory of Syntax* (Cambridge, MA: MIT Press, 1965), 30, 15–16 et passim.

67. An *ens per aliud* is an entity that exists by virtue of and is determined by another entity or entities; an *ens per se* is an entity that exists by virtue of and is determined solely by itself.—Trans.

68. Aristotle, *Categories*, 1b, 2a.

69. Ibid., category 2a.

70. Ibid., category 3a. Translation modified.

71. Immanuel Kant, *Critique of Pure Reason*, B 107, 105.

72. Ibid., B 107–8.

73. Among the Sumerians something quite similar was repeated at a high cultural level, as if in time-lapse photography. The Sumerians had the original idea of inscribing underlings' tributes to the ruler's court on clay tablets. That the making of signs and speaking have something to do with each other had been known long before that. But the Sumerians were the first to have started to provide words, in a planned way, with signs to serve them. They made signs in the form of images that followed in the footsteps of words. This was the origin of profane language—ca. 3,200 years BCE. See Christoph Türcke, *Vom Kainszeichen zum genetischen code* [From the Mark of Cain to the Genetic Code], 15ff.

74. Ferdinand de Saussure, *Course in General Linguistics*, 67, 69.

75. *Adaequatio rei et intellectus*, or "correspondence between a thing and the mind," was proposed by Aristotle as the criterion of truth and has served as a classical locus for philosophical discussion ever since.—Trans.

76. Jacques Lacan, "The Freudian Unconscious and Ours," trans. Alan Sheridan, in *The Seminar of Jacques Lacan, Book XI: The Four Fundamental Concepts of Psychoanalysis*, 17–28 (New York and London: W. W. Norton, 1981), 20. Emphasis in original.

77. Ibid., 20–21.

78. Jacques Lacan, "The Instance of the Letter in the Unconscious, or Reason Since Freud," in *Écrits*, trans. Bruce Fink, 493–41 (New York and London: W. W. Norton, 2006), 423, 429–31. Cited as "Instance."

79. Freud, *New Introductory Lectures*, 155ff.

80. Jacques Lacan, "The Function and Field of Speech and Language in Psychoanalysis," in *Écrits*, trans. Bruce Fink, 237–68 (New York and London: W. W. Norton, 2006), 262. Cited as "Functions and Field."

81. Lacan, "Instance," 524.

82. Lacan, "Function and Field," 294.

83. Ibid., 206ff.

84. Ibid., 263. Translation modified.

85. Ibid., 248.

86. Sigmund Freud, *Zur Auffassung der Aphasien: Eine kritische Studie* [On aphasia: a critical study] (Frankfurt: Fischer, 2001), 117.

87. Ibid., 109, 98.

88. See the revealing study on Freud's childhood by Franz Maciejewski, *Der Moses des Sigmund Freud: Ein unheimlicher Bruder* [Sigmund Freud's Moses: An uncanny brother] (Göttingen: Vandenhoeck and Ruprecht, 2006).

89. Josef Breuer and Sigmund Freud, *Studies in Hysteria*, 129.

90. "Primal repression" is discussed in chap. 1 ("Dreamtime" section) and chap. 3 ("Speech Acts" section).

91. That repression always has a conceptual side, which can extend to the highest reaches of philosophy, is something that Klaus Heinrich has demonstrated in numerous ways. For him, Kant's "transcendentality" and Heidegger's "Being" are star witnesses for concepts that repress, since they are constituted, from

their inception, in such a way as to make it impermissible to reflect on their own origin in mythology, which after all is the childhood of conceptuality, so to speak. Heinrich asks, "What can we learn, for a non-repressive concept of conceptualization, from the stuff that religions present us with and that interests us for the sole reason that, in it, conflicts are formulated that today have still not been laid to rest?" (Klaus Heinrich, *Arbeiten mit Ödipus: Begriff der Verdrängung in der Religionswissenschaft* [Working on Oedipus: The concept of repression in religious studies], Basel, Stroemfeld/Roter Stern, 1993, 120.) This is also the question this book raises. However, two things should be more clearly delineated than Heinrich does: the unavoidable primary repression, without which there are no concepts, and repressive concepts that unnecessarily close themselves off from their prehistory and are therefore detrimental to conceptuality.

92. Hesiod, *Theogony* 678ff.
93. Aristotle, *Politics*, trans. Benjamin Jowett, in *The Complete Works: Revised Oxford Translation*, ed. Jonathan Barnes, Bollingen Series LXXI.23–24 (Princeton: Princeton U-niversity Press, 1984) 1253a.
94. Exodus 3:17.
95. Freud, *New Introductory Lectures*, 100.
96. Josef Breuer and Sigmund Freud, *Studies in Hysteria*, 106.

AFTERWORD: HIGH-TECH DREAMTIME

1. Novalis, *Blüthenstaub* [Pollen], in *Werke*, vol. 2, ed. Hans-Joachim Mähl (Munich: Hanser, 1978), 227.
2. Theodor W. Adorno, *Negative Dialectics*, trans. E. B. Ashton (New York: Continuum, 1973), 366.
3. Christianity reiterated this type of failure in an especially significant way. "Thy kingdom come," prayed Jesus, but in place of God's kingdom came the church.
4. Hegel, *Science of Logic*, 82.
5. Freud, *New Introductory Lectures*, 78.
6. Günther Anders, *Die Antiquiertheit des Menschen* [The antiquated nature of the human], vol. 1 (Munich, C. H. Beck, 1956), 21ff.
7. For a discussion of imagination as the literal incorporation of images, see chap. 1 ("Representation" section).—Trans.
8. Sergei Eisenstein, in *Film: Auge—Faust—Sprache: Filmdebatten der 20er Jahre in Sowietrussland* [Film: Eye—fist—language: Film debates of the 1920s in Soviet Russia] (Berlin, n.d.,) 27.
9. Walter Benjamin, "Work of Art," 238.
10. Claude Lévy-Strauss, "Ein Hymnus an die Jugend" [A hymn to youth], *Frankfurter Rundschau*, March 21, 1995, 8.
11. Walter Benjamin, "Work of Art," 238.
12. Wolfgang Bergmann, "Ich bin nicht in mir und nicht ausser mir" [I am not within myself and not beside myself], in *Hyperaktivität: Kulturtheorie, Pädagogik, Therapie* [Hyperactivity: Cultural theory, pedagogy, therapy], ed. Bernd Ahrbeck (Stuttgart: Kohlhammer, 2007), 54.

13. Julia Kristeva, *New Maladies of the Soul* (New York: Columbia University Press, 1995). 9.
14. See the foreword to this volume.
15. Paul Klee, *Kunst-Lehre* [On Art] (Leipzig: Reclam, 1987], 60.
16. Benjamin, *Arcades Project*, 118. Translation modified.
17. Benjamin, *Work of Art*, 238.
18. The word *updating* is English in original.—Trans.
19. See chap. 3.
20. Hegel, *Science of Logic*, 477.
21. See chap. 2.
22. See Christoph Türcke, *Fundamentalismus—maskierter Nihilismus* [Fundamentalism—disguised nihilism] (Hanover: zu Klampen, 2003).

INDEX